East-West Conflict

This book is also in the
Studies in International and Strategic Affairs Series
of the Center for International and Strategic Affairs,
University of California, Los Angeles, and
the Institute for Political Science,
University of Bonn, West Germany.

A list of the other titles in this series can be found at the back of the book.

East-West Conflict

Elite Perceptions
and Political Options

EDITED BY

Michael D. Intriligator
and Hans-Adolf Jacobsen

Westview Press
BOULDER & LONDON

This Westview softcover edition is printed on acid-free paper and bound in softcovers that carry the highest rating of the National Association of State Textbook Administrators, in consultation with the Association of American Publishers and the Book Manufacturers' Institute.

Published in 1988 in the United States of America by Westview Press, Inc., 5500 Central Avenue, Boulder, Colorado 80301

Library of Congress Cataloging-in-Publication Data
East-West conflict.
  (Studies in international and strategic affairs series of the Center for International and Strategic Affairs, University of California, Los Angeles, and the Institute for Political Science, University of Bonn, West Germany)
  1. United States—Foreign relations—Soviet Union.
2. Soviet Union—Foreign relations—United States.
3. Elite (Social sciences). 4. World politics—1975–
1985. 5. United States—Foreign relations—1981–
6. Soviet Union—Foreign relations—1975–
I. Intriligator, Michael D. II. Jacobsen, Hans-Adolf.
III. Series.
E183.8.S65E27 1988   327.73047   87-29477
ISBN 0-8133-7520-7

Printed and bound in the United States of America

⊗ The paper used in this publication meets the requirements of the American National Standard for Permanence of Paper for Printed Library Materials Z39.48-1984.

6   5   4   3   2   1

Contents

Foreword

The publication of this book is timely. The INF accord signed at the December 1987 summit between President Reagan and General Secretary Gorbachev is truly a historic step forward in arms control and should serve as a springboard for subsequent agreements on strategic, chemical, and conventional forces. In East-West relations, we are witnessing a dynamism that few would have believed possible only a few years ago.

It would, however, be a mistake to draw exaggerated conclusions from this progress. Arms control is but one aspect of the East-West relationship. Other aspects are equally important and relate directly to the very nature and causes of East-West conflict. Glasnost and perestroika notwithstanding, we have seen little movement on the central issues of human rights in the Soviet Union and the restoration of full national sovereignty to the countries of Eastern Europe.

East-West policy requires sober analytical thought. Ideological rigidity is as much out of place as euphoria. Where possibilities for dialogue with the Soviet Union exist, we should pursue them assiduously, without, however, losing sight of fundamental Western interests and objectives. Progress in specific areas should not cause us to overlook other areas of persisting and fundamental conflict. The basic thrust of this present volume is to support such a reasonable and balanced policy.

While I do not necessarily subscribe to all of the views contained in this volume, I believe that it affords useful insights into the nature of U.S.-Soviet relations and helps the reader develop a better understanding of the concerns of one of America's key allies. Prepared jointly by German and American scholars, it is a valuable contribution to the transatlantic dialogue.

Ambassador Richard R. Burt
U.S. Ambassador to the
Federal Republic of Germany

Preface

This book is an updated proceedings of a very lively conference, with the same title, held in Bonn, Federal Republic of Germany in June 1986. The conference brought together U.S. and German Federal Republic scholars and policymakers to analyze U.S., Federal Republic, and Soviet elite perceptions of East-West conflict. It analyzed perceptions both generally and in relation to specific decisionmaker perceptions with the goal of identifying policy implications and political options. The conference was cosponsored by the UCLA Center for International and Strategic Affairs and the University of Bonn Institute for Political Science, and it was supported by a grant from the Volkswagen Foundation.

The conference was part of a regular program of institutional cooperation between the UCLA Center and the University of Bonn Institute, which has also included a workshop on "The Crisis in East-West Relations: Implications for the United States and the Federal Republic of Germany," held at UCLA in February 1982, regular exchanges of faculty and students, and an ongoing summer arms control simulation conducted by William C. Potter, Executive Director of CISA, which currently alternates between the University of Bonn and the University of California, involving students from both universities in a simulation of the U.S.-Soviet arms control negotiations in Geneva.

We would like to acknowledge the support of the Volkswagen Foundation, which made the conference possible, and the assistance provided by our colleagues William C. Potter at UCLA and Wolfgang Pfeiler of the University of Bonn, who helped us in organizing the conference. We would also like to acknowledge the superb editorial work of Ann M. Florini, the CISA Editor, on this volume.

M. D. I.

H.-A. J.

Affiliations of the Contributors

MARY N. HAMPTON is a Predoctoral Fellow at the Center for International and Strategic Affairs, University of California, Los Angeles.

OLE R. HOLSTI is George V. Allen Professor of Political Science at Duke University.

MICHAEL D. INTRILIGATOR is Professor of Economics and Political Science and Director of the Center for International and Strategic Affairs, University of California, Los Angeles.

HANS-ADOLF JACOBSEN is Professor of Political Science and Director of the Institute for Political Science, University of Bonn.

WERNER KALTEFLEITER is Professor of Political Science and Director, Institute of Political Science, Christian-Albrechts University at Kiel.

ANDRZEJ KORBONSKI is Professor of Political Science and Director, Center for Russian and East European Studies, University of California, Los Angeles.

BIRGIT MEYER is Professor of Political Science, University of Esslingen.

GOTTFRIED NIEDHART is Professor and affiliated with the Historical Institute, University of Mannheim.

WOLFGANG PFEILER is Professor of Political Science at the University of Bonn and affiliated with the Research Institute of the Konrad Adenauer Stiftung.

JAMES N. ROSENAU is Professor of International Relations and Director of the Institute for Transnational Studies, University of Southern California.

MORTON SCHWARTZ is with the Bureau of Intelligence and Research of the U.S. Department of State.

Introduction:
Perceptions and Conflict

Michael D. Intriligator
and
Hans-Adolf Jacobsen

Perceptions and Misperceptions

Social scientists interested in political decision-making have long been fascinated by Soviet and American perceptions--and misperceptions--of one another. Faulty perceptions, especially those of the political elite in both countries, have been cited by various scholars as responsible for the deterioration of East-West relations after World War II, the escalation of the nuclear arms race, and the intractibility of most outstanding international political issues. It has even been alleged that the distorted image of the United States among Soviet leaders is curiously similar to the distorted image of the Soviet Union among American leaders, and that this bleak "mirror image" may be self-perpetuating.

While there has been substantial interest in superpower elite perceptions, relatively little attention has been given to the issue of intra-alliance perceptions of the adversary and the extent to which the perceptions of elites in NATO states coincide or diverge. Even less attention has been given to the study of Soviet elite perception on NATO policy.

Purpose and Principal Themes

The major purpose of the conference on which this book is based was to bring together American and West German scholars in order to

1

analyze U.S., German, and Soviet elite perceptions of East-West conflict. The book treats several interrelated issues pertaining to perceptions and misperceptions as well as policy implications. First, it identifies the origins of misperceptions in East-West relations and the sources for perceptual change. In particular, Chapter 1, by Gottfried Niedhart, provides a historical account of perceptions and misperceptions in East-West relations, while Chapter 2, by James N. Rosenau, develops a theoretical approach to learning in East-West relations, one in which superpower leaders respond dynamically to one another and to prior experiences as habit-driven actors.

Second, the book analyzes the nature of decisionmaker perceptions. Chapter 3, by Ole Holsti, examines U.S. elite perceptions of the Soviet Union by analyzing beliefs of American leaders about the Soviet Union and Soviet-American relations over the period 1976 to 1984. Chapter 4, by Birgit Meyer, analyzes differing West German perceptions of the Soviet threat. Chapter 5, by Morton Schwartz, analyzes Soviet elite perceptions of the U.S., while Chapter 6, by Wolfgang Pfeiler, analyzes Soviet perceptions of West Germany. Chapter 7, by Andrzej Korbonski, analyzes East European perceptions of West Germany.

Third, the book attempts to assess the policy implications and political options for the West. Chapter 8, by Mary Hampton, examines West German foreign policy and its relation to Western security. Finally, Chapter 9, by Werner Kaltefleiter, considers the potential for forging a U.S.-Federal Republic consensus vis-a-vis the Soviet Union.

Broader Implications

In its broader implications, the book suggests various alternatives available to the leadership in the U.S. and the Federal Republic. These two countries clearly play the central roles in the Western alliance, the U.S. through its superpower role as leader of the West and the Federal Republic through its central role in Europe and in the NATO alliance. A clear understanding of the similarities and differences in elite perceptions in the U.S. and West Germany of Soviet foreign, political, diplomatic, economic, and military policy is essential to a correct formulation of the various political options for changing East-West relations. In particular, it is important for U.S. elites to understand Federal Republic elite perceptions and vice versa in order to improve their own perceptions of both the Soviet Union and one another and thereby to develop a more coordinated policy.

Origins of Misperception

Misperception has been identified as one of the important driving forces behind East-West conflict, particularly misperception by political leaders. But what are the sources of misperception? One source, as discussed by Rosenau, is habit-driven actors. A related source is the role of ideology, with leaders in both East and West seeing the world in terms of their own ideological preconceptions. These preconceptions may be mistaken, leading to misperceptions, but there may be certain information that tends to confirm these preconceptions. Another contributing factor is the labels used by each side concerning the other. Yet another is propaganda and disinformation, in that leaders may start to believe their own propaganda. While this point was made at the conference concerning Soviet elite perception of American and West German foreign and defense policy, it is undoubtedly also applicable to U.S. and Federal Republic elite perception of Soviet foreign and defense policy. It is essential to identify the origins of misperception in order to correct these errors; otherwise they tend to be self-perpetuating.

Sources of Perceptual Change

Perceptions and misperceptions are not static. They change over time in response to events, to decisions, and to other factors, although changes usually occur slowly. Just as it is important to study the origins of misperception, it is also important to study the dynamics of perceptual change. Among the factors that lead to changes in elite perceptions are the awareness of the decision-maker of perception and misperception, diplomacy, negotiations, meetings of officials, public statements, private discussions, and even some private groups. Technology can also change and/or accelerate the change in perceptions, via newer systems of communications, including systems using satellites and computers.

An important factor in perceptual change is the awareness of interdependence of perceptions. Western perceptions of the Soviet Union and Soviet perceptions of the West are, in fact, dependent on one another. Thus there can be a dynamic process of interaction of perceptual change, where small changes in perceptions can have feedback effects. An example is the rapid change in U.S. and Chinese perceptions of one another, with Sino-American relations changing from confrontation to limited cooperation. While perceptions usually change very slowly and tend toward continuation, there may be other situations of potentially dramatic changes occurring through the reinforcement of latent feedback effects once the process begins by an external stimulus. Of course this type of instability could as well generate adverse as positive relations, and it could create rather than destroy misperceptions. These "fast" changes in perceptions can be contrasted to "slow" changes that occur over much longer historical periods and usually stem from many interacting factors, including such systemic factors as geostrategic, political, economic, military, historical, and other such considerations and such idiosyncratic factors as personalities and attitudes of national leaders, particularly now, the leaders in the United States and the Soviet Union.

Similarities and Differences in U.S. and West German Perceptions

There are some similarities and, at the same time, some differences in U.S. and West German perceptions. For example there is agreement on the value of the alliance structure but, at the same time, disagreement on the nature and value of detente in East-West relations and on the West German policy of Ostpolitik. These differences are rooted in historical, political, economic and geostrategic factors, which require further study, including theoretical, empirical, and case studies.

1

Western Attitudes Toward the Soviet Union: Perceptions and Misperceptions

Gottfried Niedhart

In 1946, George F. Kennan described what in his view was most important when dealing with the Soviet Union: "Naturally all of us who have been working on Russian affairs have concentrated on trying to fathom the workings of the Soviet mind and to develop our knowledge of Russia to a point where we would be able to make a pretty good estimate of probable Soviet behavior in given states of circumstances."[1] To achieve proper assessments of a partner or adversary in international affairs is a permanent and essential aim of any foreign policymaker. Historically it can be traced back to the very origins of states and their interactions. Western efforts to analyze Soviet policy and conflict behavior in a systematic way started only after the Second World War when the U.S.S.R. became a recognized world power. Today there are many scholars in numerous research units dealing with the Soviet Union and collecting information about Soviet attitudes and purposes.[2]

This chapter provides an introduction into the process of image forming in the context of the East-West conflict. It goes without saying that its title is far too ambitious. What will be done is to ask some questions and raise some problems which are relevant to the subject of perceptions and misperceptions in East-West relations. First, there will be a survey of the content of images of the U.S.S.R. held in the West and of the changing importance of certain factors which formed and form Western images of the Soviet Union. The next step will be to ask for the sources of an image and to deal with the nexus between image and behavior. Finally there will be some concluding remarks on the difficult

5

but necessary task of distinguishing image and reality. Does perception always tend to be misperception? Throughout I shall concentrate on Western perceptions. One of the reasons is that we have much more and better information about the Western elites than we have about the Soviet leadership.[3]

It is important to emphasize the impact of history on present East-West relations.[4] Of course, we cannot simply ask what can we learn from history and how can we apply our historical knowledge to politics. But we can turn to history as a field not only of mistakes but also of alternatives and political processes. History reminds us constantly that things may change and do change and that we must not stick to prefabricated perspectives. Furthermore, historical experiences are consciously or unconsciously a part of our behavior. In the Soviet Union historical consciousness is traditionally very strong. With respect to East-West relations, historical experiences are not very encouraging for the Soviets. Their country has been invaded time and again. This is true not only during Tsarist times, but especially for the period after 1917. The Western intervention against the Bolsheviks during the Russian Civil War, the Polish-Soviet war in 1920 and, most important, the German attack in 1941 were traumatic experiences. Therefore national security has upper-most priority in the strategic thinking of the Soviet leadership.

Next comes what might be called ideological security. The logic of Soviet ideology necessarily leads to Soviet feelings of insecurity. All non-communist states are perceived as a threat even if the state of East-West relations is one of detente. The history of Soviet Russia is the history of permanent effort to catch up with the West. Western elites have to be aware of this predisposition of their Soviet counterparts to suffer from a feeling of inferiority and fear. Although history also shows that Tsarist or Soviet Russia always recovered from defeat and in the end became a world power, this status has to be seen in comparison with the superior potential of the Western superpower. Undoubtedly, President Reagan's Strategic Defense Initiative reminded the Soviet government of the existing asymmetry in the balance of forces.

Corresponding to Soviet fears which lead to ideological aggressiveness, one can observe similar reactions in the West which are also influenced by a collective memory. Western attitudes toward the Soviet Union still contain elements of the ideological conflict of the 19th century between the liberal values of Western political culture and the socialist or Marxist challenge; between the "bourgeois international" on the one hand and the "socialist international," the movement of international socialism or communism, on the other hand. Before the First World War this conflict was a transnational conflict, which involved social groups, not states as international actors. The international system of mostly non-aligned powers was a homogeneous system in spite of all power conflicts. This changed in 1917 with the entry of the United States into the European war and the October Revolution in Russia. By 1917 the transnational conflict of the 19th century became an international conflict. Soviet Russia was the first state guided by Marxist-Leninist ideology and thereby the "socialist international" received its political home.

From then on mutual suspicion, tension and conflict dominated the relations between the West and the East. For both sides, Soviet Russia embodied the revolution against the West. In the beginning this conflict was of marginal importance to the international system as a whole. But after the Second World War the East-West conflict moved to the very center of world affairs. The division of the industrialized world into two hostile camps was accompanied by enemy images and threat perceptions. How to achieve correct assessments of the other side and how to avoid misperceptions is one of the most crucial problems in East-West relations.

During the inter-war period Great Britain was the primary adversary of the Soviet Union, due to the United States' retreat to the Western hemisphere. After the outbreak of the Second World War the United States resumed the leadership of the West, and from then on played a leading role in shaping Western attitudes and policies toward the Soviet Union, although the British part in the beginning of the Cold War must not be overlooked.

As far as Germany was concerned, until the Second World War it belonged neither to the West nor to the East. Germany's position between East and West and a possible German-Soviet rapprochement was regarded as major problem in Western assessments of the Soviet Union's role in European affairs. It was Germany's warfare which changed relations between the West and the Soviet Union completely and also the Western perception of the Soviet Union, at least for a short time. After the Second World War, East and West wanted to prevent Germany's alignment to either side. Hence the division of Germany arose.[5]

During the war the Western allies (or a majority of the population and the political elites) had a favorable image of the Soviet Union and for the first time in East-West relations conceived a common strategy in world affairs. Even Churchill, who could not really forget his anti-communist attitudes and suspicions about the Soviet Union during the war, returned from Yalta most enthusiastically: "It is a different Russian world to any I have seen hitherto."[6] This enthusiasm did not last very long. Recent research has shown that British observers changed their attitudes towards the Soviet Union earlier than their American counterparts. In November 1945 Lord Halifax, the British ambassador in Washington, reported to London: "There persists a stubborn determination to rationalize Soviet actions whenever possible and thereby to reduce the prevailing fear of the Russians in the hope of realizing the American dream of one world."[7]

The ups and downs in East-West relations and the changing images of the Soviet Union show that the Soviet reality is never perceived in its totality. Western images of the Soviet Union are formed by different aspects of the Soviet reality. Over time the importance of certain aspects changes drastically, a process that will probably continue. Sometimes Western politicians and their advisers lay stress on the revolutionary potential of the Soviet system, on the ideological conflict between the West and the East, and on the totalitarian character of the Soviet regime. At other times this seems to be less important, and the Soviet Union is mainly perceived as a military power defining national interests just as other powers do. Occasionally economic aspects most strongly influence Western perceptions of the Soviet Union. Thus we have to deal not only with favorable or unfavorable images but also with a variety of Soviet realities which form the Soviet Union's image. There may be aspects of the Soviet reality which contribute to an unfavorable image and suggest political confrontation, and at the same time other aspects which suggest correct relations and a working partnership with the Soviet Union. However poor the relations between the United States and the Soviet Union may be, the Soviet Union remains a useful market for American farm products.

Images of the Soviets: Ideology and Policy

A major problem for Western observers of the Soviet Union has always been and still is the interaction between Communist ideology and pragmatic policy. How important is ideology in Soviet perceptions of the capitalist world? Does a Soviet politician act as a member of the international Communist movement aiming at world revolution? Or do Soviet decision-makers act like Machiavellian politicians who know their interests and options? No doubt Western elites perceive the East-West conflict in terms of both ideological and power conflict. It is impossible to isolate one of these two. On the whole, when the West perceives the Soviet Union to be an equal military power, it tends to perceive the direct Soviet threat to the industrialized countries as primarily military rather than ideological. This does not apply to Western perceptions of the threat posed by Soviet ambitions in the Third World, which are still seen as a primarily ideological threat.

After the Second World War and during the 1950s, when the U.S.S.R. was not regarded as an equal military power, the Soviet Union primarily appeared to be the center of world communism attempting to infiltrate Western societies. As early as 1945, the British Foreign Office pointed out that Moscow had to be seen not only as the center of communism but also as the organizer of a communist crusade in Europe and in the colonial territories. Especially in the Western occupation zones of Germany and after 1949 in the Federal Republic of Germany, the Soviet Union was perceived as a revolutionary power and not as a state with limited objectives. Anti-communism was the raison d'etre of the Federal Republic in the 1950s. The first Federal Chancellor, Konrad Adenauer, again and again warned of the communist threat, not because the Soviet Union wanted to launch a war but because of subversive communist activities. In Adenauer's assessment the Soviet Union was economically weak. Its leaders did not want to use the Red Army for offensive purposes. Furthermore, Adenauer thought that after a period of Western rearmament and after having regained enough strength the Soviet Union should be reassured that the West did not have hostile intentions against its territory.[8]

The more Western elites stress the importance of ideological factors in the outlook of Soviet foreign policy-makers, the less favorable is the image of the Soviet Union. People who stress the importance of ideology mostly feel disturbed by the Soviet political system and deplore the oppressive character of the regime. If ideology is regarded as less important, the Soviet policy is seen more in terms of *Realpolitik*. In this context the different Western approaches in handling human rights issues since the Helsinki Conference are of some significance.

During the 1960s and 1970s, when the Soviet Union reached military parity and when the Communist bloc lost its unity, the ideological conflict did not disappear but moved to the background. In the extreme case of General de Gaulle, ideological elements were ignored completely. In most cases, however, Western elites believed that ideological factors were still in some way relevant. In 1980 foreign policy experts in the Federal Republic were asked whether they believed in the relevance of ideological factors to Soviet foreign policy. 68 percent answered in the affirmative.[9]

More concrete than ideology is economics. The U.S.S.R. is a market for Western products and an exporter of raw materials. Therefore, the condition of the Soviet economy contributes to Western images of the Soviet Union and influences Western political strategies.

Economic cooperation or economic pressure are occasionally used as instruments to affect Soviet behavior.

Both methods — cooperation and pressure — stem from the Western conviction that the economic sector has to be regarded as a sector of enormous weight and that an adequate perception of the Soviet Union has to take into consideration the Soviet economy. The economic weakness and vulnerability of the Soviet Union — in contrast to its military power — are often misunderstood in the West. To use trade relations as a lever in Western strategies vis-a-vis the Soviet Union is certainly one of the worst miscalculations. Since the end of the Second World War any Western attempt to modify Soviet policy by means of economic offers or sanctions has proved abortive.[10]

The most important facets in any image of the Soviet Union are its armed forces and its foreign policy aims. Western assessments range from expansionism to retrenchment; Western reactions extend from confrontation and containment to cooperation.[11]

Since the very beginning the Soviet Union has not been considered a reliable partner in international affairs. The short period of alliance during the Second World War was an exception. When the harsh confrontation of the Cold War period came to an end and when the Cuba crisis was solved peaceably there was a slight improvement of the Soviet image. But when asked in 1969: "Does the Soviet Union contribute to world peace?" the majority in Western Europe answered in the negative.[12] In the Federal Republic the Soviet Union was perceived as a threat, and the Social Democratic Party/Free Democratic Party (SPD-FDP) coalition government in Bonn in 1971-72 did not regard the Soviet Union as a status quo power any longer, as it had in 1969-70. Soviet power during the 1970s was perceived as a threat because Soviet armaments grew faster than a moderate Soviet defense policy would have required. Western elites were troubled by a Soviet Union that had become an equal superpower and had changed status from a continental to a genuine world power. Although Soviet armaments are perceived as a threat, only a minority feels that war is intended by the Soviet leadership. Only 10 percent of foreign policy experts who were interviewed in the Federal Republic in 1980 suspected that the Soviet Union was planning a war against NATO.[13]

One has to distinguish between overall images which may be favorable or unfavorable and particular aspects of an image which may be more important for the decision-making process than the overall image. The period of detente in the 1970s was a period of looking for ways of cooperation, although the overall image of the Soviet Union had not changed very much. This is in accordance with the findings of Frei and Ruloff "that the East-West system has the nature of a complex system difficult to control." As they describe it the "comprehensive system" has five subsystems:

1. The security subsystem as defined by the balance of defense expenditure and arms deployment;
2. The diplomatic subsystem comprising the structure of cooperative and conflictive interactions;
3. The economic subsystem determined by the structure of exchange and cooperation in the commercial, financial and technological fields;
4. The domestic political and national environment(s) of the states participating in the evolution of East-West relations; and
5. The "bloc" structure subsystem.

All these five subsystems evolve in the absence of any coordination and, without control of any overarching logic, the processes advance with different rhythm. In the diplomatic subsystem changes can occur within a few months. The observed cycles in diplomatic climate have phase lengths of three or four years. In contrast, major shifts in defense policies require between five years and a decade. Time is running at different speeds in the various subsystems.[14]

Sources of Images

This leads us to our second and third points: the sources of an image and the nexus between an image and political behavior. It is a truism that every perception of the outside world is determined by external stimuli as well as by internal factors.[15] And it is another truism that the amount of information available when perceiving any ally or enemy is variable but always limited. One of the basic problems in dealing with the Soviet Union is the lack of information which we have at our disposal, not in the sense of knowing nothing but of having to rely on a few sources only. The Soviet leadership still has the mentality of a beleaguered people in the fortress of Communism. This results in an extremely poor communication system within the Soviet Union and even poorer towards the outside world. The initial response to the breakdown of the nuclear power station of Chernobyl is a striking example. A normal interest in the free flow of information might not be accepted by the Soviet authorities. "The more you dig, the more you draw suspicion onto yourself."[16]

Due to the restrictive information policy of the Soviet government in general, Western observers continually suffer from a severe shortage of information and much remains guesswork. The U.S.S.R. appears to be an impenetrable system. As Charles Bohlen, the American ambassador to the Soviet Union between 1953 and 1957, put it: "No one in the Kremlin would talk to a foreigner in any informative way. We had to read the newspapers carefully, exchange information with other ambassadors, and pick up gossip from American reporters, whom I saw once a week and played poker with regularly."[17] Of course, the lack of information is not the only problem when perceiving a foreign country. Even within alliances such as NATO, severe perception problems arise from time to time, notwithstanding a much better flow of information. But in the Soviet case it is more difficult than in Western countries to find a proper analytical framework for the interpretation of data which are available. Gorbachev's call for *glasnost* has not changed the problem fundamentally, even though it seems to be a promising start.

Internal and External Stimuli

Generally speaking we can say that the incoming information--even if there is no lack of information--does not reflect the entire reality. Every perception tends to be a misperception. Every perception tends to produce an image which is a fragment. If one could compare the image with the reality (which one cannot really do because of the limited amount of information) one could adjust the image of the U.S.S.R. to the Soviet reality. This is one aspect of the problem, the one concerned with the external stimuli. In the historiography of the Cold War and East-West relations in general, the concentration on external stimuli, on the Soviet side of the conflict, rather than the Western behavior in East-West relations, was the first and traditional approach to the East-West conflict.

In contrast, the so-called revisionist school of historians concentrated on internal factors and on Western conflict behavior. The revisionists maintain that the Cold War image of the Soviet Union was determined by American economic interests. Here domestic stimuli rather than external stimuli shaped the West's perception of the Soviet Union. Incoming information was selected and filtered by Western values and interests.

No doubt both approaches have to be combined. After the Second World War the American desire to create the "One World" and the Soviet refusal to be a part of this world can be described as an internal and an external stimulus respectively. This combination of an internal and an external stimulus produced a new image of the Soviet Union and henceforth determined Western perceptions of Soviet policy. To choose another example: the partial identity of interests between the superpowers during the detente period, their antagonistic cooperation, was caused by the perception of the Soviet Union as an equal military power (the main external stimulus in the Western image of the Soviet Union) and by the Western desire to avoid an arms race and to develop trade relations with the Soviet Union.

To put it in more general terms: the process of perception of the outside world is not only an isolated act of cognition by which information is collected and sorted out. Forming an image of the Soviet Union as an enemy or as a partner is always connected with the image of one's own society and interests. Every perception starts from individual beliefs, from collective mentalities, from the observer's political, social and economic system, from circumstances of the domestic and international environment. That explains why decision-makers recommend different solutions for the same problem.

In her recent book on the origins of containment, Deborah Larson suspects: "Had Dean Acheson been president, the United States would have launched the containment policy much sooner." Although U.S. decision-makers "confronted the same 'objective' circumstances and received similar information and analyses of the world situation, "they arrived at Cold War beliefs at different times, by separate paths."[18] In her "psychological explanation" of the beginning of the Cold War, Larson presents a "multilevel explanation of the origins of American Cold War policies, using variables on the level of the international system, domestic politics, and individual policymakers' cognitive processes." By taking into account categories like the international system or domestic politics she warns (in agreement with Jervis' admirable synthesis) of "over-psychologizing" and "psychological reductionism":

> Cognitive psychologists view people as 'information processors' whose behavior is largely determined by the way in which they select, code, store, and retrieve information from the environment. Consequently, a key to understanding individual variability lies in the study of cognitive processes. Still, to explain American Cold War policy entirely by individual policymakers' cognitive processes - ignoring objective U.S.-Soviet conflicts of interest or the imperatives to conflict inherent in the nature of the international system - would be patently reductionist.[19]

Images and Behavior

This brings us to the question: do the decision-makers' perceptions matter? What is the nexus between perception, image and behavior? Every perception process consists of static elements and dynamic elements. Starting from beliefs and all sorts of preconditions, outside stimuli are added and images are formed. This is a highly complex process which never stands still. Images may change or partly change or remain fairly stable. Once an image has been formed the further process of collecting data is narrowed. On the whole, images seem to be of long duration. In the political field, however, unforeseen conflicts arise and decisions have to be reached at short notice. If we simplify the problem and ask which comes first, the image on the one hand or the political conflict and decision on the other hand, we can find both answers. In a recent article Karen Mingst states, in accordance with Kenneth Boulding's pioneering study on *The Image*: "behavior depends on the image. This nexus is vitally important for elite image studies."[20] The opposite opinion, as stated by Daniel Frei, sees the East-West conflict as the result of a conflict of interests, not the result of enemy images on both sides. The conflict produces the enemy image, not the other way around. Frei adds, however, that enemy images intensify the conflict.[21]

Boulding wrote in the 1950s and criticized the immobility of politics due to the Cold War belief system. The negative image of the Soviet Union prevented any flexibility vis-a-vis the Soviet Union. As we know from Holsti's much quoted article on John Foster Dulles[22] there may indeed be a direct connection of image and behavior. A stable and rigid enemy image corresponds to a high degree of tension.

But East-West relations not only know periods of intensified hostility but also of peace initiatives and detente. As we have seen, detente was not brought about by a favorable image of the Soviet Union but by military competition and new developments in the military balance. This in turn resulted in some new aspects within the Soviet image and a certain amount of integrative structure in East-West relations. So we can conclude that one has to distinguish periods of stable and clearly defined relations between East and West, either hostile or friendly, from periods of transition and adjustment. In periods of transition we observe the interaction of political decisions, perceptive processes and long-term belief systems. Future research should be directed to the problem of the interaction between images and political actions. Actors might be driven by beliefs and images or even misperceptions but also by new facts and real conflicts.

A good example is the phase of transition from the anti-Hitler coalition in Second World War to the beginning of the Cold War. Deborah Larson shows quite convincingly that decisions were taken before a stable image had been formed. She calls into question the assumption "that policymakers consciously direct their actions to achieve larger goals." "People frequently behave contrary to their professed beliefs; their convictions are often internally contradictory; and on many important issues they have no stable preconceived notions whatsoever."[23] "The change in U.S. policy-makers' beliefs was gradual and ragged. There was no neat turning point."[24] Only *after* the formation of the Cold War belief system did the image determine the policy.

Conclusion

This paper has been mainly concerned with perceptive processes and the interaction between images and political actions. One of its basic assumptions is that it is impossible to perceive any reality in an "objective" way. Of course, this is true also with respect to the Soviet reality. Strictly speaking, any perception is misperception because our information is limited and because image-forming and decision-making necessarily go beyond this limited amount of information. It may be that our assessment of the Soviet Union changes although the Soviet Union itself does not change. Or the assessment remains unchanged whereas Soviet policy does change. If we cannot avoid misperceptions altogether we can try to avoid distortions and illusions. How can this be achieved?

To my mind there is one principal answer, and based on this there are suggestions how to move in the right direction by little steps. The principal answer is that one has to control very carefully the selection process when filtering incoming information. One must not leave out information which seems contrary to one's belief system. One has to separate one's own definition of interests from the assessment of Soviet moves. Instead of relying too much on internal factors and stimuli one should try to understand the other side in order to assess external stimuli adequately.

Hand in hand with this basic effort there are numerous practical steps which are conceivable. I mention only some of them. We should not look for simplistic solutions, for instance by dividing the world between "Goodies" and "Baddies".

We should explicitly and consciously rule out enemy images as instruments in our conflict behavior. At the same time we must not have any illusions of harmonization or convergence between the liberal West and the communist East. We should have a clear idea of the conflicting interests. We have to live with this conflict and to endure its tensions. But knowing one's adversary must not result in denouncing him as the arch-enemy.

We should keep in mind that our image of the Soviet Union is of relevance not only to our own attitudes and policies but also to the Soviet image of the West. Overdrawing the Soviet threat and using our threat perception for home consumption and armament programs must have an enormous impact on the Soviet leadership and their perception of Western strategies.

Western elites should try to help the Soviet leadership to feel less insecure and threatened. Western politicians seem to be in a better psychological position to deal with the security dilemma in East-West relations. At any rate Western economic and technological superiority should not be used to goad the Soviets.

We should stop evaluating the Soviet Union by Western standards. We do not have to accept any aspects of the Soviet value system but in order to avoid disappointments and frustrations we should be familiar with their values. Especially we should be aware of different languages in the East and the West. Key terms like "peaceful coexistence," "balance of power" or "democracy" have totally different meanings. From the Yalta Declaration on Liberated Europe to the Helsinki Conference on European Security runs the story of conflicting concepts and misunderstandings. We have to accept these conflicting concepts. In our age of nuclear warfare the Western idea that freedom and peace are indivisible is not true any longer in a global sense. It is true only for the Western world.

These principles and practical suggestions will not end the East-West conflict. But they can help to overcome a Cold-War confrontation and aim for a resolution of this conflict — in contrast to all experience in the history of international affairs — short of war. A sober perception of the Soviet Union is no guarantee for eternal peace but rather a necessary precondition for progress in world politics and for replacing war by other means of competition.

In a book which gives evidence of the combined efforts of American and German scholars, it seems appropriate to conclude with a quotation from the intellectual memoirs of a German-born American political scientist, John Herz's book *Vom Überleben* which he wrote and published in German. Herz maintains that we have to think in our adversary's categories. We have to practice the virtue of empathy: "This means, among other things, that we must learn to understand our adversary's ways of thinking and to put ourselves into his position, because we cannot permit him to do something that might doom not only himself but all of us."[25]

Notes

1. D. Yergin, *Shattered Peace: The Origins of Cold War and the National Security State* (Boston: Houghton Mifflin, 1977) p. 163.

2. See for instance R. E. Kanet, ed., *The Behavioral Revolution and Communist Studies* (New York/London, 1971); V. Gransow, *Konzeptionelle Wandlungen der Kommunismusforschung* (Frankfurt/New York, 1980); A.v. Borcke and G. Simon, *Neue Wege der Sowjetunion-Forschung* (Baden-Baden: Nomos Verlagsgesellschaft, 1980); W. Welch, *American Images of Soviet Foreign Policy: An Inquiry into Recent Appraisals from the Academic Community* (New Haven/London, 1970); M. Light, "Approaches to the Study of Soviet Foreign Policy," *Review of International Studies* 7 (1981) pp. 127-143.

3. This remains true in spite of various penetrating studies like H. Adomeit, *Soviet Risk-Taking and Crisis Behavior: A Theoretical and Empirical Analysis* (London: George Allen & Unwin, 1982).

4. On this see G. Niedhart, ed., *Der Westen und die Sowjetunion: Einstellungen und Politik gegenüber der UdSSR in Europa und in den USA seit 1917* (Paderborn: F. Schöningh, 1983); W. Link, *East-West Conflict: The Organization of International Relations in the 20th Century* (Leamington Spa: Berg Publishers, 1985).

5. For an excellent summary of recent research see J. Foschepoth, ed., *Kalter Krieg und Deutsche Frage: Deutschland im Widerstreit der Mächte 1945-1952* (Göttingen/Zürich: Vandenhoeck & Ruprecht, 1985).

6. Quoted in J. Foschepoth, "Britische Deutschlandpolitik zwischen Jalta und Potsdam," *Vierteljahreshefte fur Zeitgeschichte* 30 (1982) p. 675.

7. P. G. Boyle, "The British Foreign Office View of Soviet-American Relations 1945-46," *Diplomatic History 3* (1979) p. 313.

8. For recent research on the perception of power in Europe after the Second World War see the papers of an international conference with British, French, Italian and German participants: J. Becker and F. Knipping, eds., *Power in Europe? Great Britain, France, Italy and Germany in a Postwar World 1945-1950* (Berlin/New York: de Gruyter, 1986).

9. D. Schössler, *Militär und Politik: Das Sowjetunionbild in der sicherheitspolitischen Analyse* (Koblenz: Bernard & Graefe, 1983) pp. 182-183.

10. On this controversial matter see A. Stent, *From Embargo to Ostpolitik: The Political Economy of West German-Soviet Relations 1955-1980* (Cambridge: Cambridge Uniersity Press, 1981); H.-D. Jacobsen, *Die Ost-West-Wirtschaftsbeziehungen als deutch-amerikanisches Problem* (Baden-Baden: Nomos Verlagsgesellschaft, 1986); C. Wörmann, *Osthandel als Problem der Atlantischen Allianz* (Bonn: Eurpopa Union Verlag, 1986).

11. See for instance R. J. Pranger, "Six U.S. Perspectives on Soviet Foreign Policy Intentions," *AEI Foreign Policy and Defense Review 1* (1979) No. 5.

12. A. Richman, "The U.S. Image Under Stress: Trends and Structure of Foreign Attitudes toward the United States," in C. W. Kegley and P. J. McGowan, eds., *Challenges to America: United States Foreign Policy in the 1980's* (Beverly Hills/London: Sage, 1979) p. 228.

13. Schössler, op. cit., pp. 180-181.

14. D. Frei and D. Ruloff, *East-West Relations Vol. 1: A Systematic Survey* (Cambridge, Mass: Oelgeschlager, Gunn & Hain, 1983) p. 280.

15. Much has been published on this problem. I refer only to R. Jervis, *Perception and Misperception in International Politics* (Princeton: Princeton University Press, 1976) and to the introduction in E. R. May, ed., *Knowing One's Enemies: Intelligence Assessment Before the Two World Wars* (Princeton, 1984).

16. Nicholas Daniloff after his release from prison in Moscow. *New York Times*, September 15, 1986.

17. C. E. Bohlen, *Witness to History 1929-1969* (New York, 1973) p. 343.

18. D.W. Larson, *Origins of Containment: A Psychological Explanation* (Princeton: Princeton University Press, 1985) p. x.

19. Ibid. On many aspects of this problem see the useful survey by P. E. Tetlock, "Psychological Advice on Foreign Policy: What do we have to contribute?" *American Psychologist* 41 (1986) pp. 557-567.

20. K. A. Mingst, "National Images in International Relations: Structure, Content and Source," *Coexistence* 21 (1984) p. 187.

21. D. Frei, *Assumptions and Perceptions in Disarmament* (New York: United Nations Publications, 1984).

22. O. R. Holsti, "The Belief System and National Images: A Case Study," *Journal of Conflict Resolution* 6 (1962) pp. 244-252.

23. Larson, op. cit., p. 13.

24. Ibid, p. 341.

25. J. H. Herz, *Vom Überleben: Wie ein Weltbild entstand. Autobiographie* (Düsseldorf: Droste Verlag, 1984) p. 183. Professor Herz was so kind to give an English translation of this sentence in a letter to the author of 7th July 1986. Furthermore, I am grateful to Bill Woodward (University of New Hampshire, Durham) for support when I wrote the English version of this paper.

2

Learning in East-West Relations: The Superpowers as Habit-Driven Actors

James N. Rosenau

Three unrelated anecdotes suggest the central theme of the ensuing analysis:

(1) Seymour Hersh's recent book on the downing of KAL-007, *The Target is Destroyed*, provides convincing evidence that American intelligence chiefs and top policymakers immediately concluded, on the basis of incomplete transcripts and evidence, that the Soviet Union had knowingly fired on the passenger plane and that they reached this conclusion in spite of an initial assessment by Air Force intelligence that the attack was based on a succession of Soviet blunders, including a failure to identify the plane.

(2) The Soviet studies program at Emory University picks up and tapes Soviet TV broadcasts, including one of a press conference in Moscow held by Marshal Ogarkov to assert the Soviet perspective on the incident. At one point a questioner asked, "I'd like to inquire into a moral dimension of what happened. Suppose there had been some 2,000 rather than some 200 passengers on the plane, would it have been shot down?" The Marshall turned away from the audience and whispered something to the translator

An earlier version of this paper was presented at the Annual Meeting of the International Studies Association, Washington, D.C., April 18, 1987. I am grateful to Ole R. Holsti, Michael Intriligator, Joseph S. Nye, William Potter, and Pauline Vaillancourt for critical reactions to earlier drafts. Thanks go too to the Institute for Transnational Studies for its support.

before turning back to the microphone and replying, in effect, "I don't respond to hypothetical questions." By turning up the volume on their equipment, the scholars at Emory were subsequently able to hear what he said to the translator. He said, "Why would anyone want to put 2,000 people on an airplane to carry out a spy mission!"

(3) A recent column by conservative author William Safire summarizes his reactions to a four-hour conversation he had in Geneva with counterparts from the Soviet media during the 1985 Summit conference.[1] Stressing that he went into the meeting convinced that Soviet leaders are verbally manipulative and deceptive as they disguise their real purposes behind Marxist rhetoric, Safire relates that after vigorous debate they could "find little agreement on anything," the upshot being that "I have come to this conclusion: *They really believe all this stuff*—just as fiercely as I believe what I know to be the truth...I think they suffer not a twinge of conscience about abuse of dissidents; they in turn consider my notions of democracy absurd...I am now willing to concede that they may not be self-deceiving liars and hypocrites, but are the patriotic product of their upside-down world."

The first two of these incidents express the power of culture and habit, the rote way in which people on both sides of the relationship respond to the other. The third suggests a capacity for change, a trace of the possibility that even the most habitual actors are capable of revising their orientations through new experience. This two-to-one ratio against change is more pessimistic than the ensuing inquiry. Here I argue that the last anecdote is expressive of a potential for systemic transformation that, with time, may overwhelm the systemic inertia depicted in the first two anecdotes.

The Analyst As Critic

To assert a central theme by quantifying anecdotes, of course, is not to establish either its viability or its validity. On the contrary, such a speculative contrast highlights the need to think more systematically about the underlying dynamics of superpower relations. And the need is urgent. The rapid-fire series of events that began with General Secretary Mikhail Gorbachev's accession to power and that has continued through the Geneva summit, Chernobyl, the Daniloff affair, glasnost, Sakharov's release, Reykjavik, the Iran-Contra weakening of the

Reagan presidency, and the Soviet offer on medium-range weapons testifies to dynamics inherent in the superpower relationship that elude
easy comprehension.

Both sides have long been mired in self-perpetuating hostility,
based on elaborate belief systems in which the other is deeply embedded
as the prime threat to a secure and prosperous future. Nonetheless, the
possibility remains that all is not hopeless, that there is much at work in
the relationship which is encouraging and likely to undergo improvement in the future.[2] Such is the thrust of what follows.

The following analysis seeks to develop a perspective in which both
American and Soviet officials and publics are seen as learning entities
whose habit-driven behavior is open to change, perhaps even to a
measure of rationality that allows for convergence around shared interests. Much as the rational-actor model serves the heuristic purpose of
facilitating insights into the underlying nature of bargaining situations,
so does the habit-driven model offer a heuristic approach: that of grasp-
ing how new learning may be transforming old predispositions in a
world revolutionized by a dynamic microelectronic technology.

The Need For Theory

The problems posed by East-West relations suffer from a lack of
theorizing. There is no dearth of information on the various facets of
the subject; nor is there a lack of innovative research tools for exploring
the deeper processes at work in the relationship; and there is certainly
no scarcity of observers eager to probe each and all of these processes.
Indeed, so much has been written about the big issues of our time—
about war and peace, about conflict and cooperation, about East-West
tensions—that it can readily seem fruitless to undertake still another effort to probe such matters. Recent decades have witnessed such substantial progress on the part of social scientists toward unraveling the
bases and processes through which perceptions and misperceptions unfold, the values and mechanisms through which publics resist or
respond to the mobilization efforts of leaders, the interactive stimuli
and reinforcements through which tensions escalate and wane—to mention but a few of the relevant dynamics underlying the Soviet-American
relationship.

So social scientists might justifiably argue that East-West tensions
are not a problem of insufficient understanding, but of politicians and
citizens applying the newly-developed knowledge and adjusting their
goal-seeking energies to the constraints and opportunities inherent in
what is now known about individual and group behavior in the First and

Second Worlds. Yet, we who study human affairs cannot rest on our laurels. There is always more to learn. More importantly in the case of Soviet-American relations, there are conceptual jails to storm, entrapping formulations to escape, obsolete models to revise. We are so locked into negative theories of the relationship that we may be blind to the many ways in which a rapidly changing world is altering its foundations. This is why it seems startling to search the relationship for its positive potential.

Such theorizing serves as a counter-intuitive method for stepping aside and assessing whether our conceptual homes are located in jails or open spaces. To seek to demonstrate the positive potential in East-West relations is to meet a prime criterion of science, that of organizing the analysis around the rejection of a null hypothesis. In this case, the null hypothesis is that the superpower relationship is hopelessly mired in stalemate and incapable of change and improvement.

Notwithstanding all the progress in uncovering how cognitive processes and escalatory dynamics sustain and shape global conflicts, evolving technologies and capabilities may give rise to alterations in the value of key variables, thus requiring us to update our understanding of the structure of superpower relations. Our hard-won knowledge about the relationship is subject to obsolescence unless we continuously monitor the forces that may be transforming it as the pace of change quickens.

In short, the task is not fruitless. There is still much ground to cover and good, urgent reasons to theorize about the big issues yet again. Politicians need assistance in coping with change, in adjusting to new dynamics and to the possibility that their long-standing beliefs about the world need to be updated and refined if they are to make the most of Soviet-American relations.

The Habit-Driven Actor Model

To negotiate a break from a conceptual jail one has to have some notion of what one is trying to escape, what routes can lead to freedom, and what one wants to accomplish once the prison walls are left behind. That is, what are the core elements of the theories that are entrapping us, what organizing premises should replace them, and what propositions should the new, jailbreaking theories enable us to test? Specifically, what underlying models are locking us into a negative view of Soviet-American relations, what alternative perspective will allow us to discern the possible presence of positive trends, and what conclusions would allow us to revise the null hypothesis that the superpower relationship lacks a potential for improvement?

Let us start by indicating what needs to be demonstrated for the null hypothesis to be rejected. A rejection would be in order if it could be shown that East-West relations are undergoing change in the direction of both sides accepting the complexity of their relationship and converging around the rules that sustain and contain it. If each side is ever more capable of perceiving the dynamics that move the other, then that signifies an openness to the dynamics that mark global life in the waning years of the century. For a greater capacity to see the world through the other's eyes—to perceive its officials as aware of the limits to their own actions and to conceive of its publics as able to assess new information—paves the way for regarding the other's actions as legitimate. And to be ever more able to cast the adversary in a context of legitimacy is to create the potential for meaningful dialogue and the eventual containment, if not the amelioration, of disputes.

What would justify rejection of the null hypothesis, in short, is not the reconciliation of East-West differences or even attempts along these lines. For the relationship is a conflict-ridden one and it is likely to be marred by major disputes as far as one can anticipate into the future. But, still, a positive trend line can be expected to ensue if it can be shown that the rules governing the relationship are undergoing revision consistent with the complexity and interdependence that has come to characterize global life.

Two models—one that posits a rational, calculative actor and another that presumes a closed actor responsive to historic precedents—constitute the conceptual jails that prevent us from evaluating whether the rules governing the superpower relationship are susceptible to transformation. Those who rely on the rational actor model posit both U.S. and Soviet officials as deeply committed to goals rejected by the other, as highly conscious that the other needs to be thwarted in the pursuit of its goals, and keenly aware of the need to be cool and calculative in determining each move directed at the other. From the perspective of this rational model, the relationship is seen as a zero-sum game in which conciliatory actions are understood to be insincere deception, propaganda ploys, and/or outright bluffs. The other side, in other words, is perceived as endlessly clever in its relentless efforts to prevail.

In what might be called the historical-precedent model, the leaders of each superpower see the other not as clever and calculating, but as locked in by strategic circumstances, ideological rigidities, and power realities that continue to feed a deep reservoir of distrust which, in turn, precludes mutual understanding and accommodation. From this perspective, the superpower relationship is not so much a game as it is an inevitable collision of two powerful streams of historical development.

Although the two models can lead to different interpretations of why either superpower acts to contest the other in particular ways, they share an inability to account for change. In both cases, the dynamics of post-industrial societies and the microelectronic revolution are not seen as challenges to the predispositions of Soviet or American officials. Rather, both models assume that the elites on each side employ either their rational or historical perspectives in such a way as to interpret the dynamics of change as merely reinforcing their presumptions about the orientations of the other. Neither model allows for the officials of either superpower to reconsider whether their long-standing postures are increasingly inappropriate. That a leader of either side should pull a "Sadat" and break sharply with conventional animosity is utterly beyond the premises of either model. Risk, subtle hints of possible accommodation, acknowledgments of erroneous assumptions, trends toward shared rules of conduct—these are not viable options in either the rational or historical models. It is in this sense of not allowing for change that most prevailing models of U.S.-Soviet relations constitute conceptual jails. There may be considerable validity inherent in both the rational and historical perspectives, but through their reinforcement mechanisms they are nevertheless incarcerating, leaving us with no way of escaping from the implications of our underlying assumptions.

If we are destined to fail in pursuing the rational and historical routes to a jailbreak, what alternative paths to conceptual freedom are available? The answer developed here is a model of public affairs that lies between the dictates of rationality and those of history. For want of a better label, I shall call it "the habit-driven actor" model.[3] It assumes that officials and publics are not locked into the requirements of either rationality or historical precedent. Instead actors are conceived to be open to new learning—and thus to change—even as they are primarily driven by a tendency to undertake the same behavior as they did previously in the same context.[4]

Before elaborating on how a capacity for change can be embedded in habit, let us note that the habits which drive behavior are viewed as a composite—a habit pool, as it were, which is fed and sustained by all the diverse wellsprings of human experience. That is, decision makers and citizens strive for goals and respond to challenges in habitual ways, by which is meant that combination of past experiences, memories, beliefs, personality, role expectations, and cognitive styles to which they have long been accustomed. Depending on how these bases of behavior combine to make each act like the previous one in the same context, habit-driven actors can be flexible or rigid, innovative or conventional, defiant or compliant, power-oriented or self-sacrificing, calculative or impulsive, complex or simple—but whatever the quality and direction of their behavior, it springs from a readiness to respond to situations in a characteristic, familiar, and repetitive fashion.

This is not to say that habit-driven actors never seek to act rationally or that they never get deeply locked into historical patterns. Quite the opposite may be the case. If their customary way of getting from one moment to the next involves a careful framing of alternatives, a systematic gathering of information, a deliberative cost-benefit analysis, and a self-conscious assessment of feedback from prior decisions, then they resemble closely the prototype of the rational-actor model. Likewise, if they are used to living by the rules and conforming to the patterns of the past, then their behavior will parallel that posited by the historical-precedent model. Conceptually, however, both rational and historical actors are but a subspecies of the habit-driven family, variants that have become habituated to relying on either counter-intuitive methods or precedent-affirming routines to cope with the distortions of memory, the compulsions of personality, the biases of beliefs, the inflexibility of role expectations, and the constraints of cognitive style.

Few would quarrel with the proposition that empirically no individual manages fully to offset all the components of habit, and that rational and historical actors are only ideal types, with the result that the behavior of even the most extreme of either type is always habit-driven to some degree. In the real world, that is, the interest-maximizing conduct of rational actors and the routine-conforming responses of historical actors is but one dimension of their habit-driven nature. The other dimensions originate with either internal stimuli that can throw rational calculations off course or external stimuli that can divert historical precedents, leaving Russians and Americans alike as neither rational nor rote in their ways of filtering and interpreting the external world. As will be seen, it is here, in the vulnerabilities of rational- and precedent-bound actors, that Soviet-American relations are conceived to unfold in a learning rather than a constant context.

It is important to stress that habit-driven actors are not conceived to be equivalent to the nonrational actor. By definition they can never achieve perfect rationality, but the concept of a habit-driven actor is not merely a residual category for all behavior which is other than rational or rote. Whereas nonrationality can involve impetuous, erratic, spontaneous, and other forms of inconsistent behavior, the habit-driven actor concept posits specified and consistent dynamics that are anything but impetuous or random. On the contrary, a person's habits have normally worked in the past and served well the task of overcoming challenges. So there are good reason to be comfortable as a habit-driven actor and, as such, to eschew capricious behavior.

It follows that while different habits drive people to engage in different forms of behavior, in each case the action is a product of systematic antecedents that render probable a high correspondence with the prior act in the same context. Thus, for example, the tendencies of officials include the habits of leadership, which may be different from the habits of followership to which citizens are accustomed; but both the rulers and the ruled share the tendency to proceed from a well-established base of prior memories, beliefs, expectations, personality needs, and the like. Both act as they always have to maintain (or, in the case of dissenters and rebels, to disrupt) the equilibrium of the systems in which their actions have consequence.

It must be emphasized that the habit-driven model is not confined to single individuals. The habit-driven actor can also be a collectivity if analysis is cast at a macro level. Indeed, in a world of habit-driven individuals, collectivities and their organizations are bound to conduct their affairs through habitual processes that draw on the collective memories, beliefs, and cognitive styles which have accumulated across time. A central purpose of organizations, in fact, is precisely that of concerting effort so that outputs are consistent (i.e., habitual). To be sure, bureaucracies also design their decision-making activities with a view to maximizing rationality and the prospects of achieving their goals; but like individuals, they never have sufficient information and must perforce rely on habitual procedures to resolve their differences over goals and the meaning of the available information. Thus does it become possible to conceive of the world as dominated by habit-driven nation-states, each of which is so locked into its own history, geography, and socioeconomic circumstances as to respond in characteristic ways to events abroad. Likewise, each maintains a policy-making organization that aggregates the habits and seeks to insure (through foreign policies) that the responses are consistent with prior experiences and underlying circumstances.

Whether the focus is on individual Americans or Russians or on their respective collectivities, habit-driven actors do not draw on the same characteristics to respond to all situations. There may be some tendencies that are common to all responses, but for the most part the wellsprings of habit are conceived to be at least moderately differentiated, with some habitual behavior being appropriate to one set of circumstances while other habits are relevant to other contexts. One relies, for example, on different memories, traits, expectations, and beliefs when circumstances require action as a leader than when the situation calls for being led. To some extent, in other words, habits are derivatives of systems and their repeated performance in a systemic context helps to sustain that system.

Accounting for Change

To stress the continuities embedded in habit pools is to pose the problem of how the habit-driven actor model accounts for change. In a world of actors predisposed to repeat past patterns, how can fundamental transformations ever unfold? Are not habit-driven actors as locked into their orientations as tightly as rational and historical actors are imprisoned by theirs? The answer to this last question is crucial to the analysis that follows: no, in the habit-driven model individuals and collectivities are conceived to be capable of change even though the combination of memories, traits, expectations, and beliefs that guide them are deeply rooted sources of their behavior. Unlike their rational and historical counterparts, habit-driven actors are open to new stimuli. Some are more open than others for a variety of reasons, but none is so closed as to be immune to internal or external stimuli. They may be essentially comfortable with their habit pools, but they are not so fully content as to prevent new inputs. Why? Because among their habits is a readiness to learn from experience and to acquire new skills that may, in turn, facilitate further learning. This readiness may consist of no more than a latent tendency—a normally quiescent personality trait, a discrepant memory trace, an unresolved past experience, an unexplored flexibility in role expectations, a cultural ambiguity, or any of a number of other habit components that are vulnerable to contradiction. But whatever its origins, the readiness to learn is part of an actor's habit pool and, as such, is susceptible to activation under certain conditions. It may require stimuli on the scale of powerful trauma—such as a Pearl Harbor or a crisis over missiles in Cuba—but at some point even the most habitual actor is at least minimally open to reorientation.

Be they officials or citizens, Western or Eastern, individuals or collectivities, in other words, actors are conceived as learners and not as constants on the world scene. As learning entities, they can never fully succeed in cutting off all feedback that runs counter to their orientations. Being open to learning, they are thus capable of changing. This can occur in either of two ways: (1) when external stimuli are so startlingly new as to jolt their habitual modes and foster new patterns more appropriate to the evolving circumstances; or (2) when they develop, internally, new skills, capabilities, and/or responsibilities to a point where the old, habitual ways begin to give way. Externally-induced habit change is exemplified by the adjustments that follow the termination of international wars, while the consequences of the microelectronic revolution for the analytic capabilities of people and publics are illustrative of internally-induced habit change.[5] When basic change does occur, of course, the external and internal stimuli of it are interactive and reinforcing. Together they eventually produce new characteristic modes of coping with the problems that, in time, then evolve as new habit-driven forms of conduct.

East-West Tensions In a Learning Context

Viewed from the perspective of the habit-driven actor model, let us now probe the Soviet-American relationship for points at which old modes may be subject to alteration in response to developments within both societies and in the structure and processes of global life. Having indicated the goal of breaking out of the conceptual jails that house rational- and precedent-bound actors through an escape route populated by habit-driven officials and publics, we can now specify more precisely what would constitute encouraging indicators of change in the relationship. It will be recalled that rejection of the null hypothesis becomes feasible if it can be shown that Soviet-American relations are moving in the direction of both sides accepting the complexity of their relationship and converging around the rules that sustain and contain it.

At least twelve indicators seem worthy of exploration for evidence of new learning that could facilitate an acceptance of new relational rules. Taken together, the ensuing list of indicators makes clear that something more is meant by convergént rules of the game than a shared recognition that nuclear war is unthinkable and that processes leading to it must be cut off. The notion of new relational rules is not cast simply at the level of a hotline between the Kremlin and the White House (though such direct, institutionalized mechanisms are not precluded). Nor does it resemble the theory of détente which, as one observer has stressed, "overlooks some of the persisting and fundamental incompatibilities between Western and communist societies and contains overly optimistic assumptions about the effects of communication on behavior."[6] Rather, these relational rules involve complex, indirect, and perceptual predispositions as well as explicit goals and institutionalized mechanisms,[7] predispositions which may not be fully recognized by their carriers but which may nevertheless underlie superpower encounters in the Third World, actions in the other power's sphere of influence, trade and financial interactions, etc. What follows is far from a thorough listing of possible indicators, but it is suggestive of the broad range in which learning can occur in international relationships:

1. *More frequent fluctuations in opinions.* Shifts of this sort would indicate a flexibility that allows for reacting to the other side in terms of its behavior rather than in terms of fixed ideological precepts.

2. *The frequency of objections to particular actions by the other side diminishes with the passage of time.* Such a habit can evolve only as the rules of the relationship become looser and inhibit the accumulation of grievances that linger as ideological rhetoric. Greater agreement on the rules of the relationship, in other words, allows the other side to undertake actions that once would have been considered so outrageous as to be quickly incorporated into the litany of hostility.

3. *The tendency to bargain simultaneously over different issues in different fora expands, or at least does not contract.* This tendency can survive only if the process rules of the relationship take precedence over those pertaining to substantive issues, since otherwise arguments about a single issue could spill over into other issue areas and bring bargaining in the latter to a halt. The greater the habitual sensitivity to issue-area boundaries, in other words, the more are both sides likely to be accepting of the dynamics that move the other.

4. *A growing habit of openly stressing that some actions of the other side consist of posturing, that they are bargaining positions rather than actual plans, and that they are thus publicly expected to change after both sides have played out the bargaining scenario.* Such a pattern of positing the adversary as engaging in ploys amounts to a tacit acknowledgment that the rules of the relationship are as subject to game theoretical considerations as to the goals that underlie policies. More than that, to accept publicly such bargaining arrangements is to recognize that the game is of a nonzero sum nature, since bargaining is impossible in a zero-sum game, and that its payoffs are a reflection of the rules of play as well as the intensity and compatibility of the goals sought.

5. *A pattern wherein both sides increasingly accuse the other of acting to please public opinion.* To make such accusations is to accept that the relationship springs from domestic as well as international roots and that its rules, being enmeshed in societal processes, are neither transitory nor superficial.

6. *A diminished inclination to complain that the other side is spying or that it is encouraging defections.* A lessening of such

complaints suggests a tolerance for adversarial behavior that serves to further explicate and legitimate the rules of the relationship.

7. *A growing eagerness on the part of the elites to understand their counterparts and to revise their stereotypes.* Such a habit can evolve only if both sides are willing to accept the processes whereby the other side participates in the relationship. Stated differently, such an eagerness is reflective of legitimacy being accorded to the relationship.

8. *An increasing predisposition to express interpretations of each other's internal politics.* To seek or have an understanding of what is transpiring within the adversary is to evolve a capacity to see the world through the eyes of its officials and publics, thereby replacing wariness with acceptance and acknowledging a readiness to conduct the relationship in terms of institutionalized rules rather than ad hoc adjustments.

9. *A decreasing inclination to call for change or upheaval within the other side's sphere of influence.* Such a pattern reflects an attachment of legitimacy to the geographical boundaries of the relationship that, in turn, further legitimizes the rules that govern interaction within it.

10. *More frequent calls for a dialogue about the relationship and the shared problems and threats it subsumes.* The emergence of this habit indicates a growing security with respect to the rules of the relationship and how they can be used to expand its substantive concerns.

11. *A growing tendency on the part of the press of each side to cite identifiable or anonymous sources of the other side as a basis for interpretations.* Such a pattern could evolve only if officials on each side accept the rules of the relationship sufficiently to give off-the-record interviews in which the press of the other side participates.

12. *Traces of a habit in which the officials of each side shows signs of adopting, even copying, the behavior of their counterparts on the other side.* Such a process would further suggest a learning in which the rules of the relationship are so fully understood and accepted as to permit emulation.

It is important to emphasize that while elaborate data relevant to these indicators have not been gathered, each of them is susceptible to systematic inquiry. Several operational measures for each indicator could readily be framed and data sufficient to yield recognizable trends could thus be developed. To be sure, a number of conceptual and empirical difficulties would have to be resolved, but the results would surely justify the effort, both empirically in terms of knowledge about the underlying patterns of Soviet-American relations and theoretically in terms of how habit-driven international relationships may be affected by the dynamics of change presently at work in world politics. For the time being, however, the foregoing indicators must be viewed as a research agenda, with the test of the null hypothesis being confined to some disparate findings and insights that are suggestive but far from conclusive. Indeed, what follows is highly selective in its effort to probe for traces of learning and legitimacy in the habit-driven behavior of American and Soviet actors toward each other.

Testing the Null Hypothesis

Perhaps the most persuasive case for rejecting the null hypothesis can be made by comparing the Soviet-American relationship today with what it was between the end of World War II and Stalin's death in 1953. It does not require much reflection to appreciate that considerable change has occurred with respect to all twelve indicators since 1953 and that all of the change is in the direction of habits which involve a greater acceptance of complexity and legitimacy in the relationship. This is particularly notable for those indicators (#11 and 12) involving access to policy-making institutions. Now, for example, it is commonplace for Western journalists to refer to "reliable" sources within the Soviet policy-making organization as the basis for their accounts from Moscow, whereas in the Stalin years their interpretive efforts were confined largely to comparisons of Politburo seating arrangements at the opera and other ceremonial gatherings as a measure of shifting power alignments and possible policy shifts.[8] Equally indicative, recently high Soviet officials have begun to emulate their American counterparts by holding press conferences with Western journalists in attendance and permitted to ask questions, whereas in the earlier era any access to top leaders was highly problematic.[9] Likewise, Western scholars can now move more freely in their search for information from counterparts and bureaucrats in the Soviet hierarchy,[10] just as Soviet academics are moving more widely in American academic and government circles in their quest for information and patterns.[11] Indeed, these interactions have even reached the point where extensive contacts in Moscow enable American analysts to report at length on how the Soviet "leadership is seriously studying the domestic configuration of American political forces as they bear on foreign policy" and how the several interpretations surfaced in the Soviet deliberations have "yet to yield firm, commonly held conclusions" as to the central tendencies at work in the United States.[12] That Soviet scholars maintain similar contacts in Washington was quite evident during a panel at the 1986 Annual Meeting of the International Studies Association in Anaheim, California, where three of them candidly presented their views of the sources of American foreign policy.

Admittedly, the evolution of these habits permitting a greater availability to the policy-making processes of the other side does not form a smooth upward trend line. As one who spent an isolated week in Moscow trying to establish contacts with unresponsive counterparts who were clearly under orders to avoid interaction with USIA-sponsored speakers in the months following the placement of American missiles in Western Europe, I can testify that downturns, zigzags, and limits continue to mark the pattern depicting the habitual availability of elites to each other. But ragged as the trend line may be, it nonetheless traces an upward slope if viewed across the last three decades. The very fact that USIA officials in Moscow were reflective and tolerant, rather than offended and apoplectic, in the face of curt dismissals of their offers of visiting speakers is itself suggestive of the kind of learning that runs counter to the null hypothesis.

But comparing the present with the Stalin period, it might be argued, is a loaded test of the null hypothesis. Viewed with subsequent hindsight, such an argument would stress, the Stalin era is an anomaly, a time in Soviet development when post-revolutionary consolidation and world war conduced to dictatorial leadership. So it is hardly surprising that once the revolution was secured, superpower status achieved, and the autocratic leader dead, the Soviet system became more available to outsiders and more susceptible to emulating practices elsewhere. Such developments, this line of reasoning would conclude, do not amount to fundamental change: as an international actor the Soviet Union is still very much habituated to inaccessibility and playing by its own rules. In short, to test the null hypothesis it must be shown that practices since Stalin have moved in the anticipated direction. What are needed are not comparisons of 1947 with 1987, but of, say, 1967, 1977, and 1987.

Given an absence of sufficient data for such comparisons, of course, this form of the null hypothesis cannot be refuted. It is theoretically possible that both countries are still locked into their early Cold War rules of international play, and that the foregoing indicators of accessibility are misleading. As Nye stresses, "Not all change is learning."[13] Conceivably the politics, norms, and structures of the Soviet and

American systems have undergone substantial evolution in recent decades without corresponding changes in their handling of their super-power roles.

The nature of social systems and the powerful forces for change unleashed by the microelectronic revolution, however, make such an isolation and constancy of international variables seem highly unlikely. Social systems do not stand still as technology and industrialization introduce profound alterations in the generation and use of information or the way goods are produced and serviced.[14] Moreover, some trend data for the post-Stalin period are available for a few of the indicators (especially #1), and these all point in the direction of newly evolved habits. Poll data on American attitudes toward the U.S.S.R. between 1953 and 1982, for instance, depict considerable fluctuation that parallels the ups and downs in superpower relations and is thus more suggestive of new learning than of ideological rigidity. To be sure, there are impressive correlations which suggest that such shifts derive partly from domestic economic factors.[15] Yet it is equally clear that a goodly proportion of the variability is a response to whatever may be the degree of cordiality or hostility in the relationship at any given time.[16]

At the elite level, too, trend data depict a flexibility indicative of learning impulses rather than ideological precepts. Using a sophisticated measure of cognitive complexity and applying it to official policy statements, Tetlock has uncovered persuasive findings that point to a systematic and close interaction in which American and Soviet complexity levels influence each other.[17] Likewise, data have lately become available that delineate the presence of conflicting belief systems among elites on both sides as to the other's predispositions and goals;[18] in both cases these cleavages appear deep enough to fuel a continuous debate within both American and Soviet elite circles that seems bound to intensify their involvement with each other or otherwise sustain the processes noted above in Indicators #7 and #8. As Zimmerman and Axelrod observe, "If Western policy makers lose sight of the range of views embraced within the Soviet dialogue, their capacity to influence and shape that dialogue—and hence, Soviet policy choices—will be dramatically diminished."[19]

Unfortunately, not even systematic events and content analytic data of the sort developed by Tetlock are available for the other indicators listed above, but six of them (#2, #4, #5, #6, #9, and #10) are straightforward measures that seem plausible on the basis of anecdotal evidence. With the possible exception of Afghanistan (and even here the pattern may be evolving in the predicted direction), few issues linger long on the list of grievances both sides maintain about the other (Indicator #2). Soviet denunciations of new U.S. missiles sites in Western

Europe passed quickly from its verbal agenda, as did U.S. citations of the Soviet downing of the Korean airliner or the incarceration of Daniloff. At the least, the habit of exploiting prior offenses or blunders seems attenuated in comparison to the more vitriolic phases of the relationship in the past. Likewise, the public announcements relative to whether and when to hold a summit meeting appear to be founded on a much more explicit rhetoric of bargaining than ever before (Indicators #4 and 10). Secretary of State George Schultz's recent plea for conducting superpower negotiations privately[20] is an especially direct articulation of how both sides have come to accept that the rules of the relationship, including those that lead to posturing for the purposes of gaining a publicity advantage (Indicator #5). In the same manner, the expanding number of spies being caught (and traded) or defectors being received (or returned) appears to be growing even as the fanfare attached to them seems quite tame in comparison to the past (Indicator #6). No longer does either superpower habitually deny charges of spying, almost as if both acknowledge—and thus accept—that the rules of the relationship permit such behavior. For the same reason it seems probable that a systematic analysis of official statements since the formative years of the postwar relationship would yield the finding that both sides have progressively relinquished the habit of referring to the desirability of change occurring in the other's jurisdiction (Indicator #9).

Finally, while one indicator (#3) focuses on the extremely complex set of interactions through which issue linkages may get fashioned and may thus prove more difficult to measure, the anecdotal evidence again points to a long-term process wherein arms control issues have been sufficiently insulated within the superpower relationship to permit negotiations over them to continue even as the degree of conflict on other issues has been intense and severe. There have been brief moments, of course, when arms control talks were suspended in response to other issues, but one feels secure with the conviction that research would demonstrate an overall habit of keeping the porosity of issue-area boundaries to a minimum.[21] To cite one recent example of the relationship's extensive capacity for habitually maintaining diverse boundaries within which negotiations simultaneously proceed, in the summer of 1986 some thirteen separate sets of talks on nearly two dozen separate issues were in progress with U.S. and Soviet negotiators among those in attendance.[22] Indeed, if it is the case, as some have argued,[23] that the Reagan administration is intent upon undoing the insulation of the arms control area and maximizing issue linkages, such efforts are destined to fail if the analysis of the evolving rules of the superpower relationship developed here is accurate. Viewed from this perspective, it comes as no surprise that the incarceration of Nicholas

Daniloff by the Soviets just prior to the pending Reykjavik summit did not prove as dire as first seemed probable, that last-minute bargains were struck in order to permit convergence in Iceland and thereby preserve the insulation of arms control negotiations.

The Superpowers as Habit-Driven Actors

If this reading of the anecdotal evidence holds up when subjected to systematic inquiry, the future of learning in the superpower relationship presents several intriguing possibilities. One is the likelihood that all the tendencies promoting the acceptance of complex rules governing the relationship will increasingly converge in ever more intense interactions, thus accelerating the pace at which old habits are replaced and new ones evolved that, in turn, further stabilize and legitimize the boundaries of superpower competition. The learning process, in other words, may trace a J-like exponential curve that propels the relationship well beyond its present confines.[24] Second, since both sides know that the learning is occurring and that the habits of legitimacy are deepening, it seems quite unlikely that the direction of the learning curve can be meaningfully reversed. There can be no going back to the earlier premises of a simple strategic-military rivalry once each knows that the other accepts their tensions as rooted in and shaped by the economic, social, and political complexities that mark modern world politics.

Third, and perhaps most intriguing of all, it appears conceivable that among the new components of the habit pool will be an expanding readiness to subordinate short-run, game-theoretical maneuvers to anticipated outcomes of long-term economic, social, political, and international processes.[25] If both sides come to appreciate the internal and external dynamics that constrain the other, if both know the other understands the forces that propel them, if both recognize when the other is engaging in tactical ploys and know that their own tactics are similarly comprehended, if both accept that the other cannot be tricked into major concessions and that they are thus fated to be linked together in an endless competition, and if all this knowledge is further supplemented for both by extensive information derived from a growing capacity for precise aerial photography and detailed electronic spying, then it seems very likely that both superpowers will become habituated to patience, to waiting for long-run national and global forces to unfold, setting the limits of choice and shaping the course of action.

What lies ahead, in short, is a superpower relationship in which the balance between macro processes and micro calculations moves ever more pronouncedly in favor of the former. The perceptions of officials will still be crucial as sources of their behavior, but their perceptual habits will shift from a preoccupation with how counterparts on the other side interpret the world to how the world conditions their interpretations. The leaderships of the U.S. and the Soviet Union will thus become the followers—the implementers, as it were—of the shifting restraints, opportunities, and demands that are inherent in an increasingly interdependent world revolutionized by an explosive microelectronic technology.

At this writing signs of these new habits are everywhere. The inclination to posit one's own choices and those of the adversary as a yielding to, or at least as a prisoner of, macro dynamics has surfaced lately on both sides of the relationship. On the American side the habit has been well articulated by George Kennan, who perceives Soviet leaders as

> a group of troubled men—elderly men, for the most part—whose choices and possibilities are severely constrained. I see these men as prisoners of many circumstances: prisoners of their own past and their country's past; prisoners of the antiquated ideology to which their extreme sense of orthodoxy binds them; prisoners of the rigid system of power that has given them their authority; but prisoners, too, of certain ingrained peculiarities of the Russian statesmanship of earlier ages—the congenital sense of insecurity, the lack of inner self-confidence, the distrust of the foreigner and the foreigner's world, the passion for secrecy, the neurotic fear of penetration by other powers into areas close to their borders, and a persistent tendency, resulting from all these other factors, to overdo the creation of military strength.[26]

But Kennan has long advanced this perspective and what is new are signs of the habit being acquired by officials who have tended to ignore macro dynamics as a source of Soviet behavior and, instead, have attributed it to a quest for expanded power. Recently, for example, traces of the emergent habit have been evident in:

— the confident expectations of U.S. officials that their Soviet counterparts would eventually return to the arms control talks after quitting in November, 1983, over the placement of U.S. missiles in Western Europe;

— the equally confident reasoning as to why they would agree to a summit meeting in 1986 on U.S. terms;[27]

— Secretary of State Schultz's speech about possible long-run consequences of the microelectronic revolution and how it faced the Soviet Union and its allies with "an agonizing choice: They can either open their societies to the freedoms necessary for the pursuit of technological advance, or they can risk falling farther behind the West";[28]

— President Reagan's message to Congress on "Freedom, Regional Security and Global Peace," where he observed that "there are reasons to think that the present time is especially propitious for raising doubts on the Soviet side about the wisdom of its client ties" and that "there is no time in which Soviet policy reviews and reassessments are more likely than in a succession period, especially when many problems have been accumulated for some time";[29]

— a subsequent press conference when the President was asked .whether public denunciations of him by Gorbachev were "in the spirit of Geneva" and answered that his post-Geneva communications with Gorbachev had all been cordial and that "maybe he [Gorbachev] was speaking to a different audience at that time";[30]

— and a report on the attitudes of high U.S. officials that quoted them as citing a number of long-term factors which were turning "the dynamism" in world affairs behind the U.S. and had the Soviets "on the run."[31]

For the Soviets, of course, the inclination to ascribe causation to macro forces is a habit of long standing. It can even be viewed as the core habit of the Marxist/Leninist paradigm, a guide to the analysis of class and the flow of historical materialism. Nevertheless, traces of change in the habit as presently practiced in the Kremlin are discernible. There is some evidence of a tendency to differentiate among the macro forces seen relevant as sources of U.S. conduct. Now, for example, Soviet analysts are apparently drawing distinctions between different types of American conservatives, rather than lumping them all together as the military-industrial complex.[32] Such a tendency has even surfaced in a nationally-televised Gorbachev speech in which his expressed concern that Reagan was "unable to cope" with his right-wing "entourage," to keep "the 'hawks' in the White House in check," appears to have underlain a calculation that by calling for a quick summit meeting in Iceland he could by-pass the Washington bureaucracy.[33] In short, where the habit was once a simple process of ascribing causation to macro forces, now it may be undergoing transformation to one of seeking causation in such phenomena. Such a change is entirely consistent with the stress here on new learning that allows for the acceptance of complexity as an underlying condition of East-West relations.

Obstacles to Learning

Learning is not a linear process. Even as new predispositions evolve, so do old ones remain tenacious, parading an endless array of stimuli that can divert or arrest the readiness to learn afresh. This clash between historic patterns and current alternatives is a source of continuous tension for habit-driven actors, and nothing in the foregoing analysis is intended to suggest that either side in the superpower relationship has so fully broken with the past as to sustain their learning curves unconstrained by earlier orientations. Both sides still maintain obstacles that partially block the arteries through which new stimuli enter their habit pools.

Perhaps the most notable constraints are those embedded in ideology. Ideology and learning are antithetical. They offset each other, such that the more narrow and rigid ideological precepts are, the more is the habit pool closed to change. At its most tenacious, anti-learning best, ideology can intrude a rigidity upon the superpower relationship that prevents both sides from recognizing change in the other, that inhibits their readiness to insulate issue-areas, or that otherwise curbs all twelve of the tendencies noted above as conducing to legitimacy and stability in the relationship.

That ideology continues to limit learning in the superpower relationship can be readily demonstrated. On the Eastern side, the inclination to ascribe causation to macro dynamics is still so strong that "Soviet analysts have been blind to the impact of Soviet conduct on outcomes...they have concentrated entirely on the domestic and historical determinants of their adversary's policies and ignored the effects of their own actions on shaping those policies."[34] In effect, engaging the Soviets as rational actors who calculate moves in response to prior and anticipated moves is extremely difficult because they continue to be habituated to macro-level orientations.

On the American side, too, traces of ideological blocks to learning can be identified. Bunce, for example, examined U.S. public attitudes toward the Soviet Union across the 1948-1985 period and found evidence of increased polarization and ideological cleavage since 1974.[35] Similarly, studies of American elites between 1976 and 1984 have turned up "a dominant pattern [in 1984]...of substantial ideological and partisan polarization on a broad spectrum of questions."[36]

By way of preserving the focus on the potentials of the superpower relationship, however, it must also be noted that if the contents and dynamics of ideology are put into a context of habit formation, maintenance, and attenuation, it becomes possible to conceive of ideology as a rhetorical habit co-existing with the habits underlying the acceptance of complexity and legitimacy in the relationship. To be sure, such rhetoric is not random. It does express underlying orientations, or at least it is unlikely to be totally divorced from behavior. But neither are the two necessarily identical. Behavior has its roots in a number of orientations, drawing as it were on the habit pool in different ways as concerns and conditions shift. Thus can the habits of ideology and learning co-exist, if not easily, at least sufficiently to allow for unacknowledged changes in response to new stimuli.

Hints of such a co-existence can be discerned in the fact that the rhetoric of the Soviet leadership did not prevent them from perceiving the U.S. build-up after Vietnam and thus being "taught...an important lesson: never underestimate the United States."[37] As another astute American observer of the Soviet scene puts it, the capacity to derive such lessons exemplifies "a learning process that has led to growing sophistication and 'emancipation' from doctrinal stereotypes on the part of a relatively small number of members of the intellectual and political elites, but that has not been explicitly acknowledged nor affected the reiteration of orthodox clichés in and by the mass media and routine propagandists."[38] Indeed, there may even be change occurring with respect to the reiteration of orthodoxy at the mass level; the propaganda issued at this level now includes traces of an acknowledgment that stories about the darker side of American life do not convey a full picture.[39] Likewise, a closer look at survey data on American publics and elites highlights discrepancies between ideological rhetoric and changing habits. Despite the indications of ideological polarization in the leadership data, for example, the 1984 survey yielded a noteworthy decline in the proportion of leaders who were inclined to attribute expansionist motives to the U.S.S.R. as well as tendencies toward "moderate" assessments of Soviet behavior.

By "moderate" I mean that a large part of the leadership sample tends to accept many of the following propositions: Soviet foreign policy derives from multiple and complex motives rather than simple, unidimensional ones; relations between the United States and the Soviet Union are often characterized more accurately as non-zero-sum rather than zero-sum; and however troublesome those relations might be, the Kremlin is not the sole source of American foreign policy problems.[40]

At the mass level in the United States there are also faint signs that ideological constraints are loosening. As previously noted, poll data for the post-1976 period depict more fluctuations in public opinion toward the Soviet Union than was the case in the first years of the Cold War.[41]

As one close observer of U.S.-Soviet relations put it, "Many Americans...seem ready to have their stereotypes revised."[42] This is not to suggest that the ideological limits to learning in East-West relations are minimal or decreasing.[43] Surely they do and will continue to serve as mechanisms of mutual distortion and as blocks to mutual acceptance.

At the same time it would be erroneous to presume that the articulation of ideological rhetoric is an exact indication of the potential for and pace of learning. I would argue that the opposite conclusion is more appropriate, that further development of the perspective and indicators presented here will lead to further support for viewing the superpowers as habit-driven actors whose relationship is moving on to ever more secure footings.

Notes

1. William Safire, "Are They for Real?" *New York Times* November 24, 1985 (italics in the original).

2. For another inquiry into the positive aspects of the superpower relationship, see Nish Jamgotch (ed.), *Sectors of Mutual Benefit in U.S.-Soviet Relations* (Durham: Duke University Press, 1985). Explorations of how the positive aspects might be highlighted can be found in Marshall Shulman, "A Rational Response to the Soviet Challenge," *International Affairs* Vol. 61 (Summer 1985), pp. 375-83, and Christer Jönsson, *Superpower* (London: Frances Pinter, 1984).

3. For a more elaborate formulation of this model, see James N. Rosenau, "Before Cooperation: Hegemons, Regimes, and Habit-Driven Actors in World Politics" *International Organization* Vol. 40 (Autumn 1986), pp. 849-94.

4. For a cogent analysis from a similar perspective that elaborates on how the learning concept might be applied to a specific dimension of superpower relations, see Joseph S. Nye, Jr., "Nuclear Learning and U.S.-Soviet Security Regimes" a paper presented at the Annual Meeting of the American Political Science Association, Washington, D.C., August 28, 1986.

5. For a lengthy discussion of how the microelectronic revolution may be affecting the analytic habits of people and publics, see James N. Rosenau, "Micro Sources of Macro Global Change" Institute for Transnational Studies, University of Southern California, Los Angeles, CA, 1986.

6. Kalevi J. Holsti, "Détente as a Source of International Conflict" in Nissen Oren (ed.), *Images and Reality in International Politics* (New York: St. Martin's Press, 1984), p. 140.

7. For a cogent analysis of the interaction among the predispositional and institutionalized rules that compromise the relationship, see Alexander L. George, "U.S.-Soviet Global Rivalry: Norms of Competition" a paper presented at the XIIIth International Political Science Association World Congress, Paris, France (July 1985). For a more general discussion of the informal premises to which both sides in the relationship adhere and to which each views the other as adhering, see Paul Keal, *Unspoken Rules and Superpower Dominance* (New York: St. Martin's Press, 1983).

8. This is not to say, of course, that this form of "Kremlinological" analysis is no longer necessary to an understanding of Soviet affairs. Given the nature of political culture in the U.S.S.R., it will doubtless long be an important form of inquiry even as other, more direct forms are now possible. For a provocative discussion of the links between Kremlinology and the emergent field of semiotics, see Christer Jönsson, "Soviet Political Language: The Analysis of Esoteric Communication" a paper presented at the XIIIth Inter-

national Political Science Association World Congress, Paris, France (July 1985).

9. For an elaboration of this point, see James N. Rosenau, "Toward a Single-Country Theory: The U.S.S.R. as an Adaptive System" in Roman Kolkowicz (ed.), *Rethinking Soviet Foreign Policy* (forthcoming).

10. For a persuasive discussion of how "surprising knowledge about issues or topics in Soviet oreign policy can be obtained from open sources through basic research," see William Zimmerman, "What do Scholars Know About Soviet Foreign Policy?" *International Journal* Vol. 37 (Spring 1982), pp. 198-219.

11. The quest of Soviet scholars seeking to comprehend U.S. policy making toward their country was recently eased, at least slightly, when their Western counterparts published a book on this somewhat specialized topic. Cf. Joseph S. Nye, Jr. (ed.), *The Making of America's Soviet Policy* (New Haven: Yale University, 1984).

12. Seweryn Bialer and Joan Afferica, "Gorbachev's World" *Foreign Affairs* Vol. 64, No. 3 (1985), p. 632.

13. "Nuclear Learning and U.S.-Soviet Security Regimes" p. 11.

14. For cogent analyses of possible impacts the microelectronic revolution may be having on the Soviet system, see Ellen Mickiewicz, "Managing Public Opinion and International News in the Soviet Union" in Kolkowicz (ed.), *op. cit.; Ithiel de Sola Pool*, "The Changing Soviet Union: The Mass Media as Catalyst" *Current* (January 1966); and George H. Quester, "Transboundary Television" *Problems of Communism* Vol. XXXIII (September-October 1984), pp. 76-87.

15. In the case of the relationship between public attitudes toward the Soviets and weekly earnings in the U.S. for the thirty-year period, the correlation was .84 and the comparable figure for disposable income is .42. Miroslaw Nincic, "The American Public and the Soviet Union: The Domestic Context of Discontent" *Journal of Peace Research* Vol. 22, No. 4 (1985), pp. 351-52.

16. *Ibid.*, p. 348-49. For another analysis depicting shifts in U.S. attitudes toward the U.S.S.R., see Valerie Bunce, "Presidential Leadership of Public Opinion: The Hardening of American Attitudes Toward East-West Relations," a paper presented at the Annual Meeting of the American Political Science Association, New Orleans, LA (August 1985). For a more theoretical discussion of the fluctuations in the superpower relationship, see James N. Rosenau and Ole R. Holsti, "Public Opinion and Soviet Foreign Policy: Competing Belief Systems in the Policy-Making Process" *Naval War College Review* Vol. XXXII (July-August 1979), pp. 4-14.

17. Philip E. Tetlock, "Integrative Complexity of American and Soviet Foreign Policy Rhetoric: A Time-Series Analysis" *Journal of Personality and Social Psychology* Vol. 49, No. 6 (1985), pp.

18. See, for instance, Ole R. Holsti and James N. Rosenau, *American Leadership in World Affairs: The Breakdown of Consensus* (Winthrop, MA: George Allen & Unwin, 1984), and William Zimmerman and Robert Axelrod, "The

'Lessons' of Vietnam and Soviet Foreign Policy" *World Politics* Vol. XXXIV (October 1981), pp. 1-24.

19. Ibid., p. 21.

20. Bernard Gwertzman, "Schultz Wants U.S. and Soviet to End Public Diplomacy" *New York Times* March 31, 1986, p. 1.

21. For an analysis of the dynamics of this habit as practiced on the Soviet side, see Christoph Royen, "Change in Eastern Europe: Implications for Soviet Policy and the Scope of Western Influence" in Uwe Nerlicj and James A. Thomson (eds.), *The Soviet Problem in American-German Relations* (New York; Crane Russak, 1985), pp. 153-185.

22. The foci and locale of each set are catalogued in the *New York Times* August 31, 1986, p. 18.

23. Leslie H. Gelb, "Policy Struggles by U.S. and Soviet on Verge of Shift" *New York Times* April 5, 1986, pp. 1, 5.

24. A hint of this potential for learning and a J-like curve insofar as the Soviets are concerned is provided by these comments of a long-time observer of the U.S.S.R. (Alexander Dallin, "Fruits of Interaction," p. 44):

> There is a good deal of evidence that as a result of greater interaction a process of learning is already taking place which deserves closer study than it seems to have received to date. This is true, for instance, of arms control concepts, of empirical sociology, of concern over environmental pollution, of management techniques, of the uses of quantitative methods in the social sciences, and many other areas, large or small. There is a distinct increase in shared perceptions that would have been impossible a generation ago; for instance, the "mutual hostage" posture written into the SALT agreements, so much at variance with orthodox Leninism; or the recognition of "non-zero sum games," with the un-Bolshevik implication that not everything your adversary is for, you are necessarily against; or the occasional sense of solidarity of the superpowers vis-a-vis others, be it China or Third World countries demanding capital assistance.
>
> Often this process is bound to be unacknowledged or even denied. But in the long run, the multiplication of exposure and contacts cannot but yield cumulation of new assumptions and attitudes—an unwitting process of borrowing and learning. And—this may be critical—among other things it should promote among the next younger generation of the Soviet elite a firm conviction that it is to their own advantage to get along with the outside world. This will be true if and only if we make it worth their while.

25. For a cogent discussion of the short-run bargaining processes, see Steven J. Brams, *Superpower Games: Applying Game Theory to Superpower Conflict* (New Haven: Yale University Press, 1985). A much less theoretical (but current) assessment of these short-term processes can be found in Jeremy R. Azrael and Stephan Sestanovich, "Superpower Balancing Acts" *Foreign Affairs* Vol. 64, No. 3 (1986), pp. 479-98.

26. George Kennan, "Reflections: Two Views of the Soviet Problem" *The New Yorker* November 2, 1981, p. 55.

27. Gelb, op. cit., p. 5.

28. Bernard Gwertzman, "Schultz Says Technology May Aid In Easing East-West Tensions" *New York Times* March 22, 1986.

29. Gelb, op. cit., p. 5.

30. *New York Times* April 10, 1986, p. 14.

31. Gelb, op. cit., p. 1, 5.

32. Bialer and Afferica, op. cit., pp. 632-33.

33. David K. Shipler, "Elusive Opportunity" *New York Times* October 26, 1986, Section 4, p. 1.

34. Ibid., p. 633.

35. Bunce, op. cit.

36. Ole R. Holsti and James N. Rosenau, "Domestic and Foreign Policy Belief Systems Among American Leaders" a paper presented at the Annual Meeting of the International Studies Association, Anaheim, CA (March 1986), p. 25.

37. Bialer and Afferica, op. cit., p. 637.

38. Alexander Dallin, "The Domestic Sources of Soviet Policy," in Seweryn Bialer (ed.), *The Domestic Context of Soviet Foreign Policy* (Boulder, CO: Westview Press, 1981), p. 359.

39. William J. Eaton, "Soviets See U.S. in More Kindly Light" *Los Angeles Times* February 17, 1986, p. 1.

40. Ole R. Holsti, *The Lessons of Vietnam and the Breakdown of Consensuses on Foreign and Domestic Policy: A Study of American Leadership* (Durham: Final Report on N.S.F. Grant No. SES-83-09036, December 1985), p. 2-16.

41. Bunce, op. cit.

42. David K. Shipler, "How We See Each Other? The View from America" *New York Times Magazine* November 10, 1985, p. 40.

43. For an incisive discussion of the tension between learning and ideology on both sides of the superpower relationship, see Paul Hollander, *Soviet and American Society: A Comparison* (Chicago: University of Chicago Press, 1978) pp. 12-36.

3

What Are the Russians Up to Now:

The Beliefs of American Leaders About the Soviet Union and Soviet-American Relations, 1976-1984

Ole R. Holsti

On February 28, 1946, Senator Arthur Vandenberg asked his colleagues in the Senate, "What is Russia up to now?" He was neither the first nor the last to pose that question, as the post-World War II period has seen an almost perpetual debate on the issue. Vandenberg's question was asked at a time when many Americans believed that cooperation between leading members of the wartime "Grand Alliance" could continue, as envisaged by President Franklin D. Roosevelt in his concept of the "Four Policemen" (the United States, the Soviet Union, Great Britain, and China). Others were more skeptical. In his famous "long telegram" of 1946 and in an essay on "The Sources of Soviet Conduct" a year later, George F. Kennan wrote that Soviet foreign policy was driven largely by internal forces, including the need

Preparation of this paper was supported by National Science Foundation grant No. SES-83-09036, and the Duke University Research Council. I also wish to thank the following for their valuable assistance: Daniel Harkins for skillful computer programming; Steven Jenkins, Elizabeth Rogers and Maija Holsti for research assistance; and Jennifer Rainey and Lib Franklin for ably typing the manuscript.

for real or imagined external enemies and, therefore, that at least in the short run American offers of friendship and cooperation were likely to prove fruitless. Kennan's diagnosis of Soviet international behavior and his prescription of a "long-term, patient but firm and vigilant containment of Russian expansive tendencies" were enormously influential in providing an intellectual framework for American policy toward the Soviet Union, but they did not end the debate about the appropriate means for dealing with the USSR.

The debate has often been stimulated by external events. The invasion of South Korea; the death of Stalin, and to a lesser extent, other changes of top leadership in the Kremlin; the invasions of Hungary, Czechoslovakia and Afghanistan; Sputnik; the Cuban missile crisis; and the activities that constituted the high point of detente in 1972-73 are some of the more dramatic episodes that have intensified interest in the question posed by Vandenberg. But almost as often the debate has been aroused by American domestic politics, especially presidential election campaigns. In 1952, the concept of containment came under attack from some Republicans, notably John Foster Dulles, as too "static." Later events demonstrated clearly that its putative replacement — "roll back" — was campaign rhetoric rather than policy. In order to disarm critics in the right wing of his own party in 1976, President Ford let it be known that "detente" was no longer a part of the White House working vocabulary. Four years later the soon-to-be-nominated Ronald Reagan asserted in a long interview with a friendly newspaper that the Soviet Union was the sole source of international problems, and during the subsequent campaign he attacked detente as the cause of the "worst decade in American history."

If American policy is affected by both external and internal factors, then the state of public and leadership opinion about the Soviet Union and its foreign policy is of more than passing interest. This paper draws upon evidence generated by three nationwide surveys undertaken in 1976, 1980, and 1984, each of which resulted in well over two thousand responses from people occupying leadership positions in institutions ranging from the State Department and the Pentagon to business, labor unions, the media and churches. After a description of data and methods, the analyses to be undertaken here deal with several aspects of the Soviet Union and Soviet-American relations.

Each of the three surveys includes a number of questions dealing with the USSR, Soviet-American relations, and American foreign policy. These permit analyses of trends during the period 1976-1984 (Tables 2-4). A cluster of items in the 1984 survey focuses on the sources of Soviet foreign policy. Several of these items are used to develop a "hard-to-soft" scale of interpretations of Soviet policy (Tables 5-8). The scale is used to identify backgound factors associated with various perspectives on Soviet foreign policy, with some emphasis on party and ideology (Tables 9-22). The relationship between beliefs about Soviet foreign policy and other political beliefs — both domestic and foreign policy — is examined in the final part of the section on findings (Tables 23-26).

Data and Methods

One of the anomalies of public opinion research has been the relative lack of attention directed at the foreign policy attitudes and beliefs of opinion leaders. Since Almond's seminal study of *The American People and Foreign Policy*, it has been customary to distinguish among various strata of the public; for example, among opinion leaders, the informed public and the mass public. Yet, although the distinction among these segments of the public has been a standard part of the literature on public opinion and foreign policy for at least three and a half decades, until recently opinion surveys have rarely distinguished between leaders and the general public. On occasion the Gallup organization has surveyed a sample of persons listed in *Who's Who in America*, but not frequently enough to be of great value for gauging leadership attitudes on foreign affairs, let alone for undertaking trend analyses. Polling organizations often disaggregate the sample of respondents according to educational level — usually among those with college, high school and grammar school educations — and the evidence has consistently demonstrated that respondents with a higher level of education are more likely to have an internationalist outlook on foreign affairs. This relationship has usually carried over to more specific policies; for example, in substantially greater support for foreign aid, liberalization of trade, and assistance to allies. To some extent education may provide clues about leadership views, but it is not a wholly satisfactory surrogate measure because there is also evidence of substantial and systematic differences between the college educated and opinion leaders.[1]

The post-Vietnam period has witnessed increased interest in the foreign policy attitudes of American leaders. Surveys have been undertaken by Barton, Russett and Hanson, Sussman, and the Chicago Council on Foreign Relations.[2] These useful studies provide the kind of evidence that is unavailable for the preceding forty-year period that began with the inception of regular polling by the Gallup organization, but they are not without some limitations. The first three were one-time surveys that preclude trend analyses, and of the three, only two focus substantially on foreign affairs. The latter, on the other hand, encompass only two occupational groups — businessmen and military officers.

The CCFR surveys include samples of both leaders and the general public, but most of the primary and secondary analyses have directed their attention to the latter rather than the former. Thus, although the situation has improved significantly during the past decade, evidence about leadership opinions continues to lag far behind the mass of data on public opinion.

The Foreign Policy Leadership Project was initiated with a view to undertaking a survey of Americans in leadership positions in a broad range of occupations. The specific and immediate impetus for the project was the hypothesis that the Vietnam tragedy would precipitate an active debate about "the lessons of Vietnam" and that the debate would in fact range across virtually all aspects of America's external relations — its proper role in the world, the scope and content of its national interests, the means by which those interests should be translated into policy, and the appropriate strategies and tactics for pursuing them. The first survey, conducted in 1976, yielded responses to a long questionnaire from 2,282 leaders. Among the many findings of the resulting studies were striking signs of the deep impact of the Vietnam war in dividing Americans on a wide spectrum of foreign policy issues. A second survey, conducted four years later, just a few weeks after the American Embassy in Teheran and many of its personnel were taken captive and the Soviet Union invaded Afghanistan, resulted in responses from 2,502 leaders. The results show the existence of deep cleavages on foreign policy rather than the emergence of a "post-Vietnam consensus." The most recent survey, undertaken in 1984, includes completed returns from 2,515 leaders.[3]

The Leadership Samples

The ideal survey would have a sample that faithfully and precisely replicates the society's leadership structure. This series of studies has proceeded on several assumptions: it is not possible to construct such a sample without the expenditure of far greater resources than were available; no effort to do so would yield results that would satisfy all observers of American society; different return rates among subgoups would almost certainly skew the resulting groups of respondents in various ways; and, most importantly, the purposes of these studies do not depend upon a construction of the ideal sample. If the sole purpose were to describe the foreign policy views of leaders in the aggregate, in a manner comparable to a public opinion poll, the failure to address more precisely the structure of American leadership might pose serious problems of inference. However, the present goals are rather different, seeking to answer questions about trends, the relationship of various beliefs to each other, and of beliefs to respondent attributes.

As a consequence, the issues of whether media leaders should represent X percent or Y percent of the entire sample or whether it should include more business leaders than military officers — or vice versa — are not especially urgent. It is more important that the sample include representatives of many, if not all, major components of the nation's leadership structure and that there be enough respondents in occupational and other sub-categories to permit reliable comparisons among them. The sampling procedures were intended to satisfy these requirements.

Having eschewed the task of constructing a precise replica of America's leadership structure does not, however, imply that the sample is free of premises about American society. For example, the procedures used here clearly incorporate the pluralistic assumption that the foreign policy process in the United States is sensitive to a multiplicity of influences rather than merely to those of a narrow class or sector of society (e.g. business interests). However, because the data for various occupational and other groups are presented, readers who reject such premises may still find something of interest in the findings.

A search for a single source that identifies persons who occupy a variety of leadership roles, as well as those in sub-leadership positions who would have a high probability of occupying the top roles in the years ahead, proved fruitless. The leadership samples were therefore constructed in ways that represented several types of compromises between the ideal and reality.

One part of each sample consists of approximately 1,800 names randomly drawn from the most recent edition of *Who's Who in America*, a useful source that includes biographical material about each person. *Who's Who in America* is not without some significant drawbacks, however. Some groups are very heavily represented, especially business executives and educators. Conversely, military officers, labor leaders, the clergy, and several other important occupational groups are underrepresented. The age and sex distribution of its biographees may accurately mirror the leadership structure of American society, but the limited representation of women and younger people rendered it less adequate for present purposes.

The second part of the samples was constructed using quotas for leaders from each of several groups that are inadequately represented in *Who's Who in America*: State Department officials and Foreign Service Officers, military officers, labor officials, politicians, clergy, foreign affairs experts outside government, media leaders, and women. Names and addresses were drawn from various directories using random sampling procedures whenever feasible. In several cases the groups were sufficiently small that all members were included; for example, all chief editorial writers of newspapers with a circulation exceeding 100,000 were included in each sample, as were the presidents of all fifty state labor organizations.

One of the largest occupational groups in the 1976 sample consisted of military personnel, including both senior officers (colonels and general officers, and their naval equivalents) then serving in the Pentagon, and junior and middle grade officers attending one of the service schools. The 1980 and 1984 samples on the other hand, include students at the National War College, a higher level service school with smaller classes.

Return Rates

The leadership surveys were conducted by mail. In order to preserve their anonymity, respondents were asked to return the questionnaire to one address (a stamped, addressed envelope was provided for this purpose), and a postal card (also provided) acknowledging its completion to another. Names of those returning the postal card were then removed from the list for the next mailing.

Two thousand five hundred and fifteen of the 4,058 recipients of the 1984 questionnaire completed and returned it for an overall return rate of 62.0 percent. The comparable figures from the 1976 and 1980 surveys were 53.2 percent and 63.2 percent. As was the case in the two earlier surveys, return rates from the various groups varied rather sharply. Less than fifty percent of the labor leaders and Catholic clergy returned a completed questionnaire, whereas more than 70 percent of the foreign policy experts outside government, Protestant clergy and Jewish rabbis took part.

Respondents in each of the three surveys are described according to various attributes in Table 1. A few of the differences in the three samples are worth noting. Because classes at the National War College are smaller than those at the Naval Post-Graduate School, the number of military officers in the 1980 and 1984 samples is substantially smaller. On the other hand, the number of clergy increased. The number of women and holders of a legal degree has risen steadily whereas the proportion of veterans has declined. The ideological self-identification of respondents has remained virtually constant over the eight-year period covering the three surveys, but the proportion of those identifying themselves as Republicans and Democrats has increased.

Differences in the composition of the 1976, 1980, and 1984 samples, although not dramatic except in the case of military officers,

TABLE 1
FOREIGN POLICY LEADERSHIP SURVEYS: SELECTED BACKGROUND CHARACTERISTICS OF AMERICAN LEADERS, 1976, 1980, 1984

| | RESPONDENTS | | | | | |
| | 1976 | | 1980 | | 1984 | |
	N	%	N	%	N	%
OCCUPATION						
Business Executives	294	13	459	18	468	19
Labor Officials	74	3	89	4	81	3
Educators	565	25	635	25	616	24
Clergy	101	4	148	6	162	6
Military Officers	500	22	177	7	147	6
Public Officials	110	5	152	6	122	5
Foreign Service Officers	125	5	150	6	147	6
Media Leaders	184	8	245	10	224	9
Lawyers	116	5	146	6	165	7
Health Care	*	*	116	5	125	5
Others and no answer	213	9	185	7	258	10
	2,282	99	2,502	100	2,515	100

* Included with "others" in 1976.

	N	%	N	%	N	%
SEX						
Men	2,009	88	2,173	87	2,124	84
Women	224	10	290	12	313	12
No answer	49	2	40	2	7	3
	2,282	100	2,502	101	2,515	99

	N	%	N	%	N	%
IDEOLOGY						
Far left	18	1	14	1	16	1
Very liberal	202	9	144	6	164	7
Somewhat liberal	578	25	614	25	633	25
Moderate	576	25	648	26	662	26
Somewhat conservative	666	29	793	32	743	30
Very conservative	126	6	163	7	163	6
Far right	5	*	9	*	3	*
Other, No answer	111	5	117	5	131	5
	2,282	100	2,502	102	2,515	100

* Less than 0.5%

	N	%	N	%	N	%
HIGHEST LEVEL OF EDUCATION						
Some high school	7	*	7	*	2	*
High school graduate	32	1	98	2	20	1
Some college	141	6	135	5	131	5
College graduate	221	10	290	12	260	10
Some graduate work	487	21	339	14	288	11
Graduate degree	1,351	59	1,646	66	1,736	69
No answer	43	2	47	2	78	3
	2,282	99	2,502	101	2,515	99

* Less than 0.5%

GENERATION (DATE OF BIRTH)						
World War II (before 1924)	898	39	753	30	517	21
Korean War (1924-1932)	442	19	638	25	695	28
Interim (1933-1940)	256	11	390	16	441	18
Vietnam (since 1940)	583	26	367	15	457	18
Age not stated	103	4	354	14	405	16
	2,282	99	2,502	100	2,515	101

POLITICAL PARTY PREFERENCE						
Republican	590	26	728	29	764	30
Democrat	793	35	918	37	933	37
Independent	763	33	764	31	668	27
Other	15	1	13	1	54	2
No preference	63	3	27	1	18	1
No answer	58	3	52	2	78	3
	2,282	101	2,502	101	2,515	100

MILITARY SERVICE						
Veterans	1,500	66	1,513	60	1,375	55
No military service	737	32	943	38	1,056	42
No answer	45	2	46	2	84	3
	2,282	100	2,502	100	2,515	100

make it necessary to use some caution in comparing aggregate results for the three surveys. This poses less of a problem for cross-sectional analyses — for example, in assessments of the impact of various backgound attributes on beliefs about the Soviet Union and its foreign policies. It will suffice for the present to say that the 1984 leadership samples resembles those of 1976 and 1980 in a number of respects. It is occupationally and generationally diverse, slightly more Democratic than Republican, ideologically moderate rather than extremist, mostly male and veterans of military service, and highly educated.

The Questionnaire

Each person in the leadership sample received a 16-page printed questionnaire that included 205 closed-ended items. In several respects a mailed questionnaire may not be the ideal research instrument for probing into leadership beliefs. There is validity in the observation that elite interviews may provide more revealing information about attitudes and beliefs than questionnaires. This point is particularly relevant when the population of interest can be clearly defined, when it is quite limited in number, and when it is geographically concentrated rather than dispersed. These conditions would prevail, for example, in a study of members of a legislature or a foreign office. However, the present goal was to gain access to the occupants of a broad range of top leadership roles, and for this purpose interviews seemed out of the question. Given very limited resources, the trade-off is between a small number of interviews and much broader coverage by means of a mailed questionnaire.

In order to permit comparison with 1976 and 1980 data, the 1984 questionnaire included 96 items that had appeared in the two earlier surveys including a substantial number that deal directly with the Soviet Union. An additional seventeen items had appeared in the 1980 survey but not in 1976.

Findings

Soviet foreign policy, Soviet-American relations, and American goals

Eight items in the 1984 questionnaire, all but two of which had appeared in the two earlier surveys, deal more or less directly with the nature, motives and goals of Soviet foreign policy. Responses of leaders taking part in the three surveys are summarized in Table 2. The first three columns indicate the percentage of those who agree — either

TABLE 2
IMAGES OF THE ADVERSARY:
THE NATURE, MOTIVES AND GOALS OF THE SOVIET UNION
AS PERCEIVED BY RESPONDENTS TO THE
1976 (N=2,282), 1980 (N=2,502), AND 1984 (N=2,515)
FOREIGN POLICY LEADERSHIP SURVEYS

Please indicate how strongly you agree or disagree with each of the following statements	% Agree *			Index **		
	1976	1980	1984	1976	1980	1984
The Soviet Union is generally expansionist rather than defensive in its foreign policy goals	83	85	77	.59	.61	.47
Revolutionary forces in "Third World" countries are usually nationalistic rather than controlled by the USSR or China	60	58	69	.19	.12	.27
The Soviet invasion of Afghanistan was one step in a larger plan to control the Persian Gulf area	—	66	62	—	.36	.24

Communist nations were encouraged to seek further triumphs elsewhere as a result of Vietnam	69	68	59	.32	.30	.14
Detente permits the Soviet Union to pursue policies that promote rather than restrain conflict	57	60	45	.15	.20	-.03
American foreign policy should be based on the premise that the Communist "bloc" is irreparably fragmented	32	32	36	-.25	-.26	-.22
The Soviet Union acted in Afghanistan largely to protect itself against having a hostile regime on its borders	—	30	32	—	-.38	-.33
The tide of influence in world affairs has swung toward communism as a result of the Vietnam War	40	34	18	-.16	-.23	-.49

* "Agree strongly" plus "agree somewhat" responses combined.

** Computed by scoring "agree strongly" as 1.0, "agree somewhat" as 0.50, "no opinion" as 0.0, "disagree somewhat" as -0.5, and "disagree strongly" as -1.0, resulting in a scale of 1.0 (all "agree strongly") to -1.0 (all "disagree strongly").

Not all questions were included in all three surveys.

"strongly" or "somewhat" — with the item in 1976, 1980, and 1984. The three left hand columns summarize their responses somewhat differently; the index takes into account the intensity of both agreement and disagreement, resulting in a scale of 1.00 (all respondents "agree strongly") to -1.00 (all "disagree strongly").

The results leave little doubt that most American leaders regard the Soviet Union as an expansionist power, both in general (77 percent) and with respect to its longer-term goals in such a specific undertaking as its invasion of Afghanistan (62 percent). Conversely, relatively few of them (32 percent) accept the proposition that the Kremlin's motives in Afghanistan are essentially defensive. However, the data also reveal a rather consistent trend toward a somewhat more benign view of Soviet foreign policy in 1984, at least as compared to four years earlier. This pattern emerges not only with respect to the items cited above — in 1980, for example, 85 percent of respondents ascribed expansionist motives to the USSR — but also on several others as well. Whereas in 1980 three leaders in five agreed that "Detente permits the Soviet Union to pursue policies that promote rather than restrain conflict," four years later only 45 percent did so. Moreover, there was a tendency to regard the USSR as less menacing within the broader global context. Although only about a third of the leaders taking part in the 1984 survey believed that the communist bloc is irreparably fragmented, almost twice that many (69 percent) were inclined to regard revolutionary forces in the Third World as nationalists rather than the pawns of Moscow or Beijing. Finally, the somewhat apocalyptic consequences sometimes predicted to result from America's loss in Vietnam elicited less agreement in 1984 than they had in the two earlier surveys. The view that communist nations had been encouraged to seek triumphs elsewhere as a result of Vietnam gained agreement from just under three-fifths of the respondents, a loss of about ten percent from the previous surveys, and the proposition that, "The tide of influence in world affairs has swung toward communism as a result of the Vietnam War" gained agreement from fewer than one leader in five, a very substantial drop since 1976 and 1980.

In summary, the picture that emerges from the data in Table 2 does not sustain charges that American leaders, as a whole, are wedded to a chiaroscuro image of world affairs in general or, more specifically, of the Soviet Union. Stated somewhat differently, although President Reagan has been quite successful in obtaining support for several aspects of his program, notably with respect to tax cuts and defense spending, and his personal popularity has remained high, these data suggest that he has been less successful in persuading most American leaders on all elements of his diagnosis of world affairs.

Table 3 presents data on several items that focus on premises and policies within the context of American-Soviet relations. The format is identical to that of the previous table: the first three columns present

TABLE 3
AMERICAN-SOVIET RELATIONS
AS PERCEIVED BY RESPONDENTS TO THE
1976 (N=2,282), 1980 (N=2,502), AND 1984 (N=2,515)
FOREIGN LEADERSHIP SURVEYS

Please indicate how strongly you agree or disagree with each of the following statements	% agree *			Index **		
	1976	1980	1984	1976	1980	1984
Continuing arms control negotiations after the Soviets shot down the Korean civilian air liner	—	—	84	—	—	.57

Restoring grain sales to the Soviet Union	—	—	70	—	—	.30
The U.S. should provide increased support to rebels who are fighting the Soviets in Afghanistan	—	—	65	—	—	.20
There is considerable validity in the "domino theory" that when one nation falls to communism, others nearby will soon follow a similar path	67	63	55	.24	.17	.04
Preventing American firms from selling non-strategic equipment to the Soviet Union	—	—	45	—	—	-.06
Opposing a "nuclear freeze"	—	—	43	—	—	-.11
Any communist victory is a defeat for America's national interest	40	45	40	-.14	-.06	-.16
Soviet actions in Afghanistan do not affect vital American interests	—	24	39	—	-.43	-.20
The U.S. should take all steps including the use of force to prevent the spread of communism	33	36	33	-.29	-.23	-.29
It is not in our interest to have better relations with the Soviet Union because we are getting less than we are giving to them	29	26	11	-.33	-.36	-.65

* "Agree strongly" plus "agree somewhat" responses combined.

** Computed by scoring "agree strongly" as 1.0, "agree somewhat" as 0.5, "no opinion" as 0.0, "disagree somewhat" as -0.5, and "disagree strongly" as -1.0, resulting in a scale of 1.0 (all "agree strongly") to -1.0 (all "disagree strongly").

Not all questions were included in all three surveys

the percentage of agreement with each item in 1976, 1980 and 1984, and the three columns to the left summarize responses on a scale of 1.00 (agree strongly) to -1.00 (disagree strongly). Only four of the ten items appeared in all three surveys and another one was included in both 1980 and 1984. The trends that emerge from the results are generally congruent with those in Table 2, indicating both wariness and restraint with respect to Soviet-American relations. A declining majority (55 percent) of the respondents agreed with the "domino

theory," and almost two-thirds of them expressed a willingness to support rebels in Afghanistan (a majority of about the same magnitude that
rejected the proposition that "Soviet actions in Afghanistan do not affect vital American interests"). At the same time only one leader in nine
accepted the view that better relations with Moscow are against the national interest, and the majority rejected both a zero-sum view of communist gains or were prepared to employ all means, including force, to
prevent such advances. With respect to each of these items, the
"hardline" view had somewhat fewer adherents in 1984 than four years
earlier. However, these results may also reflect the wording of questions. In the light of changes in Sino-American relations during the
period covered by these surveys, would the substitution of "Soviet
Union" for "communism" in these questions have elicited different
responses?

Table 3 also includes several items on more specific policies that
appeared only in the 1984 survey, thus precluding trend analyses. As indicated earlier, there is strong support for assistance to rebels who are
fighting the Soviet invaders in Afghanistan, but in other respects there
is moderate to strong agreement with policies that constituted some of
the elements of detente, especially as pursued during the Nixon-Kissinger era in the early 1970s. Respondents expressed strong support for
arms control negotiations (even in the aftermath of the Soviet attack on
the Korean civilian airliner) and they divided almost evenly on the
nuclear "freeze" proposal. They also agreed strongly with resumption of
grain sales to the Soviet Union, as candidate Ronald Reagan had
promised in 1980 (and carried out during his first term) when attacking
President Carter's post-Afghanistan embargo on new grain agreements,
and a smaller majority expressed disagreement with policies to prevent
American firms from selling non-strategic goods to the USSR, as had
taken place in connection with the construction of a gas pipeline from
Siberia to Western Europe.

In summary, although substantial numbers of American leaders
take a very dim view of Soviet actions in Afghanistan, many support
both general and specific policies that bear a substantial resemblence to
the detente period of the early-to-mid 1970s. Further evidence to be
presented later will tend to offer further support for this interpretation.

A cluster of items, borrowed from the Chicago Council studies,
asked respondents in each of three leadership surveys to assess the importance of several possible goals for American foreign policy. Items in
the 1984 questionnaire concerning containment and matching the
Soviet military buildup are of special interest, and several others, dealing with arms control, the balance of power and defending allies, are
also relevant to Soviet-American relations. In order to provide a fuller,

comparative perspective on the priorities attached to these goals, Table 4 reports the results for several others as well. The format is identical to that of the previous two tables except that response options ranged from "very important" to "not important at all."

Although over one-third of the leaders taking part in the 1984 sur-

TABLE 4
GOALS FOR AMERICAN FOREIGN POLICY:
ASSESSMENTS BY RESPONDENTS TO THE
1976 (N=2,282), 1980 (N=2,502), AND 1984 (N=2,515)
FOREIGN POLICY LEADERSHIP SURVEYS

Please indicate how much importance should be attached to each goal	% Very Important			Index *		
	1976	1980	1984	1976	1980	1984
Securing adequate supplies of energy	72	78	85	.85	.88	.92
Promoting and defending our own security	85	90	83	.92	.95	.92
Worldwide arms control	66	55	71	.82	.74	.83
Fostering international cooperation to solve common problems, such as food, inflation and energy	70	73	66	.84	.86	.82
Helping to improve the standards of living in less developed countries	38	43	59	.65	.68	.78
Combatting world hunger	51	51	56	.72	.73	.76
Protecting the global environment	—	47	53	—	.70	.74
Defending our allies' security	37	44	48	.67	.71	.73
Averting financial crises arising from Third World debts	—	—	44	—	—	.69
Maintaining a balance of power among nations	44	55	43	.69	.76	.68
Matching Soviet military power	—	—	40	—	—	.63
Containing communism	39	41	38	.63	.65	.63
Promoting and defending human rights in other countries	—	27	33	—	.52	.60

Strengthening the United Nations	25	35	27	.47	.53	.46
Helping to bring a democratic form of government to other nations	7	10	18	.33	.38	.49

*Computed by scoring "very important" as 1.0, "somewhat important" as 0.5, and "not important at all" as 0.0 resulting in a scale of 1.0 (all "very important") to 0.0 (all "not important at all").
Not all questions were included in all three surveys

vey rated "containing communism" as an important goal — a response that did not vary significantly from the results in 1976 and 1980 — it did not emerge as the dominant goal of American foreign policy. As in the two earlier surveys, of the items dealing with military/ strategic issues, arms control was accorded a higher priority than containment. Indeed, 71 percent of the 1984 leadership sample gave arms control the highest importance rating, an increase of 16 percent during the four year interval since the 1980 study. The question on containment may be another case in which the wording might have affected the results. Specifically, would respondents have attributed greater importance to containment had the question been worded differently: "Containing Soviet expansion?" It is at least possible that some respondents would have been more inclined to give a higher rating to that more specific goal than to the more open-ended one implied by "containing communism." The item on "matching Soviet military power," which did not appear in the prior surveys, was rated about the same as containment. The other two strategic goals — defending allies and maintaining a balance of power — resulted in somewhat different although not necessarily contradictory results. Compared to 1980, a higher proportion of leaders rated the former as very important, but there was a rather precipitous decline in the rating for the latter. Although these results may seem somewhat incongruous, perhaps they reflect growing support for specific and finite undertakings (defending allies), on the one hand, and declining enthusiasm for more open-ended ones (maintaining a balance of power), on the other.

The results do not indicate a post-Vietnam stampede toward isolationism among American leaders as a group, but they suggest that for many the agenda of the nation's foreign policy must include quite a number of non-strategic issues, including but not limited to concerns for energy availability, international economic cooperation, the standard of living in less developed countries, hunger and famines, the global environment, Third World debt problems, and the like. Each of these goals was accorded greater importance than either containment or matching Soviet military power, and in most cases the data revealed a trend of greater concern for these issues.

The sources of Soviet foreign policy: A scale

In addition to describing trends in leadership thinking about the USSR, two other purposes of this paper are to identify the background attributes associated with various interpretations of Soviet foreign policy and to assess how these interpretations are linked to other beliefs about domestic and foreign policy. In order to facilitate these tasks it will be helpful to develop a scale on which American leaders can be placed in accordance with their beliefs about Soviet foreign policy.

Among the new items in the 1984 questionnaire is one that asks respondents to assess the sources and motives of Soviet foreign policy by expressing agreement or disagreement with six propositions, several of which address questions that have been central to the debate about "what is Russia up to?" For example, does the Soviet Union behave much like a typical great power? To what extent does its foreign policy reflect the imperatives of Marxist-Leninism ideology? The fundamental nature of the Soviet political system? Is its foreign policy driven by fear or by inherently expansionist propensities? Do Soviet leaders have a high or low propensity for risk? The distribution of responses by those taking part in the 1984 leadership survey is reported in Table 5.

To the extent that agreement emerges from the results, it tends to be on a somewhat moderate rather than either an extremely soft/optimistic or hard/pessimistic interpretation. An overwhelming majority of more than eighty percent of the respondents agreed that, "The Soviet Union and the U.S. share a number of foreign policy interests such as prevention of war, arms control, and stablizing relations between them." Almost equally large proportions also expressed agreement with the propositions that the Soviets have a low propensity for risk and that their external actions "often stem from genuine fears for Russian security." (Recall from Table 2, however, that relatively few were willing to explain the invasion of Afghanistan as a manifestation of genuine security fears.) At the same time, over two-thirds of leaders believed that Soviet foreign policy goals are "inherently expansionist" because these tendencies are built in to their system (see the similar results to a comparable item in Table 2), and a majority believe that they are guided by Marxist-Leninist ideology. Finally, only about a third of the respondents agreed with the proposition that the Kremlin's foreign policy goals are similar to those of typical great power.

TABLE 5
THE SOURCES OF SOVIET FOREIGN POLICY
AS APPRAISED BY RESPONDENTS TO THE
1976 (N=2,282), 1980 (N=2,502) AND 1984 (N=2,515)
FOREIGN POLICY LEADERSHIP SURVEYS

Please indicate how strongly you agree or disagree with each statement	% Agree Strongly	% Agree Somewhat	% Disagree Somewhat	% Disagree Strongly	% Not Sure
The Soviet Union and the U.S. share a number of interests such as prevention of war, arms control, and stabilizing relations between them	46	36	9	7	2
The Soviets will seek to expand only when the risks of doing so are relatively low	29	49	15	5	2
Soviet foreign policy goals are inherently expansionist and will not change until there is a fundamental transformation of the Soviet system	32	37	20	7	4
Soviet foreign policy actions often stem from genuine fears for Russian security	25	47	15	10	3
Soviet foreign policy is essentially guided by Marxist-Leninist ideology	16	35	27	12	9
Soviet foreign policy goals do not differ significantly from those of all major powers	9	26	24	41	1

Five of the items in Table 5 were used to construct a "hard-to-soft" scale for ranking American leaders; the exception is the question on risk-taking, which scaled rather poorly. The end points of the scale are defined in this manner.

Hard. "Agree strongly" with the fourth and fifth items, stipulating that the Soviets are inherently expansionist and that their foreign policy goals are guided by Marxist-Leninist ideology; "disagree strongly" with the first, third and sixth items, indicating shared Soviet-American interests, genuine security fears as a source of Soviet policy, and equating Soviet policy with that of all major powers.

Soft. This end of the scale is exactly the reverse of the hard end. That is, "agree strongly" with the first, third and sixth items, and "disagree strongly" with the fourth and fifth items.

The reliability rating of this scale, which will be used in much of the remainder of this paper, is .70 as measured by Cronbach's alpha. In order to assess the scale more fully, the next section examines responses to three clusters of items that focus directly on relations between Washington and Moscow.

Threats to American Security

A question first introduced in the 1980 questionnaire asked respondents to assess various threats to American security during the remainder of the millenium. Leaders taking part in the 1980 survey gave primary emphasis to threats emanating from the Soviet Union in the form of its military buildup and its expansionist activities in Third World areas. At the same time they accorded considerable importance to dangers arising from a variety of unresolved domestic issues. Less urgency was attached to the other three options in this cluster of items: the rich nation-poor nation gap, the population explosion, and American interventions abroad.

Responses to the same items in 1984 revealed quite substantial changes, most notably in a much narrower gap between the most and least widely cited threats. Soviet activities were still cited by many as a major threat, but there was a considerable reduction in those who listed a military gap between the United States and the USSR as one of the top dangers. No doubt the large American military buildup during the first Reagan Administration assuaged the fears of some respondents. Whereas in 1980 "a growing gap between rich nations and poor nations" was checked off by only about one quarter of the leaders taking part in the survey, by 1984 it emerged as the most widely cited threat. There was also a very substantial increase in the percentages of those who cited "uncontrolled growth of the world's population" and "American intervention in conflicts that are none of our business."

When leaders taking part in the 1984 survey are classified according to their interpretations of Soviet foreign policy on the scale developed from the questions in Table 6, their responses to the threat question yield a pattern that enhances confidence in the scale. Those in

TABLE 6
INTERPRETATIONS OF SOVIET FOREIGN POLICY
AND POSITIONS ON OTHER FOREIGN POLICY ISSUES;
FUTURE THREATS TO THE UNITED STATES

During the remaining years of this century, which _two_ of the following are likely to pose the greatest threat to American national security?	--------% CHECKING EACH OPTION--------		
		Soviet foreign policy: Respondents in extreme quintiles	
	All respondents	Hardest	Softest
an increase of Soviet military strength relative to that of the U.S.	38	67	13
a growing gap between rich nations and poor nations	43	22	65
an inability to solve such domestic problems as the decay of cities, unemployment and inflation, racial conflict and crime	39	24	45
uncontrolled growth of the world's population	24	15	31
American interventions in conflicts that are none of our business	21	11	38
Soviet expansion into Third World areas	35	61	8

the quintile at the "hard" end of the scale clearly perceived the greatest threats to emanate from Moscow's military strength and its expansion into Third World areas; not only did over 60 percent of them check each of these options, but none of the other four potential threats was cited by as many as one-quarter of them. In contrast, respondents in the quintile at the "softest" end of the scale as a group virtually discounted any threat from the USSR as the two items dealing with the Soviet Union ranked a distant fifth and sixth in their rankings. They attributed far greater danger to the growing gap between rich and poor nations, unresolved domestic problems, and uncontrolled population growth. Indeed, they were far more inclined to believe that American meddling in conflicts that do not concern us is a greater threat than

Soviet actions in the Third World. These results would appear to lend some credibility to scale, as well as to the internal consistency of responses by leaders who filled out the 1984 questionnaire. The striking differences summarized in the two right hand columns of Table 6 are consistent with the premise that the scale measures an important dimension of thinking about Soviet foreign policy.

Detente and arms control

Three of the foreign policy issues that dominated the 1980 presidential campaign were detente, arms control, and the appropriate level of defense spending. These issues also received a good deal of attention during the 1984 election as the two presidential candidates took rather different positions on how best to deal with them.

Leaders taking part in the 1980 survey did not, on balance, accept candidate Ronald Reagan's verdict that detente had been a snare and a delusion, resulting in catastrophic losses for America's global position during the 1970s, a decade that had seen presidents of Reagan's own party in control of the White House for over seventy percent of the time. Forty-eight percent of them rendered a favorable judgment on detente, compared to 29 percent who felt that it had been disadvantageous to the United States. Four years later, the assessment of detente was substantially more sanguine, as almost two-thirds of the respondents rendered a favorable judgment, whereas only about one-sixth of them believed that it had "contributed to a decline on American influence in the world" or, worse, "placed U.S. security in dangerous jeopardy."

However, these aggregate results reported in the left hand column of Table 7 conceal the rather striking differences between respondents at the "hard" and "soft" ends of the Soviet foreign policy scales, as summarized in the two right hand columns. Among those in the "hard" quintile, just over one-third assessed detente favorably and a like proportion judged it unfavorably. At the other end of the scale the verdict was overwhelmingly favorable, as only two percent concluded that it had harmed American interests. When all respondents, not only those at the two extreme quintiles on the Soviet foreign policy scale, are included in the analysis, the correlation between interpretations of Soviet foreign policy and assessments of detente is .50.

Despite Ronald Reagan's consistently harsh judgment about the Strategic Arms Limitation Talks and his handsome electoral victory in 1980, leaders taking part in the foreign policy leadership survey that year were, on balance, rather favorably inclined toward SALT. Only 15 percent agreed that resumption of the SALT process would "seriously jeopardize U.S. national security," whereas 68 percent felt that it would

TABLE 7
INTERPRETATIONS OF SOVIET FOREIGN POLICY
AND POSITIONS ON OTHER FOREIGN POLICY ISSUES:
DETENTE

The policy of detente pursued by previous U.S. administrations:	-------% CHECKING EACH OPTION-------		
		Soviet foreign policy Respondents in extreme quintiles	
	All respondents	Hardest	Softest
resulted in a significant improvement in Soviet-American relations	10	4	21
resulted in limited improvements in Soviet-American relations	55	32	68
had little effect, one way or the other	16	20	7
contributed to a decline of American influence in the world	10	20	1
placed U.S. security in dangerous jeopardy	6	16	1
not sure	3	7	3

Correlation, all respondents (gamma): .50

at least be a useful step in the right direction. Four years later the verdict was even more favorable, as well over nine respondents in ten offered a positive appraisal and over one-third of them judged arms control to be making "an important contribution toward a safer world." In contrast, those who viewed it as harming the nation's security fell to only two percent (Table 8).

Support for arms control among the entire leadership sample in 1984 was sufficiently high that, even among those with the "hardest" interpretation of Soviet foreign policy, more than three respondents in four gave a favorable verdict. Those at the other end of the scale were even more supportive. Ninety-six percent supported arms control negotiations and not a single person thought that it would harm American national security. The correlation between placement on the Soviet foreign policy scale and attitudes toward arms control is .39.

The third of the major foreign policy issues of the 1980 presidential campaign was the appropriate size of the defense budget. In this

TABLE 8
INTERPRETATIONS OF SOVIET FOREIGN POLICY
AND POSITIONS ON OTHER FOREIGN POLICY ISSUES:
ARMS CONTROL

If they can be resumed, Soviet-American arms control negotiations would:	-------% CHECKING EACH OPTION--------		
		Soviet foreign policy: Respondents in extreme quintiles	
	All respondents	Hardest	Softest
make an important contribution toward a safer world	38	21	56
be a useful but very limited step in the right direction	55	57	40
be of little significance	5	13	2
seriously jeopardize U.S. national security	2	6	0
not sure	1	3	2

Correlation, all respondents (gamma): .39

case, a very substantial number (58 percent) of leaders taking part in the leadership survey of that year agreed with candidate Reagan that the budget should be increased whereas only about one third that many wished to reduce it. During the next four years, a rather dramatic change of sentiment took place among those taking part in the leadership surveys. Leaders favoring an increase fell from 58 percent to only seven percent, while proponents of a reduction in budget allocations for the Pentagon included seven of every ten respondents (Table 9). Part of the shift may be attributable to a minor change in the wording of the 1984 question, and part of it may reflect a view that the President's defense buildup during the previous three years was sufficiently successful to permit reductions in future spending. Still another reason may be that the 1980 "defense consensus" is being washed away by a floodtide of red ink. The fact that half of the respondents would prefer reducing the Pentagon's allocations in order to cut the horrendous budget deficits offers some support for the latter interpretation.

Respondents in the "hardest" and "softest" quintiles expressed preferences on the defense budget that seem consistent with their views on Soviet foreign policy, although differences are somewhat muted by the overwhelming support for reduced defense spending. Among the former, the ratio in favor of reducing rather than increasing the DOD

TABLE 9
INTERPRETATIONS OF SOVIET FOREIGN POLICY
AND POSITIONS ON OTHER FOREIGN POLICY ISSUES:
THE DEFENSE BUDGET

The Administration's proposed defense budget ($305 billion) for next year should be:	------% CHECKING EACH OPTION------		
		Soviet foreign policy: % of group in extreme quintiles	
	All respondents	Hardest	Softest
Increased, and taxes should be increased to pay for it	2	3	*
Increased, and domestic programs should be reduced to pay for it	5	13	*
Maintained at about the proposed level	22	41	6
Reduced, and spending on domestic programs should be increased	20	8	34
Reduced, and the savings should be used to reduce the budget deficit	50	33	59
Not sure	1	1	*

Correlation, all respondents (gamma): .31
* Less than 0.5%

budget was 42 percent-16 percent whereas among the latter the ratio was more than 100-1. Among all 2,515 leaders, the correlation between placement on the Soviet foreign policy scale and attitudes on the defense budget was .31.

The results summarized in Table 6-9 buttress confidence in the "hard-to-soft" Soviet foreign policy scale. Each of several analyses indicated that differences among leaders at various points on that scale fit a consistent pattern; moreover, that pattern has a certain degree of face validity.

Background Attributes and Beliefs About Soviet Foreign Policy

The analysis now turns to the association between beliefs about Soviet foreign policy and the background attributes, including ideology, party, occupation, generation, gender, military service, education, and foreign travel, of American leaders taking part in the 1984 survey. Which if any of these characteristics are associated with "harder" or "softer" interpretations of Soviet foreign policy, and how strong are the relationships? To what extent do any of the cleavages that divide American leaders on questions of Soviet foreign policy overlap or cut across divisions on other issues? Do they resemble differences among the general public? For example, public opinion polls have revealed growing partisanship on foreign policy issues, but consistent evidence of a "generation gap" remains rather elusive. Are leaders similar to or different from the public at large in these respects? Because earlier analyses of the leadership survey data have indicated that ideology and party are among the stronger correlates of foreign policy beliefs, and these may also have greater direct political significance than some of the other background characteristics, they will receive somewhat more detailed attention.

Ideology

A substantial majority of respondents in the 1984 leadership survey described themselves as in the center of an ideological scale ranging from "far left" to "far right." Almost four-fifths of the respondents identified themselves as "somewhat liberal", "moderate", or "somewhat conservative." Because there are so few leaders in the "far left" (N=16) and "far right" (N=3) groups, in the analyses that follow they are combined with the "very liberal" and "very conservative" groups, respectively. Thus, the original seven-point scale has been collapsed to five categories.

The relationship between ideology and beliefs about the sources of Soviet foreign policy is summarized in Table 10, employing a format which will also be used in subsequent tables dealing with other respondent attributes (Tables 14, 18-23). The second column provides a group index score on a scale of 0.00 (all "hard line" interpretations of Soviet foreign policy) to 1.00 (all "soft line" interpretations). The two columns on the right indicate the percentage of each group (left, somewhat

TABLE 10
BACKGROUND ATTRIBUTES ASSOCIATED WITH INTERPRETATIONS
OF SOVIET FOREIGN POLICY:
IDEOLOGY

	N	Index*	Soviet foreign policy: % of group in extreme quintiles	
			Hardest	Softest
Left	180	.69	3	53
Somewhat liberal	633	.62	5	30
Moderate	662	.51	19	16
Somewhat conservative	743	.42	32	6
Right	166	.33	54	1
All respondents		.51	21	19

Correlation, all respondents (gamma): .52

* On a scale of 0.00 (all hardest line responses) to 1.00 (all softest line responses)

liberal, etc.) that may be found in the "hardest" and "softest" quintiles of the Soviet foreign policy scale.

The data summarized in Table 10 reveal that interpretations of Soviet foreign policy are strongly associated with ideology. As indicated in the second column, respondents who identified themselves as on the left are close to the "soft" end of the Soviet foreign policy scale, those on the right are about equally near the "hard" end of the scale, and the three middle groups are arrayed between them. These differences are also clearly evident in the two right-hand columns. The most conservative respondents are overwhelmingly (54 percent) among the staunchest adherents of a hard interpretation of Soviet foreign policy and few of them are found within the "softest" quintile. The pattern among the most liberal leaders is precisely the reverse, as a majority (53 percent) of them hold the "soft" view on the sources of Soviet external policy. These figures focus on leaders at the end points of the Soviet scale, but even when all respondents are included in the analysis, the correlation (gamma) between ideology and the Soviet scale is a rather strong .52.

Because data from the 1976 and 1980 leadership surveys uncovered strong links between ideology and a broad spectrum of foreign policy beliefs, it may be useful to undertake more detailed analyses of the 1984 responses to other items centering on the Soviet Union and Soviet-American relations, more specifically, the questions that first appeared in Tables 2-4.

Table 11, listing eight items on the nature, motives and goals of Soviet foreign policy, reveals very substantial differences between

TABLE 11
IMAGES OF THE ADVERSARY:
THE NATURE, MOTIVES AND GOALS OF THE SOVIET UNION
AS PERCEIVED BY RESPONDENTS TO THE 1984 [N=2,515]
FOREIGN POLICY LEADERSHIP SURVEY,
CLASSIFIED BY IDEOLOGY

Please indicate how strongly you agree or disagree with each of the following statements	% AGREE		
	Most Conservative	Most Liberal	Gamma**
The Soviet Union is generally expansionist rather than defensive in its foreign policy goals	96	47	.48
Revolutionary forces in "Third World" countries are usually nationalistic rather than controlled by the USSR or China	32	93	.53
The Soviet invasion of Afghanistan was one step in a larger plan to control the Persian Gulf area	90	26	.46
Communist nations were encouraged to seek further triumphs elsewhere as a result of Vietnam	92	33	.45
Detente permits the Soviet Union to pursue policies that promote rather than restrain conflict	86	12	.53
American foreign policy should be based on the premise that the Communist "bloc" is irreparably fragmented	18	57	.31
The Soviet Union acted in Afghanistan largely to protect itself against having a hostile regime on its borders	21	49	.24
The tide of influence in world affairs has swung toward communism as a result of the Vietnam War	45	6	.33

**"Agree strongly" plus "agree somewhat" responses combined.

**Computed for all 2,515 respondents.

liberals and conservatives. Indeed, all but the last two items find a majority of the most conservative leaders on one side of the issue and the most liberal on the other, and the differences between them are consistently large, reaching over sixty percent on four of the questions: the nature of revolutionary forces in the Third World, Soviet motives in the Persian Gulf, the impact of Vietnam on communist nations, and Soviet uses of detente. But the strong relationship between ideology and these issues is by no means confined to the leaders at the ends of the ideological spectrum. The correlations for the entire groups of 2,515 leaders are generally quite strong, as indicated in the right hand column of Table 11.

Table 12 focuses on Soviet-American relations, including the same items that appeared earlier in Table 3. The results reveal once again the strong ideological base underlying assessments of foreign affairs. In two cases — the decisions to restore grain sales to the USSR and to continue arms control negotiations after the Soviet destruction of the Korean civilian airliner — most conservative and liberal leaders offered support (although in rather different proportions), and a majority of conserva-

TABLE 12
AMERICAN-SOVIET RELATIONS AS PERCEIVED BY RESPONDENTS TO THE 1984 [N=2,515] FOREIGN POLICY LEADERSHIP SURVEY, CLASSIFIED BY IDEOLOGY

Please indicate how strongly you agree or disagree with each of the following statements	% AGREE *		
	Most Conservative	Most Liberal	Gamma**
Continuing arms control negotiations after the Soviets shot down the Korean civilian air liner	56	96	.38
Restoring grain sales to the Soviet Union	55	84	.12
The U.S. should provide increased support to rebels who are fighting the Soviets in Afghanistan	87	39	.35
There is considerable validity in the "domino theory" that when one nation falls to communism, others nearby will soon follow a similar path	92	11	.63

Preventing American firms from selling non-strategic equipment to the Soviet Union	75	20	.35
Opposing a "nuclear freeze"	75	8	.56
Any communist victory is a defeat for America's national interest	83	7	.56
Soviet actions in Afghanistan do not affect vital American interests	21	66	.32
The U.S. should take all steps including the use of force to prevent the spread of communism	77	4	.56
It is not in our interest to have better relations with the Soviet Union because we are getting less than we are giving to them	37	3	.44

*"Agree strongly" plus "agree somewhat" responses combined.

** Computed for all 2,515 respondents

tives and liberals disagreed with the propositions that, "It is not in our interest to have better relations with the Soviet Union because we are getting less than we are giving to them." The other seven items uncovered very strong differences between the most liberal and most conservative leaders, with the gulf between them reaching over eighty percent on assessments of the "domino theory". With the exception of the item on grain sales, correlations between ideology and issues of Soviet-American relations are consistently in the moderately-high to high range.

Five of the possible foreign policy goals listed in Table 13 touch, more or less directly, upon American policy toward the USSR: containment, matching Soviet military power, arms control, defending allies, and maintaining a balance of power. To understate the case, liberals and conservatives rated the importance of these goals rather differently. The gaps between responses of the most liberal and conservative leaders are exceptionally large on containment (78 percent), matching Soviet military power (85 percent), and arms control (53 percent). Comparable differences characterize responses to several of the non-strategic issues, including human rights abroad, hunger, Third World development, and the environment. The evidence reveals that the liberals and conserva-

TABLE 13
GOALS FOR AMERICAN FOREIGN POLICY:
ASSESSMENTS BY RESPONDENTS TO THE 1984 [N=2,515]
FOREIGN POLICY LEADERSHIP SURVEY,
CLASSIFIED BY IDEOLOGY

Please indicate how much importance should be attached to each goal	% VERY IMPORTANT		
	Most Conservative	Most Liberal	Gamma*
Securing adequate supplies of energy	93	70	.27
Promoting and defending our own security	99	56	.59
Worldwide arms control	39	92	.50
Fostering international cooperation to solve common problems, such as food, inflation and energy	40	86	.42
Helping to improve the standard of living in less developed countries	28	84	.44
Combatting world hunger	30	85	.47
Protecting the global environment	25	82	.46
Defending our allies' security	61	24	.23
Averting financial crises arising from Third World debts	32	56	.17
Maintaining a balance of power among nations	52	23	.23
Matching Soviet military power	84	6	.55
Containing communism	82	7	.58
Promoting and defending human rights in other countries	10	61	.46
Strengthening the United Nations	9	57	.40
Helping to bring a democratic form of government to other nations	24	20	.01

* Computed for all 2,515 respondents

tives have distinctly different foreign policy agendas that only rarely overlap to any significant extent.

The results summarized in Tables 10-13 have indicated repeatedly that assessments of the Soviet Union are strongly associated with ideological differences that extend to diagnoses of the sources of Soviet foreign policy, the significance of specific actions by the USSR (for example, the invasion of Afghanistan), assessments of the relationship between Washington and Moscow (for example, detente), and prescriptions on how best to cope with the Soviet Union. The significance of this pattern may be enhanced or eroded by the extent to which similar cleavages characterize party identification. That is, do ideological differences on the Soviet Union and Soviet-American relations overlap with partisan cleavages, or do they cut across party loyalties?

Political Party

Two generalizations about American politics, if valid today, would lead to the expectation that party affiliation is at best weakly linked to foreign policy beliefs. The first is that the two major parties are broad coalitions that cut across rather than between ideological orientations. The second stipulates that, however divided Americans may be on domestic issues, bipartisanship rather than partisanship is the rule on foreign policy issues; that is, "politics stops at the water's edge."

Although both of these generalizations are no doubt at best oversimplifications, available public opinion data indicates that, during the two decades after World War II, many significant foreign policy issues elicited rather similar patterns of approval or disapproval from Republicans and Democrats among the general public.[4] In the absence of comparable leadership surveys during that period, one can only speculate about the presence or absence of strong partisan cleavages at the leadership level. During the post-Vietnam era, however, bipartisanship has lost its status as a sacrosanct symbol. By 1979, when the Democrats controlled the White House and both houses of Congress, a leading Republican Senator called for its demise and for a return to a frankly partisan foreign policy stance. These developments are also reflected in public opinion polls of the past decade and a half which have consistently found rather substantial differences between Democrats and Republicans. Moreover, although American political parties may be less ideological than many of their European counterparts, there is at least some evidence of an increasing relationship between party affiliation and ideology. For example, among leaders taking part in the 1984 leadership survey, 65 percent of the Democrats identified themselves liberal to some degree and only 9 percent placed themselves somewhere on the conservative end of the scale; the comparable figures among Republicans were two percent and 80 percent, indicating that the liberal Republican has become something of an endangered species. The correlations (gamma) between party and ideology increased steadily through the three leadership surveys: 1976 (.66), 1980 (.70), and 1984 (.82). Although one should be cautious about generalizing too extensively from such limited data base, there is also evidence that the increasing connection between party and ideology may be found among members of the House and Senate.[5]

The sample of leaders taking part in the 1984 survey differs substantially from the general populations with respect to most attributes, including age, occupation, gender, military service, international travel, and education. But the distribution of political party preferences among the respondents — about three-eighths Democrat, one-third Republican, and slightly over one-quarter Independent — roughly approximates that among the entire American population. These figures also reflect the widely-noted erosion of loyalty to the major political parties, although the proportion of Democrats and Republicans rose slightly between the 1980 and 1984 leadership samples.

Among those taking part in the 1984 survey, the relationship between party affiliation and interpretations of Soviet foreign policy is moderately strong. As summarized in Table 14, Republicans were more inclined to accept a "hard line" interpretation of Soviet foreign policy, whereas Democrats were somewhat to the the "soft" end of the scale, and Independents were squarely between members of the two major parties. Among the entire sample of 2,515 leaders, the correlation between party and placement on the Soviet scale is a moderately high .39.

As in the case of ideology, the importance of partisanship suggests

TABLE 14
BACKGROUND ATTRIBUTES ASSOCIATED WITH INTERPRETATIONS OF SOVIET FOREIGN POLICY:
PARTY

	N	Index*	Soviet foreign policy: % of group in extreme quintiles	
			Hardest	Softest
Republican	764	.39	39	5
Democrat	933	.60	9	29
Independent	668	.52	16	18
All respondents		.51	21	19

Correlation, all respondents (C): .39

*On a scale of 0.00 (all hardest line responses) to 1.00 (all softest line responses).

the value of going beyond the results in Table 14 to examine the impact of party on the broader range of questions, introduced in Tables 2-4, relating to the Soviet Union.

Several patterns emerge from the data on images of the Soviet Union and its foreign policy, as summarized in Table 15. On each of the eight issues the Independents are, as a group, arrayed between members of the two major parties. Invariably the Republicans tended to be more pessimistic and critical than the Democrats about the nature, motives and goals of the USSR, but partisan differences, although clearly tracing a pattern similar to those defined by ideology, are somewhat less stark than ideological ones. Half of the issues found Republicans, Democrats and Independents on the same side, although with varying levels of agreement. They agreed that Soviet foreign policy is expansionist rather than defensive, and they rejected the propositions that the USSR acted out of defensive motives in Afghanistan, that the communist "bloc" is irreparably fragmented, and that the tide of influence in world affairs has swung toward communism as the result of the outcome in the Vietnam War. The other four items found sharper differences among respondents, as well as higher correlations between partisanship and responses, notably on the impact of detente on Soviet external behavior and the connection between Moscow (and Beijing) and revolutionary forces in the Third World. Because the latter propositions are at the core of current controversies on such issues as conflict in the Middle East, Africa, and Central America, these results do not suggest an easy or early reconstitution of bipartisanship.

Assessments of Soviet-American relations, summarized in Table 16, reveal a somewhat similar pattern of partisan differences. In varying degrees a majority of Republicans, Democrats and Independents supported arms control negotiations, resumption of grain sales, and aid to Afghan rebels, and they disagreed with the propositions that Soviet actions in Afghanistan have no impact on American interests and that improving relations between Washington and Moscow would be against American interests. The other five items revealed sharp differences rooted in partisanship, notably on the validity of the "domino theory", the value of a "nuclear freeze", the impact of any communist victory, and the steps to prevent such an outcome. Again, the questions most consistently dividing Republicans and Democrats are precisely those that appear to have the most direct bearing on such currently contentious issues as arms control, and the Soviet role in and the proper American response to various Third World conflicts.

Responses by Republican and Democratic leaders to a series of possible goals for American foreign policy are summarized in Table 17. The figures indicate that members of the two major political parties

TABLE 15
IMAGES OF THE ADVERSARY: THE NATURE, MOTIVES AND GOALS OF THE SOVIET UNION AS PERCEIVED BY RESPONDENTS TO THE 1984 [N=2,515] FOREIGN POLICY LEADERSHIP SURVEY, CLASSIFIED BY PARTY

Please indicate how strongly you agree or disagree with each of the following statements	% AGREE*			
	Republican	Democrat	Independent	C Coeff**
The Soviet Union is generally expansionist rather than defensive in its foreign policy goals	90	69	76	.32
Revolutionary forces in "Third World" countries are usually nationalistic rather than controlled by the USSR or China	46	83	73	.37
The Soviet invasion of Afghanistan was one step in a larger plan to control the Persian Gulf area	82	45	62	.35
Communist nations were encouraged to seek further triumphs elsewhere as a result of Vietnam	77	42	59	.31
Detente permits the Soviet Union to pursue policies that promote rather than restrain conflict	68	26	44	.36
American foreign policy should be based on the premise that the Communist "bloc" is irreparably fragmented	21	46	37	.26
The Soviet Union acted in Afghanistan largely to protect itself against having a hostile regime on its borders	24	38	32	.18
The tide of influence in world affairs has swung toward communism as a result of the Vietnam War	28	10	18	.23

**Agree strongly" plus "agree somewhat" responses combined.
** Computed for all 2,515 respondents

rated the importance of most goals rather differently; with the exception of the first (energy) and last (promoting democracy abroad) items,
the differences in "very important" ratings are all in the double digits,
ranging as high as forty percent.

The goals dealing most directly with the Soviet Union tended to
bring out some of the largest gaps between Republicans and Democrats.
Among the former, 63 percent rated both containment and matching
Soviet military power as very important foreign policy goals for the
United States, whereas the comparable figures among Democratic

TABLE 16
AMERICAN-SOVIET RELATIONS AS PERCEIVED BY RESPONDENTS TO
THE 1984 [N=2,515] FOREIGN POLICY LEADERSHIP SURVEYS,
CLASSIFIED BY PARTY

Please indicate how strongly you agree or disagree with each of the following statements	% AGREE *			
	Republican	Democrat	Independent	C Coeff**
Continuing arms control negotiations after the Soviets shot down the Korean air liner	74	91	87	.24
Restoring grain sales to the Soviet Union	69	71	72	.06
The U.S. should provide increased support to rebels who are fighting the Soviets in Afghanistan	76	57	65	.20
There is considerable validity in the "domino theory" that when one nation falls to communism, others nearby will soon follow a similar path	83	34	52	.42
Preventing American firms from selling nonstrategic equipment to the Soviet Union	57	35	43	.26
Opposing a "nuclear freeze"	66	25	42	.37
Any communist victory is a defeat for America's national interest	65	22	37	.38

Soviet actions in Afghanistan do not affect vital American interests	26	47	41	.23
The U.S. should take all steps including the use of force to prevent the spread of communism	56	19	30	.35
It is not in our interest to have better relations with the Soviet Union because we are getting less than we are giving to them	19	6	11	.25

*"Agree strongly" plus "agree somewhat" responses combined.
** Computed for all 2,515 respondents

leaders were only 23 percent and 24 percent, respectively. Conversely, the goal of arms control, while rated as very important by majorities among members of both political parties, clearly elicited substantially greater support among Democrats. Somewhat smaller partisan gaps emerged on the other two strategic issues — defending allies and maintaining a balance of power — but in each case Republicans assigned a greater importance to the goal.

Although most of the other goals listed in Table 17 touch much less directly on American-Soviet relations, responses suggest more clearly some of the differences among adherents to the two major political parties. Whereas security/strategic issues consistently received a higher priority among Republicans, Democrats were much more inclined to stress economic/development and related concerns, including international economic cooperation, the standard of living in less developed nations, world hunger, the global environment, human rights, and the like. Thus, while there are clearly some areas of common concern (energy, U.S. security, arms control), the foreign policy agendas of Republican and Democratic leaders are rather different. When combined with the results of the preceding three tables, the data in Table 17 suggest substantial difficulties facing those who would support a restoration of bipartisanship on foreign policy.

Occupation

Leaders taking part in the 1984 survey were classified into eleven occupational groups: military officers (N=146), business executives (466), lawyers (165), clergy (162), State Department officials (147),

TABLE 17
GOALS FOR AMERICAN FOREIGN POLICY: ASSESSMENTS BY RESPONDENTS TO THE 1984 [N=2,515] FOREIGN POLICY LEADERSHIP SURVEY, CLASSIFIED BY PARTY

Please indicate how much importance should be attached to each goal

	% VERY IMPORTANT			
	Republican	Democrat	Independent	C Coeff**
Securing adequate supplies of energy	89	81	86	.10
Promoting and defending our own security	96	76	82	.23
Worldwide arms control	53	82	74	.27
Fostering international cooperation to solve common problems, such as food, inflation and energy	51	74	70	.21
Helping to improve the standard of living in less developed countries	44	70	60	.22
Combatting world hunger	40	69	55	.24
Protecting the global environment	36	66	56	.26
Defending our allies' security	57	45	44	.11
Averting financial crises arising from Third World debts	39	50	45	.10
Maintaining a balance of power among nations	54	37	44	.15
Matching Soviet military power	63	24	40	.33
Containing communism	63	23	33	.35
Promoting and defending human rights in other countries	16	47	35	.30
Strengthening the United Nations	15	37	28	.28
Helping to bring a democratic form of government to other nations	19	18	18	.03

*Computed for all 2,515 respondents

labor leaders (81), public officials (122), educators (616), health care professionals (126), and chief editorial writers of major daily newspapers and other media leaders (224). The remaining 260 respondents, including the self-employed, scientists, and those who did not identify their occupations are grouped together in the "others" category.

Earlier surveys revealed some significant differences in foreign policy beliefs among members of these occupational groups. Military officers, clergy and labor leaders ranked highest on three quite distinct ways of thinking about contemporary foreign affairs, Cold War Internationalism, Post-Cold War Internationalism, and Semi-Isolationism, respectively. (These terms will be defined and discussed in a later section of this paper.) Conversely, the clergy, educators, State Department officials, and media leaders were least inclined toward Cold War Internationalism, whereas military officers ranked lowest on the other two perspectives.

The relationship between occupation and responses to the items constituting the Soviet foreign policy scale are summarized in Table 18. Systematic differences among occupational groups emerge from the data but they tend to be somewhat muted compared to those derived from ideological or partisan classifications of respondents. This is reflected in the narrower range of group index scores, the distribution of leaders in the "hardest" and "softest" quintiles, and the overall correlation (.29) between occupation and interpretations of Soviet foreign policy. Nevertheless, a discernible pattern does emerge from findings and in many respects it appears consistent with findings from the two earlier leadership surveys. Business executives, military officers and lawyers are, as a group, somewhat to the "hard" end of the scale, educators, State Department officials, labor leaders and the clergy tend toward the "soft" end, and the remaining occupational groups are closely bunched very near the mid-point of the scale. Even within this pattern, however, it should be stressed that, at least with respect to interpretations of Soviet foreign policy, there is a good deal of diversity even within the occupational groups that rank highest and lowest on the scale.

Gender

Few predictions about social changes seem as safe as the proposition that women will play an increasingly important role in leadership positions. However one may judge the pace of change in this respect, there can be little disagreement about the trend. If that premise is valid, how will this development affect politics? Will it bring a higher standard of probity to the political process? A more humane set of concerns into the formulation of political agendas? In the realm of external affairs,

TABLE 18
BACKGROUND ATTRIBUTES ASSOCIATED WITH INTERPRETATIONS
OF SOVIET FOREIGN POLICY: OCCUPATION

	N	Index*	Soviet foreign policy: % of group in extreme quintiles	
			Hardest	Softest
Business executives	466	.42	33	8
Military officers	146	.46	21	11
Lawyers	165	.47	27	12
Public officials	122	.50	23	17
Health care	126	.50	23	17
Media	224	.52	17	17
Clergy	162	.55	17	23
Labor leaders	81	.55	12	23
State Department	147	.57	7	20
Educators	616	.58	13	30
Others	260	.49	23	16
All respondents		.51	21	19

Correlation, all respondents (C): .29

*On a scale of 0.00 (all hardest line responses) to 1.00 (all softest line responses).

will it give rise to a more serious concern and a higher priority for undertakings that often fall outside the purview of those espousing or practicing realpolitik diplomacy? These questions imply that women may bring to the political process a set of beliefs or world views that differ systematically from those of their male counterparts.

These are interesting and important questions for which the evidence is both sparse and inconclusive. Although the literature on women in politics is not insubstantial and has grown dramatically in recent years, much of it is concentrated in several areas, including background attributes and political participation, socialization, voting behavior, and the like. Other questions, including foreign policy beliefs of women in leadership positions, have received less attention. For example, foreign policy surveys undertaken by the Chicago Council of Foreign Relations in 1974, 1978, 1982, and 1986 included both leaders and members of the public at large. Summaries of the finding do not even report the results for men and women separately, much less analyze the similarities and differences between them. The available information is not only scanty; it has also yielded rather contradictory conclusions.

It is possible to develop at least two different lines of reasoning concerning the foreign policy beliefs of American women in leadership positions. According to one, their beliefs will differ significantly from those of their male counterparts. More specifically, women will tend to have more benign and optimistic views of the international system, to give priority to social, economic, and humanitarian issues rather than to political-strategic concerns, and to be less inclined toward the use of military capabilities and force as means of dealing with global issues. This viewpoint conforms to a long tradition which depicts women as the less belligerent half of the species. It also finds some sustenance in more recent evidence. For example, a summary of polls on the Vietnam War found that women consistently provided less support for the American war effort, and they were stronger advocates of withdrawal from Southeast Asia.[6]

Another review of Gallup and Harris surveys revealed that these results were not confined to the Vietnam issue; women were generally found to be less inclined to seek military solutions to international, problems.[7]

It is important to recall, however, that these findings are derived from surveys of the general public rather than of individuals in leadership positions. The premise is that sex-role experiences constitute such a potent force that their effects persist throughout the populations, including those who have achieved positions of leadership in various institutions.

According to an alternative line of reasoning, the foreign policy beliefs of women leaders do not differ significantly from those of men in comparable roles. Whatever the differences among women and men in the entire population, their views converge at the leadership level. According to this thesis, leaders have more in common with each other than they have with members of their own gender in the public at large. This line of reasoning is also supported by some evidence, but empirical studies of gender differences among leaders are quite scarce. A survey of leaders attending a 1958 conference on national security revealed that any differences among men and women disappeared after controlling for occupation and party preference.[8]

Although gender gap has been cited as a significant source of post-Vietnam cleavages on foreign and defense issues, the 1976 leadership survey revealed scant evidence of gender-based differences among American leaders. Multivariate analyses also indicated that women tended to respond to a broad range of issues much as their occupational colleagues did. For example, female military officers held views similar to those of their male counterparts whereas the foreign policy beliefs of female media leaders also resembled those of their male colleagues. The 1980 leadership survey data also failed to provide stronger evidence of a gender gap among American leaders. If anything, the associations between gender and foreign policy declined during the period between the

TABLE 19
INTERPRETATIONS OF SOVIET FOREIGN POLICY AND OTHER
POLITICAL BELIEFS: GENDER

| | N | Index* | % of group in extreme quintiles | |
			Hardest	Softest
Men	2,124	.52	19	19
Women	313	.48	28	15
All respondents		.51	21	19

Correlation, all respondents (C): .08

*On a scale of 0.00 (all hardest line responses) to 1.00 (all softest line responses).

two surveys. Thus, while the term "gender gap" has become a common term in contemporary political discourse, neither of the previous leadership surveys uncovered much systematic evidence in support on gender-based differences on foreign policy issues. Even when this item or that found a significant gap between men and women, the differences rarely fit a consistent pattern. For example, on items that dealt with possible uses of force, in some cases women were slightly more prone to support such efforts, whereas in other instances they were less inclined to do so. Certainly the popular image of a gender gap pitting "hawkish men" versus "dovish women" found little corroboration in either of the two earlier leadership surveys.

Data on the relationship between gender and interpretations of Soviet foreign policy, summarized in Table 19, reveal only minor differences between men and women taking part in the 1984 survey. The thesis that the domestic and foreign policies of the Reagan Administration would enhance manifest gender differences and activate latent ones does not receive much support in these results. Indeed, although the overriding conclusion that emerges from Table 19 is that women and men do not vary much in assessing the sources of Soviet foreign policy, what differences do exist indicate that women are somewhat more inclined toward a "hard" interpretation whereas men lean slightly toward a "soft" one. Nineteen percent of men can be found in each of the extreme quintiles, but almost twice as many women are in the "hardest" (28 percent) as in the "softest" (15 percent) quintile.

Generation

Because there has been so much speculation about a "generation gap" as a primary source of cleavages on foreign affairs, it is worth a more extended discussion. Some years ago, Karl Mannheim suggested that generation is one of the more important factors shaping social beliefs and action:

> The fact of belonging to the same class, and that of belonging to the same generation or age group, have this in common, that both endow the individual with a common location in the social and historical process, and thereby limit them to a specific range of experience, predisposing them for certain characteristic mode of thought and experience, and a characteristic type of historically relevant action.[9]

Mannheim's injunction has not gone unheeded. In recent years the concept of generation has played a central role in analyses ranging from the political right in inter-war Finland to a proposed new paradigm for the entire course of American history, and from the Sino-Soviet conflict to the political views of American students. Even the recent turmoil in Poland has been explained by reference to generational differences.

American involvement in Vietnam and its attending domestic conflict have generated a good deal of speculation about generational differences and, more specifically, about the divergent lessons that Americans of different ages have drawn from the most salient foreign policy episodes they have experienced. "Generation gap" has thus joined those other famous gaps — gender, bomber, missile and credibility — in the vocabulary of many foreign policy analysts. The most visible lines of cleavage have quite often been described a falling between persons whose views were shaped by events leading up to World War II, on the one hand, and, on the other, those whose outlook has been molded by the war in Southeast Asia. The interpretation that links contemporary dissensus on matters of foreign policy to the lessons that each generation has adduced from dramatic and traumatic episodes has been summarized by a former White House National Security Adviser:

> There is a tendency in America to be traumatized by international difficulties. The generation of the Nineteen-forties was always thinking about the failure of the League of Nations. I'm talking about leadership groups now. The leadership of the sixties was always thinking about Munich. Now there is a generation worried by Vietnam, with consequences of self-imposed paralysis, which is likely to be costlier in the long run.[10]

To be more specific, the "Munich generation versus Vietnam generation" thesis usually takes some variant of the following line of reasoning. Those who experienced the bitter fruits of appeasement and American isolationism during the 1930s tended to identify the 1938 Munich Conference as the paradigmatic example of how not to deal with expansionist totalitarian regimes. When faced after World War II with the Soviet occupation of Eastern Europe, the absence of any liberalization within the USSR, as well as periodic crises in Berlin and elsewhere, persons of this generations were prepared to support an active American foreign policy to meet challenges from the Soviet Union and its satellites.

In contrast, according to this thesis, persons of a more recent generation — for whom World War II and its genesis, as well as the origins of the Cold War, are merely distant historical events rather than episodes experienced at first hand — are more likely to look to the war in Southeast Asia as a source of guidance on the proper and improper conduct of foreign relations. According to this description of contemporary American society, then, what the parents regard as indispensable commitments to maintain a viable world order their offspring view as indiscriminate (if not incriminating) undertakings against ill-defined, often phantom threats that have no intimate connection to legitimate American interests, let alone the propagation or preservation of democratic values and institutions abroad. Unencumbered by the memories and ideological baggage accumulated during World War II and the Cold War, the new generation is sometimes described as concerned with not only the physical safety of the nation, but also of this fragile spaceship earth; as ready to give up the hidebound political shibboleths of their elders in favor of a more enlightened world-view; as eager to renounce a materialistic life-style that eats up a disproportionate share of the world's resources in favor of simpler pleasures; and as inclined to respond to the sound of falling dominoes with a bored, "so what?" To some, this is a harbinger of better days to come, and to others it is no doubt a profoundly threatening one. This is, of course, a vastly oversimplified summary of a rather complex line of reasoning. Nevertheless, even if it is something of a caricature, it does capture some central elements of the thesis that in important respects the cleavages on foreign policy issues in this country represent a confrontation of two distinct world-views, each rooted in and sustained by the experiences of different generations.

The generational thesis, if valid, has some important implications for the future conduct of American foreign policy because it suggests that members of the "Vietnam generation," as they achieve positions of leadership and influence during the next several decades, will bring to their roles an intellectual baggage radically different from that of the leaders they are replacing. Under these circumstances, moreover, the prognosis is that as the next generation of leaders replaces those currently in positions of influence, a new consensus reflecting the sensibilities of the younger group will emerge in the not-too-distant future.

Recall that persons who had reached voting age at the time of the Munich Conference will reach retirement age during the current decade.

However plausible the generational interpretation of foreign policy differences may be, it is not universally accepted. Both survey and voting data suggest that, at least within the public at large, cleavages do not fall quite so nearly along age lines. Thus, the image of a "dovish" or new-isolationist generation of students demonstrating on campuses to protest the excessive foreign policy commitments of their elders provides, according to some observers, a skewed, if not inaccurate, picture of contemporary American society. For example, analyses of the 1974 Chicago Council on Foreign Relations poll failed to reveal striking differences among age groups. Of those under the age of 30, 30 percent were classified as "liberal internationalists," 32 percent as "conservative internationalists," and 38 percent as "non-internationalists." Indeed, compared to the 30-64 and over 64 age groups, those of the youngest generation were the most evenly distributed among these three categories.[11]

Even the more specific proposition that ties generational conflict to the war in Vietnam receives little support from polls conducted during the decade prior to the 1973 Paris agreement that was to have ended the war. Indeed, these surveys revealed that, compared to their elders, the younger respondents were usually more inclined to support American policy in Southeast Asia, as well as to oppose withdrawal. However, at least some advocates of the generational thesis suggest that, whatever may be true of the public at large, it describes accurately the cleavages among elites, actual and emerging.

To assess the effects of age on foreign policy beliefs, the entire sample of respondents to each leadership survey was divided into four groups based on year of birth. In the absence of any standard guidelines for identifying generations, the designation of cutting points is an arbitrary decision, based on two premises. The three wars in which the United States has been involved since 1941 were assumed to provide significant benchmarks. The "Munich generation versus Vietnam generation" thesis also identifies two of these wars as watershed points in American thinking about external affairs. The second premise is that late adolescence and young adulthood may have special significance. Because that period encompasses for many the beginning of eligibility for military service, consciousness of and interest in foreign affairs may be enhanced when prospects for personal involvement hinge upon the outcome of foreign policy undertakings. More generally, those years in the life cycle have often been identified as especially crucial in the formation and development of political beliefs.

Following this reasoning, three cutting points, 1923-4, 1932-3, and 1940-1, divided the respondents into four groups. Even the youngest of the World War II generation — those born in 1923 — had reached at least the age of 18 when the attack on Pearl Harbor brought the United States into World War II. By the end of that war they would have been likely, if otherwise eligible, to have experienced military service. But even those who were not on active military duty could scarcely have lived through the war without having taken cognizance of it. Leaders born between 1924 and 1932 would at least have reached the age of 21 during some part of the Korean War. The older among them would also have been young adults during World War II, but for this group the Korean War would presumably have been an especially salient experience. Persons born between 1933 and 1940 would, if inducted into the armed forces, most likely have served during the period following the Korean armistice of 1953 and before the rapid escalation in 1965 of the Vietnam conflict. Hence this group is labeled the "interim generation." Finally, those born after 1940 have been designated as the "Vietnam generation." Even the oldest persons in the groups would have been only 13 years old when the fighting in Korea ended. For them "the war" almost certainly refers to the conflict in Southeast Asia. The "Korea generation" constitutes the largest group (28 percent of all leaders in the 1984 survey), followed by the "World War II generation" (21 percent), "Vietnam generation" (18 percent), and interim generation (18 percent). The remainder did not reveal their year of birth.

The 1976 survey data did not provide much support for the thesis that cleavages on foreign policy issues in the United States are essentially generational in origin. More importantly, there is little evidence of a consistent pattern of cleavages that arrays the youngest group of leaders against their elders. Even when some generational differences emerged on this issue or that, they did not consistently fit the pattern suggested by the "Munich hawks versus Vietnam doves" hypothesis. The finding that generational differences accounted for little of the variance in foreign policy beliefs received further support from the 1980 survey data. Indeed, the correlations between age and beliefs was even weaker than it was four years earlier.

Despite the seeming appeal of the generational thesis, repeated efforts to find support for it in leadership survey data have thus yielded a very limited harvest. As was the case with the "gender gap" theory, even in the rare instances when differences related to age emerged, they did not fit a consistent pattern; in some cases the youngest respondents took a more "hawkish" position on an issue whereas in others it was the oldest who did so. Moreover, analyses of data from the general public

TABLE 20
BACKGROUND ATTRIBUTES ASSOCIATED WITH INTERPRETATIONS
OF SOVIET FOREIGN POLICY: GENERATION

	N	Index*	Soviet foreign policy: % of group in extreme quintiles	
			Hardest	Softest
Vietnam (born since 1940)	457	.51	20	19
Interim (born 1933-1940)	441	.52	16	17
Korean (born 1924-1932)	695	.50	22	19
World War II (born before 1924)	517	.51	23	19
All respondents		.51	21	19

Correlation, all respondents (gamma): .01

*On a scale of 0.00 (all hardest line responses) to 1.00 (all softest line responses).

have generally found a relatively weak generational basis for foreign policy attitudes.[12]

The paucity of data supporting the generational theory is also evident in assessments of the sources of Soviet foreign policy. The results summarized in Table 20 indicate that when respondents to the 1984 survey are classifed by age, the resulting groups are virtually indistinguishable in their interpretations of the USSR. The absence of clear differences rooted in age is evident not only in the index scores, none of which deviates significantly from the mean for the entire sample of 2,515 leaders, but also in the distribution of respondents in the extreme quintiles and in the overall correlation of an infinitesimal .01 between generation and the Soviet foreign policy index.

Education

A leadership survey may not be the ideal instrument for assessing the impact of education on foreign policy beliefs because any sample of American leaders is virtually certain to be skewed toward the high end of an education scale. That is unquestionably the case with the respondents to the 1984 leadership survey (as well as with the two earlier studies). Recall from Table 1 that almost seventy percent of the respondents held graduate degrees, whereas less than one percent were without some level of college experience. Even when all leaders with less than a BA/BS degree are combined into a single category, it accounts for only six percent of the entire group.

As revealed in Table 21, there is a modest relationship between education and responses to items in the Soviet foreign policy scale.

TABLE 21
BACKGROUND ATTRIBUTES ASSOCIATED WITH INTERPRETATIONS
OF SOVIET FOREIGN POLICY: EDUCATION

	N	Index*	Soviet foreign policy: % of group in extreme quintiles	
			Hardest	Softest
Less than college graduate	153	.42	35	5
College graduate	260	.46	28	14
Graduate work	288	.48	23	12
Graduate degree	1,736	.53	18	22
All respondents		.51	21	19

Correlation, all respondents (gamma): .23

*On a scale of 0.00 (all hardest line responses) to 1.00 (all softest line responses)

Lower levels of education are associated with a "harder" interpretation and each higher level of education corresponds with moderate changes toward the other end of the scale. However, even this modest pattern must be interpreted with some caution. For example, levels of education are not wholly independent of occupation, an attribute already shown to have some connection with interpretations of Soviet foreign policy (Table 18). Virtually all educators (a group found to be toward the "soft" end of the Soviet scale) could be expected to have some type of graduate degree whereas high-ranking military officers (more typically at the other end of the scale) are most likely to receive advanced training at service schools that do not offer conventional academic degrees to its graduates. Thus, further analyses of the data, to be undertaken later using multivariate techniques, may well reveal that the independent impact of education is somewhat less than suggested by the figures in Table 21.

Military Service

Military service is often thought to have a significant impact on political attitudes. More than in most organizations, socialization in the military emphasizes national security and the role of the armed forces in its maintenance, both historically and at present. Hence the often asserted thesis that those with military experience will tend to take a "harder line" on questions of foreign and defense policy, a viewpoint that is likely to carry over to interpretations of Soviet foreign policy and its sources. Helping to sustain this image is the fact that organizations claiming to represent veterans, notably the American Legion, have usually adopted predictably hard-line positions, not only on veterans'

TABLE 22
BACKGROUND ATTRIBUTES ASSOCIATED WITH INTERPRETATIONS
OF SOVIET FOREIGN POLICY:
MILITARY SERVICE

	N	Index*	Soviet foreign policy: % of group in extreme quintiles	
			Hardest	Softest
Veterans	1,375	.50	21	17
Non-veterans	1,056	.52	20	21
All respondents		.51	21	19

Correlation, all respondents (C): .06

*On a scale of 0.00 (all hardest line responses) to 1.00 (all softest line responses)

benefits and related concerns, but also on such issues as the proper level of the defense budget, conscription, containment, and the like. Evidence on the impact of military service is rather mixed, however. Most studies have focused on the professional military, and those comparing veterans and non-veterans among the general public yielded somewhat contradictory findings.

A substantial proportion of the 1984 leadership sample has served in the military. Among the entire group, almost fifty-five percent have done so and even when professional military officers are excluded from consideration, veterans constitute well over one-half of the sample. As indicated by the results summarized in Table 22, military service has virtually no impact on interpretations of Soviet foreign policy. By only the slightest of margins are veterans more inclined toward the "hard" end of the scale, and if career military officers were taken out of the analysis, even that small difference would disappear. Thus, the mere fact of military service (as distinguished from a military career) is not a significant factor in assessments of Soviet foreign policy. The finding conforms to a more general pattern that emerged from other analyses of data from the three leadership surveys, all of which indicated that veterans do not significantly differ from non-veterans with respect to foreign policy issues.

Travel

The cliche that "travel is broadening" suggests that it may have a liberalizing impact, making those who visit other countries less inclined to hold narrow, parochial views and to be more understanding of, if not necessarily more sympathetic with, foreign cultures, mores, and institu-

TABLE 23
BACKGROUND ATTRIBUTES ASSOCIATED WITH INTERPRETATIONS
OF SOVIET FOREIGN POLICY: INTERNATIONAL TRAVEL

| | N | Index* | Soviet foreign policy: % of group in extreme quintiles | |
			Hardest	Softest
None	490	.48	25	16
Limited	515	.51	21	19
Moderate	525	.51	22	18
High	412	.53	17	20
Very High	254	.51	22	18
Extremely High	319	.54	14	23
All respondents		.51	21	19

Correlation, all respondents (gamma): .07

Travel to USSR or E. Europe

	N	Index*	Hardest	Softest
Yes	562	.54	18	23
No	1,880	.50	21	17
All respondents		.51	21	19

Correlation, all respondents (C): .08

*On a scale of 0.00 (all hardest line responses) to 1.00 (all softest line responses).

tions. Whether or not the cliche is true, dictatorships often seem to make policy as if it were. The question to be addressed here is whether foreign travel is systematically associated with beliefs about the sources of Soviet foreign policy.

Those taking part in the 1984 leadership survey were classified into six groups according to the extent of foreign travel. The resulting analyses, presented in Table 23, indicate that travel has a rather limited impact on interpretations of Soviet foreign policy. Except for the two end categories it is hard to discern any impact. Respondents who had never travelled abroad were slightly more prone to adopt a "hard" interpretation, whereas those who had been abroad most extensively were a bit more inclined toward the other end of the scale, but as the overall correlations of .07 between travel and positions on the Soviet Union indicates, the relationship is quite weak.

Because respondents were asked to check the areas to which they had travelled, it is also possible to identify those who had visited the USSR or Eastern Europe, the areas that are more directly relevant to assessments of Soviet foreign policy. A substantial group of leaders, totalling more than one-fifth of the entire sample, had been in that area at least once. However, the impact of travel abroad there was apparently no greater than that of other experiences abroad. Only by the slightest of margins were leaders who had travelled in the USSR or

Eastern Europe more likely to hold "softer" views on the Soviet foreign policy.

A thorough and convincing effort to assess the impact of travel cannot be undertaken with the limited data available in the leadership survey questionnaire. Some type of "before-after" analysis would be required to determine whether attitudes are affected, how much, and in what direction. Because at least some kinds of travel are a matter of choice, do persons who choose to visit the Soviet Union (or other countries) do so because of pre-existing attitudes that differ from those held by others? Does the travel reinforce pre-existing antipathies or sympathies, or does it challenge them sufficiently to result in attitude changes? Because questions of this type cannot be answered with the data at hand, these results are at best suggestive rather than a definitive analysis of the impact of travel abroad.

Interpretations of Soviet Foreign Policy and Other Political Beliefs

The preceding pages examined how views on Soviet foreign policy are related to some of the background characteristics of leaders taking part in the 1984 survey. A parallel analysis to be undertaken here focuses on the links between assessments of the USSR and positions on a broader range of political questions about both domestic and foreign policy. More specifically, what are the connections with more general conceptions of foreign relations and of America's appropriate role in the international system? With policy preferences on an issue that straddles foreign and domestic politics — protectionism? With a wide range of economic and social domestic issues?

Three perspectives on foreign affairs

Extensive analyses of the 1976 and 1980 foreign policy leadership data revealed the existence of three quite distinct ways of thinking about foreign affairs. As these have been described in some detail elsewhere it should suffice to provide relatively brief summaries of them here.[13]

Cold War Internationalists are inclined to view the international system as bipolar in structure. A relentless Soviet drive against the United States and its allies, buttressed by a rapid military buildup in the USSR, is thus the primary threat. Although seemingly muted during periods of detente, Moscow's determination to expand its influence by whatever means is the unvarying driving force behind Kremlin policies. In order to forestall the threat, it is vital for the United States and the West to maintain a high level of military capabilities, a determination to match or exceed increases in Soviet force levels and a willingness to use military power if necessary to discourage adventures by the USSR.

Post-Cold War Internationalists tend to view the international system and primary threats to its stability in terms of North-South issues, including but not limited to the growing gap between rich and poor nations, threats to the environment, population, resources, racial conflict, trade, Third World debts, and other international economic issues. Although not unmindful of East-West tensions, they are inclined to view problems between Moscow and Washington as tractable. Detente, arms control, and other such measures can not only stabilize relations between the superpowers but also permit some of the resources that have, for example, gone into arms races to be used for dealing with the longer-range threats to mankind. As the richest and most powerful nation in the world, the United States has both a vital interest and an obligation to play an active role in eradicating obstacles to the creation of a just and stable world order.

Whereas the two internationalist schools of thought locate the primary threats to American security and interests in elements of the international system, the Semi-Isolationists believe that excessively internationalist American policies, whether to cope with East-West or North-South issues, are themselves the major threat to the United States. By taking on the role of the world's policeman, the world's do-gooder, or the world's conscience — with only selective success at best — the United States has squandered vast material and non-material resources that are vitally needed to deal with a long agenda of neglected domestic problems. Indeed, some Semi-Isolationists have revived a theme with venerable roots in American political thought — that the ability to nurture and sustain democratic institutions at home is inversely related to the scope of the nation's commitment abroad. Thus, they counsel a recognition that American vital international interests are finite, as are its resources. What is needed is not tinkering at the margins of contemporary foreign and defense policies, but a more realistic assessment of resources and a basic redefinition of vital interests. The former should define the latter rather than vice versa.[14]

Responses to several questions that appeared in both the 1976 and 1980 surveys were used to construct an index for each foreign policy belief system. The same items were included in the 1984 questionnaire, permitting the same index to be used.

The relationship between respondents' positions on three foreign policy scales and the Soviet "hard-to-soft" scale is summarized in Table

TABLE 24
INTERPRETATIONS OF SOVIET FOREIGN POLICY
AND OTHER POLITICAL BELIEFS:
FOREIGN POLICY ORIENTATION

Respondents highest on	N	Index*	Soviet foreign policy: % of group in extreme quintiles	
			Hardest	Softest
Cold War Internationalism	743	.34	50	1
Post-Cold War Internationalism	637	.61	10	34
Semi-Isolationism	629	.62	10	37
All respondents		.51	21	19
Correlations, all respondents (gamma)				
Cold War Internationalism		.70		
Post-Cold War Internationalism		.35		
Semi-Isolationism		.36		

*On a scale of 0.00 (all hardest line responses) to 1.00 (all softest line responses)

24. The results indicate a rather close connection and, as in previous analyses involving the three foreign policy scales, the relationship is especially strong for Cold War Internationalism. Leaders ranking highest on the CWI scale were also consistently toward the "hard" end of the Soviet scale, with half of them in the "hardest" quintile and only one percent in the "softest" category. When all leaders rather than only those at the end categories are considered, the result is a very high correlation of .70.

Results for the other two foreign policy scales — Post-Cold War Internationalism and Semi-Isolationism — indicate that they are both associated with a "soft" interpretation of Soviet foreign policy, whether measured by the index scores, the distribution of respondents in the two extreme quintiles on the Soviet scale, or the correlation coefficients. In neither case, however, does the strength of the relationship match that for the CWI scale. These findings are not unexpected because they are consistent with the nature of the three perspectives on foreign policy. The essence of Cold War Internationalism is its focus on dangers and opportunities arising from East-West relations and, more specifically, from an inherently expansionist Soviet Union. On the other hand, the other two foreign policy perspectives attribute somewhat less urgency to Soviet-American relations and to the extent that they do, it is to stress the possibilities for accommodation between Washington and Moscow on such issues as arms control, crisis prevention, and the like.

Protectionism

During much of the first quarter century after the end of World War II the goal of free trade enjoyed rather widespread support among American leaders. Many agreed with Cordell Hull that protectionism had contributed to the international economic chaos of the decade immediately preceding the war and thus, had helped to bring on the conflict. American economic strength was also at its zenith relative to competitors, reducing domestic pressures for protectionist measures. The "Nixon economic shock" of 1971 signalled the end of an era, however, and since that time trade issues have become an increasingly visible and contentious element of American domestic politics.

The 1984 leadership survey includes an item that asked respondents how strongly they agreed or disagreed with, "Erecting trade barriers against foreign goods to protect American industries and jobs." Support for protectionism among American leaders is rather limited, especially when compared to responses on the issue among the general public. Other analyses have also shown that protectionist sentiments tend to be independent of positions on most other domestic and foreign policy issues. Moreover, positions on the question of increasing trade barriers are not closely connected to ideological, partisan or other background characteristics. The only clear exception arises in connection with occupation, as labor leaders stand out in their strong support for protectionism.[15]

As indicated in Table 25, leaders who support raising trade barriers also tend to have a somewhat "harder" interpretation of Soviet foreign policy. Although the relationship is not very strong — the correlation is a modest .18 — three times as many advocates of protection may be found in the "hardest" as in the "softest" quintile on the Soviet scale, whereas opponents of protectionism are about equally distributed in the extreme categories. In light of the strong protectionist sentiments among labor leaders, one might guess that they account for a good deal of the pattern, but in fact the labor leaders took a somewhat "soft" view of Soviet policy (see Table 17). Another possible explanation, that protectionism and a "hard" interpretation of Soviet foreign policy may reflect an underlying isolationism arising from a shared suspicion of things foreign, may not be especially tenable either. Recall that those two ranked high on Semi-Isolationism tended to accept a "softer" view of Soviet diplomacy (Table 23). Perhaps subsequent analyses will reveal more convincing interpretations, but it is also well to repeat that the relationship described in Table 25 is rather weak.

TABLE 25
INTERPRETATIONS OF SOVIET FOREIGN POLICY
AND OTHER POLITICAL BELIEFS:
PROTECTIONISM

Respondents who	N	Index*	Soviet foreign policy: % of group in extreme quintiles	
			Hardest	Softest
Support protectionism	584	.44	30	11
Oppose protectionism	1,873	.53	18	21
Not sure	58	.58	14	29
All respondents		.51	21	19

Correlation, all respondents (gamma): .18

On a scale of 0.00 (all hardest line responses) to 1.00 (all softest line responses)

Domestic conservatism and liberalism

Unlike the 1976 and 1980 surveys, that undertaken in 1984 included a number of questions on domestic policy. These included not only some of the conventional "pocketbook" issues that focus on the economy, taxation, income redistribution, environmental and economic regulation, the budget and the like, but also some of the so-called "social issues" that have become a visible and controversial part of American political debates during the past few years. Among the latter are questions relating to abortion, school bussing, tuition tax credits, school prayer, capital punishment, and treatment of minorities or the traditionally disadvantaged. Analyses of these items revealed that almost without exception responses to them could be accurately described by a "conservative-to-liberal" scale.[16] A further distinction between economic and social issues indicated that responses to the latter tended to cluster a little more tightly, but the dominant pattern for both types of issues could be described by a conventional ideological scale.

The connection between positions on domestic and foreign policy issues is not obvious. Most of the early research on public opinion and voting behavior revealed very weak correlations at best. This conclusion is a fairly typical summary of many studies: "Across our sample as a whole in 1956 there was no relationship between scale positions of individuals on the domestic and foreign attitudinal dimensions."[17] At the same time there were some hints in the literature that perhaps the correlations between domestic and foreign policy issue was stronger among leaders than among the general public.[18] Another study of the question using the 1984 leadership survey data found a rather consistently strong correlation between responses to questions in the two policy areas.

The relationship between positions on domestic issues and interpretations of Soviet foreign policy is summarized in Tables 26 and 27. Each of the tables reports results for three domestic measures based on economic issues, social issues, and a composite measure that combines both types of issues. The results point to a clear and consistent pattern in which domestic conservatism is associated with a "hard" interpretation of Soviet foreign policy, whereas domestic liberalism is linked to a "softer" assessment. The pattern is not sensitive to the type of domestic issue, as the social, economic and composite scales yield essentially similar results. Nor do the results vary according to the type of analysis. The index scores and distributions of respondents in the extreme quintiles of the Soviet scale focus upon the most conservative and most liberal leaders taking part in the survey. Both of these measures reveal quite clearly how differently domestic conservatives and liberals interpreted Soviet foreign policy. The correlation coefficients, on the other hand, include all respondents and they confirm the result of the other measures.

The results summarized in Tables 24-27 indicated that interpretations of Soviet foreign policy are quite closely connected with a broader range of political beliefs. Stated somewhat differently, the cleavages that divide American leaders on many foreign policy and domestic is-

---

TABLE 26
INTERPRETATIONS OF SOVIET FOREIGN POLICY
AND OTHER POLITICAL BELIEFS:
DOMESTIC CONSERVATISM

Respondents highest on	N	Index*	Soviet foreign policy: % of group in extreme quintiles	
			Hardest	Softest
Composite conservatism	497	.37	45	4
Social conservatism	447	.36	47	3
Economic conservatism	524	.38	41	5
All respondents		.51	21	19
Correlations, all respondents (gamma)				
Composite conservatism		.49		
Social conservatism		.48		
Economic conservatism		.40		

*On a scale of 0.00 (all hardest line responses) to 1.00 (all softest line responses)

TABLE 27
INTERPRETATIONS OF SOVIET FOREIGN POLICY
AND OTHER POLITICAL BELIEFS:
DOMESTIC LIBERALISM

Respondents highest on	N	Index*	Soviet foreign policy: % of group in extreme quintiles	
			Hardest	Softest
Composite liberalism	468	.67	4	47
Social liberalism	580	.66	4	43
Economic liberalism	501	.66	6	44
All respondents		.51	21	19
Correlations, all respondents (gamma)				
Composite liberalism		.53		
Social liberalism		.50		
Economic liberalism		.49		

*On a scale of 0.00 (all hardest line responses) to 1.00 (all softest line responses)

sues tend to overlap rather than cut across answers to the questions, "What are the Russians up to now — and why?"

Conclusion

Owing the flood of tables presented in the preceding sections, it may be useful to recapitulate briefly some of the findings, first for aggregate results and then for differences within the leadership sample, before assessing their implications.

In several respects the four year interval between 1980 and 1984 witnessed some mellowing in perceptions and interpretations of Soviet foreign policy. To what might this be attributed? Perhaps the brutal Afghanistan invasion just prior to the 1980 survey, combined with the absence of a similarly dramatic event in 1984, was a factor. This explanation would assume that the destruction of KAL flight 007 some eighteen months prior to the later survey had had only a short-term impact on most American leaders. Alternatively, it may be that at least some respondents were reacting negatively toward some of the harsh rhetoric that had marked White House statements about the USSR and Soviet-American relations during the previous three years. However, it is also important to remember that these surveys cover only a small fraction of the post-World War II period, and even a smaller part of the seven decades since the establishment of the Soviet regime in Russia. In the absence of comparable elite data for the first three decades after 1945, assessments of long-term trends can at best be incomplete. Public opinion data reveal very substantial volatility in assessments of the Soviet Union and its foreign policy, and public images of other major international actors, for example, China, have also changed several times since World War II. Whether elite attitudes, which are presumably grounded in far better information about other nations, would reveal somewhat less volatility is a plausible hypothesis which cannot be tested given the available data.

In the aggregate, American leadership assessments of the Soviet Union appear "moderate." That label is advisedly placed in quotation marks because it will certainly evoke considerable disagreement. Those who believe that the Soviet Union is a uniquely aggressive and expansionist power which would destroy its adversaries at the first sign of weakness on the part of the West will surely not accept that judgment. Nor will those who believe that the USSR is just another major power which has only acted defensively in the face of a hostile environment dominated by those determined to undo the results of the 1917 revolution. By "moderate" I mean that a large part of the leadership sample tends to accept many of the following propositions: Soviet foreign policy derives from multiple and complex motives rather than simple, unidimensional ones; relations between the United States and the Soviet Union are often characterized more accurately as non-zero-sum rather than zero-sum; and however troublesome those relations might be, the Kremlin is not the sole source of American foreign policy problems. In a number of respects these views are not unlike those of the "realist" school of international relations theory.

It would be fascinating to replicate exactly this survey among Soviet elites to determine the extent to which their perceptions and assessments of American foreign policy parallel or diverge from those held by American leaders. Unfortunately that is not possible, and the handling of information about the nuclear accident at Chernobyl and the Daniloff case are stark reminders of how unlikely it is that we shall soon have data which would permit such cross-national comparisons.

In a number of respects many leaders taking part in the 1984 survey expressed preferences for policies that bear considerable similarity to those pursued during the Nixon-Kissinger period; that is, detente. Not only did this emerge with respect to assessments of detente itself, but also through substantial support for arms control negotiations, removal of trade barriers, and the like. On the other hand, the most troubling aspects of the detente period, conflict in Third World areas, continues to be a source of substantial division among American leaders.[19]

Although any single label is likely to be somewhat misleading, "cautious internationalism" appears to describe the views of many leaders, especially with respect to strategic issues and conflict or potential trouble spots in the Third World. There appears to be somewhat greater support for several of the items on the Post-Cold War Internationalist agenda of social, economic and environmental issues. These are in general issues which are only at the periphery of Soviet-American relations, especially as the USSR has often made it clear (e.g. at the Rome World Food Conference in 1974 and elsewhere) that it bears no responsibility for such problems and therefore that it has no obligation to assist in their resolution.

The summary above reports some central tendencies among the 2,515 respondents to the 1984 survey and it fails to disclose the rather sharp differences in views of the Soviet Union and its foreign policy that emerged when respondents are classified by several background characteristics, including other political beliefs.

As was the case with many previous analyses of the leadership surveys, a number of background attributes failed to account for much of the variance in assessment of Soviet foreign policy. These included generation, gender, military service, and travel abroad (including travel in the Soviet Union or Eastern Europe). The impact of occupation and education was somewhat greater but the leadership sample is so highly skewed toward the high end of the education scale that it might raise some questions about the latter finding.

There was a much stronger association between ideology and party preferences, on the one hand, and assessments of the Soviet Union, on the other. This finding is in line with other analyses that indicate strong and growing ideological and partisan cleavages on a much broader range of foreign policy issues.[20]

With the exception of attitudes toward protectionism, views of the Soviet Union and its foreign policy are rather strongly associated with other political beliefs on both foreign and domestic issues. The closest links are between: a "hard" interpretation of the USSR, Cold War Internationalism, and a conservative position on economic and social domestic issues. Conversely, a "softer" interpretation is associated with Post-Cold War Internationalism or Semi-Isolationism and a liberal position on domestic issues.

Although there are a number of areas in which it might be appropriate to talk about a "consensus" among American leaders, the cleavages would appear to dominate the areas of agreement. Several features of those cleavages would tend to suggest that a broad foreign policy consensus is not likely to be achieved in the very near future. First, the differences clearly have a strong and growing ideological basis. Second, partisan cleavages appear to be growing and they are reinforced by ideology.[21] Both of these trends parallel divisions that may be found among the public at large.[22] Third, cleavages on interpretations of the Soviet Union overlap rather than cut across other political beliefs, including views on a broad range of domestic issues. In short, the rather different ways of assessing the Soviet Union are rooted in and sustained by many other aspects of thinking about politics.

How, when and why might these American leadership perceptions and interpretations of the Soviet Union change? Both theoretical and empirical reasons suggest that dramatic changes will not occur in a short period of time. Leadership images tend to rest on a stronger base of factual information and to be more firmly embedded in and supported by coherent belief systems. Compared to the general public, whose views are often quite volatile, there is likely to be greater persistence in those of leaders. Other analyses of the leadership surveys described in this paper indicate that even the rather dramatic events of 1979 — the invasions of the American Embassy in Teheran and of Afghanistan by the Soviet Union — tended to reinforce rather than alter beliefs about many aspects of international affairs.

This is not to suggest, however, that foreign policy beliefs are impervious to the impact of events. An extended period of successful agreements on confidence-building measures would no doubt have an impact. The evidence cited in Tables 8 and 9 indicates that there is already rather substantial support for arms control measures and for reduced defense spending. Other areas might be cited, but these two related issues would appear to provide a good starting point. Whether the INF Treaty of 1987 will be the prelude to further arms control agreements remains to be seen.

But events can also result in less benign American leadership images of the Soviet Union. Indeed, as Kenneth Boulding[23] observed many years ago, while it may take a long time to create and nurture favorable images of others, unfavorable ones can develop much more rapidly. The history of Soviet-American relations during the past four decades would seem to provide plenty of empirical support for Boulding's rather dolorous observation about the human condition. The invasions of Hungary, Czechoslovakia, and Afghanistan, the destruction of KAL 007, the arrest of Nick Daniloff, and other such actions suggest an almost uncanny Soviet ability to do precisely those things that will sustain the most malign interpretations of Russian policy. And to be fair, such American actions as failure to ratify SALT II, President Reagan's harsh rhetoric about "the evil empire," and the like, no doubt nurture the hardest-line proponents in the Kremlin.

The longer-term implications of these findings will differ depending on one's perspectives about political life. Leaving aside the general tendency of many liberals and conservatives to find virtue in ideological consistency when they control the levers of power and to see greater merit in cross-cutting cleavages (which can serve as a brake on the implementation of the other side's program) when they do not, there is a deeper issue here. Critics who lament the lack of ideological consistency in American politics point to the consequent difficulties of governing under those circumstances, as ad hoc coalitions must be assembled to deal with each issue and the resulting policies may lack clarity and coherence. Critics to the right of the Reagan Administration, for example, Norman Podhoretz and those who vilified the president for signing the INF Treaty, have not hesitated to attack it for permitting gaps between campaign rhetoric and policy decisions to develop.

Others are less sure that the benefits of greater ideological consistency outweigh the costs. For example, would it reduce tolerance of minority views? Would the possible benefits of greater foreign policy coherence over the short run be more than offset by sharp changes when the mood swings from one end of the ideological spectrum to the other? More fundamentally, does ideology provide a sound basis from which to derive basic national interests? These and related questions are, of course, the stuff of eternal debates about the relationship between democratic politics and foreign policy.

Notes

1. William C. Rogers, Barbara Stuhler, and Donald Koenig, "A Comparison of Informed and General Public Opinion on U.S. Foreign Policy," *Public Opinion Quarterly*, 31, 1967, pp. 242-252.

2. Allen H. Barton, "Conflict and Consensus Among American Leaders," *Public Opinion Quarterly*, 38, 1974-75, pp. 507-530; Bruce M. Russett and Elizabeth C. Hanson, *Interest and Ideology* (San Francisco: Freeman, 1975); Barry Sussman, Elites in America (Washington: Washington Post, 1976); John E. Rielly, ed., *American Public Opinion and U.S. Foreign Policy, 1975, -79, -83, -87* (Chicago: Chicago Council on Foreign Relations, 1975, 1979, 1983, 1987).

3. For copies of the questionnaire and further details on methods, see Ole R. Holsti and James N. Rosenau, *American Leadership in World Affairs*, (Boston and London: Allen & Unwin, 1984); and Ole R. Holsti, *The Lessons of Vietnam and the Breakdown of Consensuses on Foreign and Domestic Policy: A Study of American Leadership*, Final Report on N.S.F. Grant No. SES-83-09036, December, 1985.

4. Ole R. Holsti, "Public Opinion and Containment," in Terry L. Deibel and John Lewis Gaddis, eds., *Containment: Concept and Policy* (Washington: NDU Press, 1986).

5. *ADA Today*, 41, No. 1, January, 1986.

6. William Lunch and Peter Sperlich, "American Public Opinion and the War in Vietnam," *Western Political Quarterly*, 32, 1979, pp. 21-44.

7. Naomi Lynn, "Women in American Politics: An Overview," in Jo Freeman, ed., *Women: A Feminist Perspective*, (Palo Alto, CA: Mayfield Publishing Co., 1975).

8. James N. Rosenau, *National Leadership and Foreign Policy* (Princeton: Princeton University Press, 1963).

9. Karl Mannheim, *Essays in the Sociology of Knowledge*, ed. by Paul Kecskmeti, (London: Routledge and Kegan Paul, 1952), p. 291.

10. Brzezinski, quoted in Elizabeth Drew, "A Reporter at Large (Brzezinski)," *New Yorker*, May 1, 1978, pp. 116-117.

11. Michael Mandelbaum and William Schneider, "The New Internationalisms: Public Opinion and Foreign Policy," in Kenneth A. Oye, Robert J. Lieber, and Donald Rothchild, eds., *Eagle Entangled: U.S. Foreign Policy in a Complex World* (New York: Longman, 1979).

12. Michael Maggiotto and Eugene Wittkopf, "American Public Attitudes Toward Foreign Policy," *International Studies Quarterly*, 25, 1981, p. 601-631; Ole R. Holsti, op. cit., 1985; but cf. David Garnham, Life Stage and Hawkishness: Effects of the "Graying of America," Paper for the Annual Conference of the International Studies Association, 1986.

13. Ole R. Holsti and James N. Rosenau, op. cit., 1984, pp. 108-139.

14. For critiques of this tripartite division, see William O. Chittick, "The Three-Headed Eagle Reconsidered," mimeo., 1986; and Eugene R. Wittkopf, "On the Foreign Policy Beliefs of the American People: A Critique and Some Evidence," *International Studies Quarterly*, 30, 1986, pp. 425-446. Using his own elite data base, Chittick found the same three dimensions, but others as well. Wittkopf argues that the tripartite division ("Three Headed Eagle") may better be described by two dimensions, each with two poles. For further analyses of the 1976, 1980, and 1984 data along these lines, see Ole R. Holsti, "The Structure of Foreign Policy Attitudes," Paper for the Annual Meeting of the American Political Science Association, 1987.

15. Ole R. Holsti and James N. Rosenau, "Domestic and Foreign Policy Belief Systems Among American Leaders," *Journal of Conflict Resolution*, Vol. 32, 1988.

16. Ole R. Holsti and James N. Rosenau, op. cit., 1988.

17. Angus Campbell, Philip E. Converse, Warren E. Miller, and Donald E. Stokes, *The American Voter* (abridged edition), (New York: Wiley, 1964), p. 113; see Bernard R. Berelson, Paul F. Lazarsfield, and William N. McPhee, *Voting* (Chicago: University of Chicago Press, 1954); and V. O. Key, Jr., *Public Opinion and American Democracy* (New York: Knopf, 1961) for similar conclusions.

18. Philip E. Converse, "The Nature of Belief Systems in Mass Publics," in David E. Apter, ed., *Ideology and Discontent* (New York: Free Press, 1964); Bruce M. Russett and Elizabeth C. Hanson, op. cit., 1975.

19. Ole R. Holsti and James N. Rosenau, op. cit., 1988.

20. Ole R. Holsti op. cit., 1985; Ole R. Holsti and James N. Rosenau, op. cit., 1988.

21. For a further discussion of this trend see I. M. Destler, Leslie H. Gelb, and Anthony Lake, *Our Own Worst Enemy* (New York: Simon and Schuster, 1984).

22. Ole R. Holsti, op. cit., 1986.

23. Kenneth Boulding, *The Image* (Ann Arbor, Michigan: University of Michigan Press, 1956).

4

FRG Perceptions of the Soviet Threat

Birgit Meyer

Introduction

There is a long historical tradition of Western perceptions of a threat from the East. These conceptions play an important role in the assessment of Soviet policy and in the planning of Western strategies.

"It is what we think the world is like, not what it is really like, that determines our behavior." This classic statement by Kenneth E. Boulding spells out the connections among social reality, our perception of social reality, and our conduct towards it. In an age where mass annihilation has become possible, it is of great importance to be able to appraise the possible motives and alternative courses of action of one's political and military adversary in order to shape one's own policies accordingly. Perception, which is both an observation of reality and implicitly an interpretation, has become an essential determinant of international politics.

In dealing with this topic, we find ourselves confronted with a conflict: either we talk and speculate generally—too generally—about overarching threat-perceptions, or we examine very concretely, perhaps too concretely, certain detailed aspects of threat-perceptions. There is an abundance of interesting historical and social-psychological synopses in the area of perceptual studies, that depict the continuity or the change of threat-perceptions. Yet there is a lack of sufficient scientific evidence supporting major theories. This paper attempts to discuss both the big picture and the more specific evidence with the necessary concentration and brevity.

Most Western observers of the Soviet Union and the East-West conflict are concerned with comprehensive questions. How threatening/expansionist/imperialist/peace-seeking etc. is the Soviet Union really? What potential does it have ideologically, economically, politically, and militarily to threaten and possibly attack its adversaries? The revolutionary heritage of the Soviet Union and its concept of peaceful coexistence, which proclaims political and economic cooperation to be simultaneous with ideological conflict, provide just grounds for mistrust and caution regarding the Soviet Union. Domestic political repression and foreign military adventures (Afghanistan, Poland) further undermine the Soviet Union's self-described image as a freedom- and peace-loving state, as does the enormous arms build-up of the 1970s and 1980s, which Western Soviet experts have assessed as economically destructive and politically counterproductive.

The question we are pursuing in this context—the West German perception of the Soviet threat—therefore concerns not the reality of the present Soviet threat, but rather images of the Soviet Union in the Federal Republic of Germany and what their prominent features are. In addition to the nature of these images, we are interested in the significance of the threat-perception, that is, what different political interests and viewpoints can be found behind the respective portrayals of the Soviet Union, and whether the threat-perceptions have changed in the course of the past twenty years, the timespan before and during the detente pursued by the social-liberal government with its Eastern neighbors.

To begin with, I have found three different ideal-type perceptual positions in the FRG. These three positions regarding the Soviet Union can be politically classified:

1. conservative position
2. liberal position[1]
3. leftist position

These positions reflect the politically relevant opinion-spectrum found in the FRG, and more specifically, in the West German political party system and the media. In terms of political parties, the conservative position is to be found in major parts of the Christian Social Union/Christian Democratic Union (CSU/CDU) coalition as well as minor parts of the Free Democratic Party (FDP) and Social Democratic Party (SPD). Former Chancellor Helmut Schmidt and his followers belong to this latter minority. The liberal position corresponds to the FDP, whereas the leftist position is associated with the majority of the SPD and recently parts of the Greens. For the national German media, position 1 is traditionally taken by *Die Welt* or the *Frankfurter*

Allgemeine Zeitung, position 2 by the *Suddeutsche Zeitung* and *Die Zeit,* and position 3 by the *Frankfurter Rundschau and Der Spiegel.*

These three positions each has a completely different image of the Soviet threat, and more specifically of the Soviet regime, Marxism/socialism in general, and Soviet militarism.

Each of these three positions not only holds a different conception of the Soviet Union, the nature of which is of interest, but also links these images with certain self-images (autostereotypes). And these self-images reflect how the holders of each perception comprehend their own political role on the one hand, and how they view the cultural and political situation of the FRG on the other.[2]

Foreign Images

The Soviet regime

In the image the conservative position conveys of the Soviet regime, the name of former dictator Stalin repeatedly arises. By characterizing the actions of Soviet officials as "stalinist," a historical continuity of political tyranny and repression is presented and set against the political and military resistance of the "free West." The conservative position also underscores the suggestion of threat by emphasizing the "Asian element" in Soviet politics. The danger of the Asiatic lies in its foreignness, backwardness and hostility to western culture.

Whereas the conservative position depicts the Soviet decision-makers primarily as power-politics-oriented and omnipotent, the liberal position emphasizes the contradictions within the Soviet regime. The Soviet leaders are not generally characterized as barbaric, brutal or ruthless, but rather as inconsistent and hesitant. The liberal position describes continuous cycles of liberality and repression in the Soviet Union. The depiction of ambivalences and various group interests among the Soviet leadership serves the purpose of putting stereotypes about the "monolithic bloc" or the "brutal USSR" into perspective.

Comment on the political developments in the Soviet Union from a pro-socialism perspective was still typical for the late 1960s for the liberal position. However, apart from criticism of the repressive measures of the Soviet regime, such a perspective is rarely heard today.

The leftist position accentuates internal Soviet processes of changes and imbues them with hopeful implications. Leftists point out the various emancipatory and liberalizing tendencies within the Soviet Union, which especially in the early 1970s were thought to have gained a broad social and political base. In addition, the leftist position views the post-stalinist development of the Soviet Union as the difficult process of doing away with oppression and political tyranny.

Even the invasion of Afghanistan appears not to have created any fundamental change in perceptions. Political use of force is depicted as "foolish" for the realization of the Soviets' own goals: internal Soviet repression hinders the domestic political discussion necessary to deal with the stalinist past and threatens the stability of domestic order.

These views, as well as the tendency to interpret even indications of stronger political discipline as expression of the weakness of the regime, indicate a desire to empathize to some extent with the conduct of Soviet leaders. The leftist position does not assign sole responsibility for the perceived political repression to the brutality of individual leaders; nor does it consider Soviet marxism to be simply a deceptive ideology which serves to prop up the regime. This perceptual position identifies the reasons for the repressive structure of the political apparatus as being deeply rooted in the structure of Soviet society: in the heritage of czarist intolerance and in skipped-over historical phases such as the Renaissance, Humanism, the Reformation, and the Enlightenment.

This point of view represents a type of convergence theory, according to which the degree of political freedom should increase both in democratically-organized welfare states and in socialistic states adhering to Marxist-Leninist ideology. And the political freedoms exercised in both social systems should become increasingly similar.

The view of Marxism/socialism in general

In discussions initiated by either the conservative or the leftist viewpoints, the fundamental problems of Marxism/socialism play a relatively major role, but from opposite premises. The conservative position reflects a consistent anti-communism, which is openly presented in the form of anti-Sovietism. It is founded on the conviction that Soviet Marxism was not deformed through Stalin's dictatorship, but must be looked on as the heritage consistent with marxist doctrine and the "reign of terror" envisioned by Lenin.

In this regard the conservatives are able to play on deeply rooted German prejudices against "the Russians" and "communism." Whereas national socialism was able to combine anti-Semitism and anti-Bolshevism to produce a highly irrational enemy-image, anti-communism, "cleansed" of its anti-Semitic aspects, was collectively rediscovered in the post-war consolidation phase of the FRG. The anti-Sovietism produced appealed explicitly to already-existing traditional threat-perceptions.

The leftist position, on the other hand, though critical of repression by Soviet officials, advocates a socialism open to reform, in which liberal freedoms such as individual freedom of opinion and freedom of the press should be possible. This perspective attempts to assign the responsibility for the shortcomings of Soviet socialism not to marxist principles, but rather to the specific conditions in the Soviet Union under which marxism is to be realized. Because it does not acknowledge Soviet reality as the realization of the idea of marxism or socialism, this perceptual position continues to hold a positive image of socialism or at least of socialist theory.

It is noteworthy that the liberal position does not link any fundamental comments on Marxism/socialism in general with the threat-image.

Soviet militarism

The conservative position sees a clear threat emanating from the Soviet offensive military strategy, and believes that Moscow uses economic and political East-West cooperation to gain unilateral military advantages. In this view the goals of Soviet militarism are:

— the division of NATO;
— the expulsion of the American military presence from Europe;
— the neutralization of the FRG; and
— the expansion of military and ideological power throughout the entire world.

The ability, if not the intention, to carry out a nuclear war as a "means of politics" is still ascribed to the Soviet Union. Its military potential is perceived to be offensive. The completely excessive Soviet arms build-up is seen as compensation for the loss of prestige suffered as a result of the imperialist moves in Afghanistan and Poland. The conservative position also envisions an acute threat through Soviet military intervention in and export of ideology to Africa and in the thereby threatened raw material supplies of the Western world.

Hence the conclusion drawn by the conservative position is the necessity of confronting the Eastern threat-politics of "the red army" with an adequate NATO defense. Eastern military endeavors face Western "half-heart-edness" in this regard. The military threat analysis, constructed primarily under a "worst-case" perspective, leads to calls on the West to strengthen its military and political defenses. Therefore the conservative position consistently and strongly supports the NATO dual-track decision of December 1979 as indispensable for the maintenance of NATO defense strategy.

The liberal position sees the threat from Soviet militarism as variable. On the one hand, Afghanistan and Poland confirmed the liberals'
worst fears about Soviet aggression and imperialism.[3] On the other
hand, Western Europe and the Atlantic alliance are not directly
threatened by Soviet expansionism as are, for example, the countries of
the Third World. Africa is considered a particular target of Soviet activity.

In liberal portrayals, the mediocrity and counterproductivity of
Soviet armament endeavors are repeatedly pointed out. The refusal to
dramatize becomes apparent. in the estimation of Soviet offensive
capacities and intentions. Comparisons with NATO capacities overwhelmingly come out in favor of the Western alliance. The liberals judge
Soviet militarism to be a less acute threat than do the conservatives.

The leftist position does not find in either in proletarian internationalism or in the principle of peaceful coexistence an ideological
support for Soviet militarism which directly threatens Western Europe.
Soviet expansionist policies are seen to be directed primarily against
Africa, and the primary function of the Soviet military is domestic
political integration. Only since 1980—after the Soviet intervention in
Afghanistan—have threats from the Soviet military been perceived and
increasingly commented upon. Yet the leftists' discussion tends to mini-
mize Soviet military strength—especially when the established conventional Soviet superiority is set against the high technical know-how of
the West. Indirect threat-perceptions prevail—even when, for example,
at rearmament discussions, the nature of the SS-20 is examined—and
the British and French nuclear weapons are considered to provide a possible counterweight to the Soviet eurostrategic potential.

Self-Images

The following will show 1) how the images of the Soviet Union
held by the three positions are related to each one's self-image, 2) how
the holders of each perception comprehend their own political role, and
3) how they view the cultural and political situation of the FRG. In
other words, this analysis demonstrates how these images of the Soviet
Union reflect the various political viewpoints found in the sociopolitical
spectrum of the country.

In the threat-analysis of the conservative position, there are consistent depictions of an extreme polarization of the political scene in the
FRG, with the irreconcilable positions "left" on one side and "conservative" on the other. In this panorama, the conservatives speak of a cultural and political "leftist trend" in the FRG which is portrayed as high-

ly threatening. The traditional values of Western European civilization have become corrupted through "leftist ideas." Norms like "religious ethics" or "self-discipline" have been critically devalued as moral categories of human behavior and social interaction.

By linking the external enemy, the socialist Soviet Union, with the internal enemy, the West German left, the conservative position incriminates socialist thought and produces a deceptive self-image of the FRG: a society free of conflicts, which could calmly face the political tasks of the future if it could only succeed at warding off the socialist enemies from without and within.

The self-image of the liberal position is characterized by its advocacy of freedom of opinion and publication and of the protection of the individual person's private life from interference by the state. This understanding of liberalism is rooted in the tradition of the emancipated middle class of the 19th century, which ensured the legally guaranteed inviolability of such classic freedoms in Germany. This perspective separates the domestic political controversies of West Germany from its portrayal of the Soviet Union.

In terms of the leftist position, the linkage of foreign image with self-image produces less easily characterized rhetorical patterns. There is a tendency towards careful consideration before judging phenomena in East and West. The leftists fear, however, that criticism of Soviet repression will activate an affective anti-communism. Evidently the leftist position faces the problem that the German "Right" (the "cold warriors," as the *Frankfurter Rundschau* for example calls them) could use the obvious indications of repression in the Eastern bloc for its own political objectives. Here, a fear of making contact with anti-Soviet forces in the Federal Republic becomes noticeable, as well as the resistance against jointly criticizing Soviet repression in a common front.

The political right in the FRG clearly constitutes the political force opposing the leftists. In some instances comparisons can be drawn between the measures taken by Soviet leaders and those of the Adenauer administration and its intellectual descendants. The tactic, to demonize the domestic political opponent by casting him into the camp of the political and ideological enemy, has been used by conservatives as well.

Ideology and Domestic Politics

The image of the Soviet Union conveyed by the national press and the major parties in the Federal Republic of Germany fulfills certain ideological functions[4] in domestic politics. These are:

a) answering of major unresolved questions of the time;
b) integration of groups;
c) justification of power structures; and
d) designing of a norm-hierarchy.

The conservative position[5]

The all-determining question is defined to be the unresolved East-West conflict. The contrasting of East and West, of unfreedom and freedom, of dictatorship and democracy is pointed out with almost eschatological pathos as being the critical question of the survival of Western civilization. The conservative position regards this conflict not only as the confrontation of two bloc-systems, but also as a critical domestic political problem. All tensions, potentials, conflicts and political policy disagreements in the FRG are seen as being directly related to the East-West confrontation.

For the conservative position, the confrontation of the superpowers is also the confrontation of divergent ideologies which are reproduced in the domestic politics of each social system and are represented through social groups. In this context, two political camps are constructed. On the one side, there is the political left, i.e. Marxists, communists, socialists, system-changers, leftist intellectuals, and some SPD/FDP politicians. On the other side are Christian non-Marxists, conservatives, and CDU/CSU politicians. Such an image, with social groups confronting each other, has as its primary purpose the separation of domestic political friend-foe groupings.

Since the conservative position suggests that the threat facing Western values emanate from an ideology founded on Marxism/Leninism and characterizes socialists as threatening, the conservatives support all those values, political structures, institutions, and interest groups that want to prevent the infiltration of such forces and ideas. These interests support the present unequal distribution of cultural, political and financial goods, the private ownership of the means of production, and the latitude of decision-making of political and economic elites that is being threatened by participatory demands.

This legitimation of prevailing power-structures occurs through an implicit hierarchy of norms. The hierarchy of norms and values can be traced back to the philosophy of the counter-Enlightenment tradition, which would prefer to see the achievements of the liberal middle class limited to the economic sphere. For the political and cultural spheres the conservatives want to restore traditional values and norms:

— obligation of the individual to "love of the homeland," to patriotism;

— willingness to sacrifice, obedience and respect towards the larger whole;

— freedom of the individual within the frame of action determined by his or her economic circumstances;

— protestant work ethic, sense of duty, discipline;

— rediscovery of pre-rational values of the individual, like heart, soul, feeling, loyalty, obligation; and

— willingness to defend and support a strong state.

The liberal position

The liberal position does not place its image of the Soviet Union in the context of a major, unresolved question of the time. This does not mean that they do not have an ideology, but the liberals neither hold a fixed image of the development of Western Europe nor do they present a fixed historical philosophy regarding the present. They do not always interpret social phenomena in the context of major unresolved questions, as the conservatives do. Rather, this perceptual position describes the phenomena in the various social orders as inherent to the specific system. It does not have to interpret all internal Soviet developments in light of a single tendency or question.

The fact that the liberal position does not link any fundamental statements regarding Marxism/socialism in general with its image of the Soviet Union indicates its relatively minimal interest in using the Soviet Union as an example for its own pro- or anti-socialist commitment. The liberal position apparently does not see the confrontation of superpowers with divergent ways of looking at the world as the decisive conflict or the unresolved question of our time. Presumably for this reason, the liberal position does not project the world conflict to West German domestic politics where friend/foe groupings would be formed.

The liberal position accepts claims to legitimacy from both systems. Thus liberals cannot be unequivocally said to be trying to justify power structures, either those of German society or those of the Soviet Union. Its commentaries reveal respect for the historical development of every nation and in the case of the Soviet Union, the liberal position explicitly does not advocate a counter-revolution. Liberals criticize both social systems and confront them with their own cultural-historical tradition and political philosophy or aims.

The liberal approach is oriented around the conception of liberalism held by the enlightened middle class of the 19th century. This perceptual position conceives its primary goal to be the emancipation of the individual and it aims to defend a legal system which renders individual emancipation possible and protects it. The portrayal of the

Soviet threat offered by the liberal position is not founded primarily on a political norm-hierarchy, but rather on a moral system of norms, in which the individual functions as both the source and the object of morality.

The leftist position

For the leftist position, the large unresolved question of the time is how the emancipatory potential, which initiated socialist movements in the last century, can be realized in the political systems of the present— i.e., how to realize liberal and social human rights in capitalist as well as in socialist systems.

The leftists perceive two sets of political orientations within both the Soviet Union and the Western democracies. On the one side are those who advocate the realization of these individual freedoms. In the West such people would be primarily political representatives of wage-dependent workers and in the East the critics of the elite, bureaucratic government. On the other side are those who want to preserve the social status quo, i.e. foreign and domestic political conservatives in the West and the party, state, and military elites in the East. The leftist position intercedes for the solidarity of those without rights, the disadvantaged, and the humbled. Thus, this image allows the leftists to combine political positions with moral beliefs.

The leftist position avoids serving as a legitimizing authority for either capitalist or socialist systems. Rather it acknowledges the power structures that have become established as the result of given historical developments. Though the leftist position believes that the realization of individual freedoms is inherently possible in both Eastern and Western social systems, it fundamentally considers such promised freedoms better guaranteed by Western democracies than by socialism as actually practiced in Soviet-dominated systems.

The leftist position does not design an explicit hierarchy of political and moral norms and values that would coincide with any specific philosophy of life. Rather, leftists often conceive of themselves as the critical voice within these systems regarding unfulfilled emancipatory promises. This attitude is attributable to the radical-democratic tradition of the part of the middle class that wanted to see attained democratic rights of political liberalism carried over to the economic sphere, and thus the leftist position assumes an unusual stance between the radical-liberal and the socialist movements.

Conclusion

In an international political situation characterized by serious superpower confrontation and the stagnation of efforts at negotiation, the danger of escalation has become acute. In such a climate it is important to realize that conflicts not only exist among nations but can be called forth and reinforced through the distorted images countries have of one another. Misunderstandings, misjudgements, distorted perceptual patterns, and ideologically-projected images can have a conflict-reinforcing effect on international relations which, in a time of increased international political tensions, can threaten world peace.

In this situation political parties and the press should assume the task of supplying information on international political relations without distorting reality. They should avoid exacerbating confrontational interpretations regarding foreign policy.

Whereas some observers speak of a deceptive detente-euphoria in the 1970s[6] and blame politicians of the detente period for having underestimated the Soviet Union, the empirical results of press and party analyses point to a different conclusion. The investigations I considered depict a surprising constancy and continuity in the perception of the Soviet threat over the past twenty years. Even in a time that, in terms of its foreign policy, was characterized by the paradigm of relaxation of East-West tensions, the only support detected for this detente in the FRG showed different features and remained on a very small scale.[7]

The conservative position has at all times, before, during, and after the East-West detente, warned of the Soviet threat and has emphasized many aspects of this threat. The liberal position has always pointed out the contrasts between the Soviet and the Western systems while clearly leaving open the hope of change through the expansion of individual liberties in the respective social systems. The leftist position has not, even after the invasion of Afghanistan in 1979 or the Polish crisis of 1981, perceived an explicit threat from the Soviet Union.

These briefly presented theses are not to lead to the conclusion that the perception of the Soviet threat did not at all depend upon the conduct of the Soviet Union. An image and its object are clearly correlated. My purpose here, however, was to specify and consequently point out the self-perpetuating nature of threat-perceptions.

According to Henry Kissinger, a man who ought to know, politicians in office have little time to acquire additional knowledge. This is where scholars assume an important, practical political task: to warn of the dangerous cycle of newly provoked and mutually reinforcing enemy-images in international politics and thus work to reduce the potential for conflict in foreign as well as in domestic politics.

Notes

1. There does not exist a better translation for the German expression "liberal."

2. My arguments are supported by data from my own research published in my book: *Das Bild der sowjetischen Dissidenten-Bewegung in der westdeutschen Presse. Zur ideologischen Auseinandersetzung zwischen West und Ost (The Image of the Soviet Dissidents in the West German Press)* (Campus Verlag: Frankfurt & New York) 1981; and by two Ph.D. dissertations on the topic of the "FRG-Perception of the Soviet Threat," and one research project on: "The Perception of the USSR in West German Parties 1980-1984."

3. "The Beaten-Down-Spirit of Helsinki", *Süddeutsche Zeitung* December 22, 1981.

4. In this summarizing evaluation I will not refer to the ideology-concept of everyday language, in which "ideological" is always only understood as what the political opponent says or does. Rather, the description of characteristic put forth by Peter Christian Ludz serves as the more appropriate definition of the concept. Accordingly, a nation-image is to be considered ideological if it does not orient itself on the self-logic of the adversary but rather serves the following functions: answering of major unresolved questions of the time/integration of larger/smaller groups/justification of power structures/designing of a norm-hierarchy. See: Peter Christian Ludz, "Ideologieforschung. Eine Rückbesinnung und ein Neudeginn," in: *Kölner Zeitschrift für Soziologie und Sozialpsychologie*, H 1/1977, S. 1-31.

5. For the following conclusions see my dissertation named above.

6. In Europe today most observers of the East-West relations speak of the "end of deterrence."

7. In the U.S., we have similar results: a poll, published in the *New York Times* before the meeting in Genf, showed that 44 percent of the U.S. citizens who were asked did not know that Soviets and Americans were allies in World War II. 28 percent thought that the Soviet Union was a war enemy of the U.S. Primarily the media transport these images. *Der Spiegel* quotes George Kennan: "The images of the Soviet Union we find in the media and in the government are far away from reality—to such an extent that it is dangerous, if they are the basis of political decisions." *Der Spiegel* 2.12. 1985.

5

Gorbachev's America Problem

Morton Schwartz

Despite Mikhail Gorbachev's April 1985 assertion that he did not "look at the world solely through the prism" of U.S.-Soviet relations, the General Secretary has concentrated his foreign policy attention on this issue to the near exclusion of all others. The foreign policy section of his Political Report to the 27th Party Congress was devoted overwhelmingly to the United States. In fact, several Third World leaders spoke openly of the Kremlin's lack of attention to regional problems. Even when speaking to other audiences, as for example in raising the question of a world security system or in arms control discussions with Britain and France, his eye remains primarily on the U.S.

Gorbachev's personnel choices—the promotion of Moscow's most experienced Americanist, Anatoliy Dobrynin, to head the International Department of the Communist Party of the Soviet Union (CPSU), of long-time observer of the American scene, Aleksandr Yakovlev, to head the Party's Propaganda Department and to the Politburo and of Yuli Vorontsov, Dobrynin's protege (he was his deputy in Washington from 1966 through 1977) to the post of First Deputy Foreign Minister—are further evidence of Gorbachev's priorities. Finally, his main policy concerns, in terms of specific proposals and official doctrine, have focused on the peace issue, which clearly impinges directly on relations with the U.S.

Though Gorbachev may have been tempted initially to treat U.S.-Soviet relations with a measure of "benign neglect"—an Administration spokesman expressed similar views during the early days of the Carter

119

Presidency—"life itself," as the Soviets like to say, imposed a different set of priorities and reaffirmed, to both leaderships, the centrality of the bilateral relationship.

The Challenge of the Reagan Administration

Gorbachev's focus on relations with Washington reflects in no small measure a continuing uncertainty in his ability to manage the Reagan Administration. While loath to confess such concerns openly, Soviet spokesmen regard the Reagan Administration as the most problematic they have ever confronted. Though Soviet military power and socio-economic development is vastly greater than ever before, this American President has proven a formidable competitor. Soviet propagandists have, at times, used personally abusive language in their treatment of the President. However, they do not consider him to be irresponsible. As Gorbachev told Algerian journalists, "I think that Washington has good idea as to what nuclear war is."[1] The Soviets, nonetheless, take the President seriously.

Soviet observers see the Reagan Presidency as presenting Moscow with multiple challenges, both domestic and in the international arena.

1. *Military/Security.* The Kremlin leadership is particularly concerned about the U.S. military buildup and especially its strategic modernization program. Having begun in the last years of the Carter Administration, such efforts were greatly broadened and accelerated under President Reagan. In the Soviet view, the recent Pentagon weapons programs have been developing at such a pace as to endanger Soviet security interests. The correlation of military forces—especially strategic force trends—are seen to be moving sharply against the USSR. These programs are seen to reflect an effort by the Administration to achieve military advantage over the USSR in order "to squeeze the Russians" internationally and "to wear them out" by exhausting the Soviet economy.

Such, indeed, is seen to be the main objective of the President's Strategic Defense Initiative (SDI). While expressing belated concern about the instabilities associated with the development of new weapons systems, Moscow sees SDI as the technological centerpiece of a broad global U.S. political, military and economic challenge. Having invested billions of rubles in their strategic missile forces, the Soviets confront the possible development of a defense-oriented strategic environment which, in effect, will negate the effectiveness of their strategic arsenal. Moscow is also apprehensive about its ability to compete; the Soviets are concerned that the U.S. will successfully exploit its technological edge. Chernenko's reference to SDI as a new U.S. Manhattan project indicated a concern that with a concentrated effort, the technologically-sophisticated United States will once again leave the rest of the world behind and thus endanger the USSR's superpower status.[2]

2. *Assertiveness in the Third World.* Soviet leadership statements have highlighted their concerns regarding the Reagan Administration's "neoglobalism." U.S. policy toward Grenada and Libya as well as the support given to the "freedom fighters" in Angola, Kampuchea, Nicaragua and Afghanistan are seen as evidence that, in contrast to the period of the "post-Vietnam syndrome" of the Carter era, the United States is again willing to use military force to enhance its own interests. Further, the U.S. is seen as attempting to resume a role as world policeman, the arbiter of regional issues. U.S. "neoglobalism" is also seen to be an attempt to contain the USSR, i.e., to challenge Soviet activities outside the traditional spheres of Soviet interest—especially the Middle East, Southeast Asia and Latin America.

3. *The Ideological Challenge.* The Reagan White House's rhetorical assertiveness and openly anti-Soviet style, not surprisingly, has attracted considerable Kremlin attention. Though Soviet publicists often suggest that U.S. political leaders all harbor such views, even if they do not openly express them, the President's unconcealed hostility towards the USSR in the early years of his Administration came as a shock. Gorbachev told the editors of *Time* in an August 1985 interview that "we are indignant" about the Administration's "abusive words."[3] Such concerns continue to this day. Referring to a series of U.S. films and television advertisements, the General Secretary complained in an April 8, 1986, speech in Kuibyshev that "shortly after Geneva, an anti-Soviet campaign was relaunched with new force in the United States, full of every type of fabrication and insult to our state."

Soviet hypersensitivity was again on display in the reaction to Chernobyl. Western criticism of the Soviet handling of the nuclear accident was denounced in a *Pravda* editorial on May 17, 1986 which charged that this "dishonest and malevolent fuss" which is "disguised by a veil of sham 'concern for people,' 'alarm about their health,' and 'anxiety about the shortage of information'" was part of an "unbridled anti-Soviet campaign." "The entire history of our state testifies," the editorial concluded, "that there are no means which the Soviet Union's enemies would not use in their effort to besmirch our country."[4]

Given Moscow's perpetual worries about the wicked ambitions of political adversaries—few powerful states are excluded from this category—the assertive style of the Reagan White House was regarded with suspicion. It was seen to reflect not only a fundamental ideological hostility toward the USSR but, at the beginning, a determination by some in the Administration to promote fundamental political and economic change in Soviet society. While Gorbachev seems considerably more self-confident than his predecessors about the durability of the Soviet system, suspicions in Moscow linger.

4. *The President's Political Strength.* Further compounding Moscow's problems is that, as Soviet observers reluctantly admit, the President is very effective politically. While charging that he resorts to political showmanship and arm-twisting, Soviet commentators grudgingly acknowledge that he is enormously popular and politically effective. They are particularly attentive to the fact that he is very successful in dealing with Congress whose support he consistently manages to obtain for expensive defense programs, military aid to the Afghan rebels and, most recently, to Saudi Arabia. Though the President is seen as having been weakened by "Irangate," the Kremlin agreed to a compromise on the issue of intermediate nuclear forces on the assumption that the President could and would win Senate ratification for an INF treaty.

The President is also seen to be unusually skilled in dealing with U.S. allies who, despite occasional misgivings, have been generally supportive of U.S. policy on INF deployment, SDI, and countering Libyan terrorism. Soviet commentators saw the 1986 Tokyo summit statement on terrorism—and the European follow-through since its adoption—as further evidence of the President's leadership abilities. The Kohl government's willingness to resolve the issue of the Pershing IA missiles—which made the INF agreement possible—is viewed as U.S. alliance-management at its very best.

The Gorbachev Response

The problem confronting Gorbachev is how to best approach management of a militarily resurgent, combative, essentially antagonistic, and politically skillful adversary. The Soviets are obviously frustrated. As *Izvestiya* commentator Aleksandr Bovin put it on April 1, 1986, while the American partners are "too unreliable" to deal with, the Soviets have no choice but "to deal with those who are given by history and destiny."

The Gorbachev response, thus far, has been largely in the realm of public diplomacy. In order to neutralize the challenge presented by the Administration, he has put together a team of experienced public relations officials and experts on the United States—Aleksandr Yakovlev, Anatoliy Dobrynin, and Foreign Ministry press spokesman Gennadi Gerasimov—to organize a political counteroffensive. Their main function has been to orchestrate a public relations campaign designed to intensify political resistance in the West to Reagan Administration policies.

Yakovlev and associates recognize that they are operating under two major disadvantages. First, the President and others in his Administration have considerable experience in communications and public relations. While the Soviets themselves are practiced in public diplomacy on arms control issues, they occasionally note that they are competing with a formidable competitor. The failure in their head-to-head confrontation with the Reagan Administration in Western Europe on INF deployment undoubtedly had a serious impact on their self-confidence.

Even more problematic is their awareness that they are burdened by a very poor international reputation. While proud of their ideological heritage, the Soviets are aware that, going back to the earliest days of the regime, Bolshevik support of revolutionary movements in various countries engendered abiding suspicion of Soviet activities and ambitions. While insisting that they, in principle, oppose the "export of revolution," the Soviets are aware that such benign interpretations of "proletarian internationalism" are not universally shared. Others are alarmed by the enormous size of the USSR's strategic and conventional capabilities and the Kremlin's demonstrated readiness to use such forces. Here, too, pride in Soviet accomplishments is tempered by an awareness of the impact of such capabilities on the USSR's international reputation. Kremlin propagandists fully understand that Soviet political effectiveness is hindered by what Gorbachev referred to as "the vicious myth about a Soviet military menace." The widespread dissemination of such beliefs, they often note, foster a political climate in which policies inimical to Soviet interests—from the formation of NATO in 1949 to SDI—are nurtured and encouraged.

Building a New Soviet Image

The first major responsibility of Yakovlev and associates is to encourage world opinion to think about the USSR in new ways. Gorbachev gave some indication of his concerns when he stated in his Congress speech that "in the military sphere we intend to act in the future so that no one has any ground for fears, even if they are imagined, for their security." In short, the "myth of the Soviet threat" must be falsified.

The overarching theme of the Soviet public relations campaign is the Soviet Union's commitment to the cause of world peace. Appealing to the West Europeans, Gorbachev told the congress of the East German Socialist Unity Party (SED) on April 18, 1986: "Do not believe the allegations about the aggressiveness of the Soviet Union. Our country will never under any circumstances begin armed operations against Western Europe unless we or our allies become targets of a NATO attack. I repeat, never."[5] The USSR, he asserts is peaceable. Its military doctrines are defensive as are its military forces. Further, its domestic system—especially now—requires peace. The USSR's "challenging domestic plans," he said in his *Time* interview, require peaceable conditions. The USSR, Soviet spokesmen tirelessly reiterate, "needs peace" to heal its economic ills.

While noting in his Congress speech that it is not possible to solve the problem of international security "with one or two even very intensive peace offensives," Gorbachev and his allies have introduced modifications in Soviet political rhetoric and even Party doctrine designed to foster a new Soviet image.

1. *The Struggle for Peace—The Historic Vocation of Socialism.* Soviet media and Party officials are now claiming that the issue of peace is of greater importance than the pursuit of traditional class objectives. The main problem, according to one commentator, is the "preservation of the human species." This goal, we are now told, "has undoubted priority over all others."[6] Class struggle apparently has taken a back seat to the more urgent goal of securing a stable peace.

This linguistic shift, implying the muting of the traditional emphasis on the struggle between socialism and capitalism in favor of the need to avert nuclear war, underlines Gorbachev's basic concern with repairing the USSR's international reputation. He has repeatedly suggested that Moscow seeks normal, fruitful, mutually-advantageous "civilized relations" with all states, not enmity and confrontation. To underline Moscow's quest for respectability, a *Pravda* article commemorating May Day stressed "the peace-making content of proletarian internationalism" arguing that, in our days, "the worldwide historic mission of the working class is not only to emancipate society from social and national oppression but also to save mankind from nuclear destruction."[7]

2. *"New Political Thinking" and Interdependence.* To further buttress his argument, Gorbachev and other Soviet spokesmen eagerly depict the USSR as committed to new, more sophisticated, more relevant approaches to international problems. In contrast to Washington's "Stone Age thinking," its exclusive reliance on military

force, Moscow, it is claimed, now understands that the solution to security problems are no longer possible by unilateral efforts to increase military capabilities. Such efforts only make one's adversaries nervous, and they, in response, counter-arm. What is needed is not more arms—which decreases rather than increases security—but arms agreements. "It is impossible to think of unilateral security," wrote Bovin. "The keys to Soviet security are kept not only in Moscow but also in Washington. The converse is also true: U.S. security is guaranteed not only by what is done in Washington but also by what is done in Moscow."[8]

Security, according to Soviet commentators, is interdependent and can be achieved only by cooperation. This is said to be true in other areas as well. Thus, Foreign Ministry press spokesman Lomeyko, commenting on Chernobyl in a press conference on May 12, 1986, said that the nuclear accident "raised with a new acuteness the question of seeking a common language of cooperation between the two different societies—socialist and capitalist. It must be a joint search and must presuppose restraint, great flexibility and reciprocal compromises." Other commentaries have noted that the scientific-technical revolution, especially the emergence of mass communication and worldwide contacts, have brought about extensive internationalization in all spheres (trade, economic, cultural, scientific) requiring increasing cooperation.

Conclusion

Moscow is now engaged in what Stanislav Kondrashov referred to as "the great work of convincing and persuading the world public and, in particular, the U.S. public, the work of winning people over and re-educating them."[9] As Gorbachev told the Togliatti automobile workers in a speech in Kuibyshev on April 8, 1986, world opinion is an enormous force that has an interest in preventing war. "For that reason we must not fold our arms. We have to put pressure on, and hard!... This is where all our strength is forged."[10] Moscow's basic objectives were set forth by Kondrashov with striking clarity when he described Soviet public relations efforts as designed to ensure that "sensible people in the West trust us more," that they "pin their hopes on our openness, flexibility, and constructiveness, and our persistence and staunchness in our efforts to introduce a new way of thinking in international life."

Thus, Gorbachev and his supporters have devised a new image for the USSR, one which they believe will result in tangible policy gains. By generating a reputation for peaceableness and responsible concern for the interests of others, the old image of the secretive, menacing Russian bear will wane and Soviet views and arguments will receive a better hearing. Acceptance of the image of a "new USSR," it is believed, will in time encourage those, especially in the West, to moderate policies adopted during the heyday of the old image (e.g., the post-Afghanistan, post-martial law economic sanctions). A more benign view of the USSR will help promote greater Western responsiveness to Soviet arms control initiatives such as the proposed ban on nuclear testing, a space weapons ban, and the proposal for the demilitarization of the Mediterranean Sea.

And to demonstrate that Moscow's commitment to "new thinking" is more than rhetorical, Gorbachev and his colleagues have undertaken some unprecedented initiatives. They have, for example, after long years of resistance, accepted the principle of on-site inspection to verify compliance with arms control agreements. Thus, by the terms of the December 1987 INF Treaty, Moscow has agreed to allow stationing of U.S. inspectors at a Soviet missile-production plant. Additionally, a delegation of U.S. Congressmen was recently granted permission to visit the USSR's radar facility at Krasnoyarsk (which is believed to be in violation of the ABM treaty), a U.S. military team was allowed to carry out a surprise inspection of Soviet military exercises in Belorussia (requested by Washington according to the terms of a "confidence-building" agreement recently signed by both sides), and Western diplomats and experts were permitted to tour a Soviet chemical weapons facility. (Though it has the world's largest chemical arsenal, the Soviet Union did not admit that it possessed such weapons until April 1987.)

The impact of Gorbachev's public relations offensive—along with his much-heralded program of "perestroyka" (restructuring) and "glasnost" (publicity)—has been considerable; poll data in Western Europe and in the U.S. (especially after the Washington summit), has begun to reflect a decided improvement in the Soviet image. However, a truly significant change in the USSR's reputation, one which could result in enhanced political leverage, awaits more substantial evidence that Gorbachev is willing to address fundamental Western security concerns. A consistently responsible policy towards such crucial issues as arms control (nuclear and non-nuclear), regional conflicts (Afghanistan, the Middle East, Cambodia), bilateral relations (including human rights), as well as global problems—e.g., terrorism, nuclear energy, control of AIDS—would help promote a more credible international image for the USSR than a high-profile public relations campaign, however artfully managed.

Notes

1. *Pravda*, April 3, 1986.

2. TASS, February 1, 1985: reprinted in Foreign Broadcast Information Service *Daily Report, Soviet Union*, February 1, 1985, p. AA1.

3. *Pravda*, September 2, 1985, p. 1.

4. *Pravda*, May 17, 1986, p. 1.

5. Carried on Radio Moscow, April 18, 1986. Reprinted in Foreign Broadcast Information Service, *Daily Report Soviet Union*, April 18, 1986, p. F8.

6. Yu. Krasin, "A Strategy of Peace is the Imperative of the People." *Mirovaya Ekonomika: Mezhdunarodnaya Otnosheniya* (World Economy and International Relations.), No. 1, January 1986, p. 3.

7. *Pravda*, April 29, 1986, p. 4.

8. *Izvestiya*, April 23, 1986, p. 3.

9. *Izvestiya*, March 17, 1986.

10. Moscow T.V., reprinted in Foreign Broadcast Information Service, *Daily Report Soviet Union*, April 9, 1986, p. R3.

6

Soviet Perceptions of the Federal Republic of Germany

Wolfgang Pfeiler

Images that political elites have of other nations form part of the foundation on which political decision-making is based. These images usually are the result of a process of image-building which is more dependent on historical traditions than on actual, personal knowledge. Education and 'Groupthink' have more influence on this process than individual experience. Most characteristics of such images, therefore, tend to be stable and invariable for generations. That also holds true for the political elites of Soviet Russia.[1]

Traditional Views of Germany in Soviet Perception

From the very beginning, Russian communists have had great respect for Germany and, in particular, the German Social Democracy. Marx and Engels, Lassalle and Bebel were viewed as the great theorists of the expected Socialist Revolution and the ensuing brilliant future. The German Social-democratic party appeared to be the prototype for the whole world's socialist movement. The party's numerical strength, its political struggle, and its organizational capabilities were admired. This model seemed to hold out promise for eventual success also for backward Russia.

Not only Germany's socialist movement, but Germany and German society in general appeared progressive in comparison to the structure of Russia's autocratic system. Many Russian socialists even expected that, in case of war between Russia and Germany, the German army would come as liberator to their country, as the French army did when it came to Germany a century ago.[2] German was supposed to be the language of the revolution and most Russian socialists tried to learn at least some German.

The internationalists within Russia's Social-democratic party, the Bolsheviks, had a particularly strong propensity to follow the example of their German comrades. Since their leader, Vladimir Lenin, and his works still play a great role in the process of Soviet socialization and education, it seems worthwhile to deal with his perceptions of Germany. He had been deeply influenced by German philosophy. He had sufficient command of German, had lived for some time among Germans and had read widely on Germany and by Germans. His extensive writings on Germany reveal a clear-cut picture of how he evaluated the German factor.

What impressed Lenin first and foremost was the organizational structure of the German state with its highly qualified civil servants. The citizens of this state appeared to him as very disciplined and extremely accustomed to legality.[3] The absence of corruption in its administrative machinery and the efficiency practiced by the whole administrative apparatus were admired and seen as a model to be followed in the Bolshevik party. He regarded Germany as one of the three leading countries in the world: Germany, Britain and the United States, in that order.[4]

In the course of World War I, when hatred against Germany surged throughout Russia, Lenin warned his comrades against such emotions: Russian socialists were supposed to stick to the alliance with the German workers. And they should learn from the Germans.[5] The repeatedly occuring slogan "Learn from the Germans" appears to be the verbal essence of Lenin's evaluation of Germany. Several times he declared that German cultural standards were among the highest in the world. Lenin repeatedly reminded his party that "Germany is the most developed, most progressive country of Europe."[6] The majority of the following generation of Soviet leaders shared Lenin's predominantly positive assessment of Germany. Josef Stalin in particular held Germany to be of exceedingly high importance.[7]

Thus, the traditional image Soviet leaders have of Germany is predominantly positive. Its salient elements are: organizational abilities, technical talents, honesty and neatness, order and discipline. German culture and especially literature are well-known and are held in high esteem. Extreme admiration, however, goes to the German willingness to work. When Mikhail Gorbachev attended the XIth Congress of the

Sozialistische Einheitspartei Deutschlands (East Germany's ruling party) in the spring of 1986 he explained to his East German TV audience that the characters of the abbreviation for Deutsche Demokratische Republik—DDR—are read in the Soviet Union as: Davai, Davai, Rabotat (Let's go, let's go, let's work). To transfer German workaholism to Soviet workers remains one of the unfulfilled desiderata of present Soviet leaders.

But there are negative elements in this picture: Germans are not to be trusted and have an inclination towards hypocrisy; their political elites are prone to overestimation of their own power and possibilities, while at the same time underestimating or misperceiving the political interests of other nations; and they show an inability to evaluate political situations correctly. These negative features seem to have their historical roots as well. A comparison of the two Russian encyclopediae published at the turn of the century with Soviet writing in the last decades shows many similarities in this respect.[8]

Particularly, the concept "Drang nach Osten" (drive for the East, for Lebensraum or "living space") has long since been a constituent term of Russian political language and in Russian writings need not be translated from the German. Historical reminiscences of this kind, together with the experience of the Second World War and German occupation, have laid the background for an attitude which may be best depicted as a mixture of admiration, liking, and mistrust.

The Perception of the Federal Republic

The aforementioned dichotomy of the traditional Soviet perception of Germany determines to a large extent the perception of the Federal Republic and everything that occurs there. This applies not only to information propagated by the Soviet media in accordance with the guidelines of the Central Committee, but also to the perceptive processes of Soviet journalists who work in the Federal Republic and Soviet citizens who travel there. These images of Germany are embedded in their minds, and this above all determines the perception. Also, any changes that take place in the Federal Republic are viewed in the context of these deeply-rooted assumptions. Even the changes that set the Soviet learning process in motion and eventually lead to an alteration in their perception of Germany can only be viewed in the framework of the original perception.

There is, in this context, an additional factor of particular importance. As single members of a society are reduced to an object-class ("the French," "the Poles," "the Arabs"), so too are entire nations, peoples or countries reduced to object-classes. For the Soviet perception of Germany, this means that the Germans in the Federal Republic today are viewed as part of the object-class "western world" or "capitalist world," while the Germans in the GDR belong to the object-class "socialist countries." Many Soviet leaders view the GDR as "our Germany," while the Federal Republic is perceived as the Germany of the West. The terms West Germany and West Germans often appear in colloquial language.

The "western world" includes the U.S., Britain, Japan, France, Italy, Sweden, Switzerland, Benelux and several others. There is a multitude of Soviet works which consider these countries to be one class in which characteristics and trends are practically the same. The image that the Soviets have of the Federal Republic is not confined to an isolated nation, but rather is part of the object-class "capitalist world."

The "FRG" as Part of the Western World

The analyses carried out by the Institute for World Economy and International Relations (IMEMO) in Moscow and the Institute for Politics and Economy (IPW) in East Berlin reflect this view of the Federal Republic as an integral figure in the politics and economics of the West.[9] It is particularly emphasized that the FRG is the leader in relation to other European countries in external trade relations. At this point, an additional methodological characteristic becomes apparent. The relations with these countries and the relations with the United States are handled separately. At the same time, this separation reflects the Soviet leadership's expectations that the contradictions within the Western world will increase. The Soviets believe that the U.S. aims to take advantage of the economies of its capitalist allies. In this way, and through the utilization of its technological superiority, the U.S. is seeking leadership in the West and the obedience of its allies in foreign affairs. In the long term, however, the Soviets believe that this policy is doomed to fail. The U.S. will not be able to change the world according to its own wishes.[10] The Soviets hope to use these contradictions to their own advantage.

Even in Moscow, it is clear that Western unity is not yet broken. The mistake of past Soviet policies serve as a partial explanation. By concentrating too much on relations with the U.S. and the Western European public, Moscow overlooked the European governments.[11] This must change. Theoretically, the Western alliance would continue to function since both the "centrifugal" and the "centripetal" forces among the three imperialist groupings have increased. Finally, as a

result of the inner logic, in the long term one could expect an intensification of the contradictions.[12]

Although there is a tendency to adhere to the fundamental perceptions, there has been a shift in the viewpoint in relation to the role of
the Federal Republic in this power play. In the early 1980s, it was assumed in Moscow that West German policy had maintained a certain
degree of independence vis-a-vis the United States. The various attempts of presidents Carter and Reagan to force the Federal Republic to
follow the American line had been successfully opposed.[13]

Many in the Soviet elite believed that the Federal Republic would
gain a fair degree of independence not only in trade policy but also in
the area of security. At times, it was expected that Bonn would attempt
to serve as an intermediary between East and West in the area of
security policy.[14] Some Soviet politicians hoped to break the German-
American security policy with the help of the West German peace movement.

Other Soviet observers realized at the time that there existed an
independent West German interest in the strengthening of the NATO
alliance. "The FRG played the deciding role in the acceptance of the
NATO decision of 1979 to deploy new nuclear medium-range missiles in
western Europe. Moreover, the acceptance of this decision was a direct
result of West German initiative."[15] A former official of IMEMO spoke
of "cooperation and competition in the military-industrial sphere,"
where the U.S. and the Federal Republic compete world-wide. Notwithstanding this competition, the West Germans at the same time advocate a strengthening of the NATO alliance when they pursue their
own long-range goals. The German-American War-Time-Host-Nation-
Support Agreement of April 1982 was in this sense, according to this official, the most important military-political document since the entrance
of the Federal Republic into the NATO alliance.[16]

In Soviet eyes, in the last three years the Federal Republic has witnessed a shift away from growing autonomy. The alliance policy of the
Kohl government and the failure of the peace movement may have contributed to the shift. The impact of American global policy was the main
factor. One must recognize that the German-American common interests were not broken by Soviet policy and propaganda. Security policy,
and the debate over SDI cooperation in particular, pointed out to Soviet
observers that among all West Europeans, West Germany is the closest
American ally.[17] The Soviet propaganda has in the meantime adjusted
to this relationship. As a result of its loyalty to the alliance (its Nibelun-
gen loyalty to Washington),[18] the Federal Republic is attacked for acting as a yes-man in the face of American policy.

This type of development in the NATO alliance does not serve Soviet interests. Former Soviet Ambassador to West Germany Valentin Falin believes that Bonn has failed to achieve anything positive in the realm of East-West relations:

> Naturally, Bonn must decide for itself which policy is preferable. Although I must say that it seems strange that Bonn would consider the following acceptable: Nixon's policy in 1972-73, Ford's policy, who publicly doubted detente in 1976, Carter's policy and Reagan's policy as well! But Reagan's policy is the renouncement of the Nixon years of 1972-73. How can one agree with two or more conflicting policies?[19]

Neither here nor in any other written Soviet sources is there any mention that Soviet behavior in the 1970s and early 1980s contributed to a growing threat commonly felt by the Western countries.

There have also been considerable changes in the Soviet perception of the German role in the unification of Western Europe. Although the European Economic Community was viewed with some skepticism in the late 1950s, it was proven in the 1960s that the EEC did indeed function. The striving of major West German companies to achieve dominance in a unified Europe was considered to be a deciding factor in Western European integration. In order to receive France's consent for the continuation of integration, the Federal Republic was forced to make a series of concessions, especially in the agricultural sector. Moscow observers believed that the aims of German industry went beyond pure economic gain: The predominant West German aspiration was political hegemony in a unified Western Europe. This hegemony appeared ever more as a means for territorial expansion in the East. "Leading circles" in the Federal Republic considered hegemony in Western Europe to be the instrument of long-term German policy toward reunification.

It was the expectation in Moscow that in the long run, the other Western European countries would not accept such a policy. A reunified Germany would be stronger than England and France put together and could again pose a threat to the United States. Out of their own interests, these countries would do everything in their power to prevent the development of a political integration under German leadership.

While this was the view held by the majority in the Soviet Union in the early 1980s, there were a few observers who believed that Western Europe was indeed in the long process of being unified. The point made by Leonid Brezhnev during his visit to Germany became one of growing importance in the eyes of the Soviets: the Soviet acceptance of the European Economic Community.[20]

If Western Europe were to become unified, the question would arise of how the Soviet Union should react. Some Soviet observers recommended the development of friendly relations with a unified Europe, although such a process would take many years. The establishment of relations between the Council on Mutual Economic Assistance (CMEA) and the EEC appeared to be a promising option. Such an economic policy seemed beneficial to the long-term security orientations of the Soviet Union.

Mikhail Gorbachev has stressed the Western European orientation of the Soviet Union. He has not only spoken of the establishment of effective relations between economic blocs, but has also expressed long-term political expectations: "In that the countries belonging to the EEC act as a political 'unit,' we are prepared to engage in a common dialogue also regarding concrete international problems."[21]

Thus, the Soviet Union will view the process of West European intregration in terms of the role played by the Federal Republic and the various political options that could develop.

The Western European orientation of the USSR has been further strengthened by the failure of Soviet policy toward the United States. Because of its close alliance with the U.S., the Federal Republic cannot be the main target of Soviet policy toward Western Europe. This will hold true as long as the Federal Republic clings to partnership with America. Boris Yeltsin, a candidate member of the Politburo, expressed such a view during his visit to Hamburg:

> We consider the FRG to be an important political partner. However, it must be understood that a partnership requires a loyal peace-keeping policy. Bonn's political course has continued to move further away from such a policy. This impedes the development of our relations, which could otherwise be very fruitful. The FRG could reveal her own profile in foreign policy, but she does not do so. She prefers to portray herself as Washington's twin. For this reason, it is difficult for us to improve our relations.[22]

This does not mean that Moscow will overlook the Federal Republic. It was no secret that in 1985, its economic growth superceded that of all the leading Western countries.[23] As a result, domestic political and economic developments in West Germany have attracted a great deal of attention.

West German Capitalism and its Perspectives

One theorem of historical materialism states that the social development from capitalism to socialism is predetermined. Today, such an expectation would be expressed in only vague or general terms. The Soviets speak not only of a growing crisis and the inherent contradictions of capitalism, but also of the considerable reserves at its disposal. They no longer hope that the Federal Republic might become a socialist state in the foreseeable future. Everything that is written on West German society in the USSR is based upon the expectation that the social order in the FRG will remain capitalist for a longer period of time.

Instead, the Soviets emphasize the aforementioned role of the Federal Republic in the Western community. Equally important are the considerations about the resulting political and economic trends and the effect these could have on Soviet policy. After all, the Federal Republic is the most important Soviet trading partner in the West, surpassing even the United States.

The successful development of German-Soviet trade, especially during the 1970s, has been emphasized in Soviet literature. "From year to year, there has been an increase in the rate of trade between the USSR and the FRG. In the decade between 1970 and 1980, the rate of foreign trade between the two countries increased by ten and a half times."[24] In this regard, the Federal Republic is ahead of the other Western countries. The twenty-five-year agreement of May 1978 has been a major catalyst for long-term economic and industrial cooperation. The political significance of this trade has been repeatedly emphasized in spite of the fact that it represents less than five percent of overall foreign trade.[25] However, the imbalance in German-Soviet trade persists. Energy and natural resources make up two-thirds of Soviet exports, while the imports consist mainly of machines and industrial equipment.

The Soviets take particular note of West Germany's strong export-oriented capital goods sector: "Exports take up about a half of the entire production of the engineering industry and the export quota for the remaining branches of the capital sector (automobile, manufacturing, precision mechanics, optics, electronics, etc.) compose over a third of the gross output."[26] During the past few years, it has been emphasized that the external market has been the cornerstone of West German economic activity, while the domestic market has remained weak.[27]

The West German economy is undergoing long-term structural changes. This applies above all to the high growth rate of the industries which have brought in new technologies. Here it is stressed that in spite of stagnating industrial production, this sector has actually witnessed an increase in investment. Only a small percentage of the investments have flowed into capacity expansion. Most of the investments have served to increase efficiency and productivity.[28]

These structural changes are also viewed in the context of the so-called "transnational corporations" (TNC), the majority of which are headquartered in the U.S. A Soviet observer who represents the position of Mikhail Gorbachev believes that the aims of economic policy have altered under the influence of the TNC:

> In the past, the main objective of state monopolistic regulation lay in the reduction of social tension achieved by the maintenance of a relatively high growth rate, with the result of minimal unemployment. Now the main objective of the state—serving the interests of the TNC—is the securing of maximum profits even during a period of stagnation and negligible growth.[29]

These trends are seen as an essential aspect of West German Chancellor Helmut Kohl's economic policy. His strategy has included an increase in private investment in order to modernize the West German economy and make it more competitive. This requires above all an increase in the profit rate. The economic policy of the Kohl government has received a positive assessment from the Soviets: In 1984 alone, the government was able to reduce the federal deficit by one third. There has also been a considerable improvement in the competitive capacity of German goods on the world market. This also accounts for the positive trade balance.[30] Much of this success can be attributed to the increased competitive capacity of the West German armaments industry. West Germany is fourth among the leading exporters in the capitalist world and has achieved a stronger position in relation to the United States. In the space of five years, the ratio of imports from the U.S. and exports to the U.S. has been reduced from 40:1 to 5.9:1.[31]

From the Soviet point of view, Kohl's successful economic policy has been accompanied by negative results in the social sector. His government has failed to develop an effective program to combat rising unemployment.[32] "There has been an uninterrupted proletarianization of one part of the bourgeois and middle classes: In 1961, 70.8 percent of the population belonged to the working class. This figure rose to 75.5 percent in 1980."[33] Proletarianization is the process in which farmers, craftsmen or retail traders lose their self-sufficiency and become wage laborers.

These shifts inspire Soviet hopes for a gradual shift in the social sector which may be in the interest of long-term Soviet policy. As in the past, there are high hopes for the various mass movements, especially the "antiwar movement."

The Political System of the Federal Republic

The early Marxist conception that the bourgeoisie serves as the instrument of the ruling class was abandoned twenty years ago. Today, Marxists speak of an interdependence between the state and monopoly capital. Scientific progress, economic growth, increasing concentration of capital and stimulation of foreign trade can all be encouraged without questioning the functioning ability of the capitalist system. In Marxist words: the relations of production can be suited to the position of the productive forces and thus preserve private ownership. In other words, Marxists have accepted the fact that capitalism works, at least for the foreseeable future.

From the Soviet perspective, West German monopoly capital has been particularly successful in this regard, especially with the American assistance after the war. The West German "ruling circles" include not only this monopoly capital and finance oligarchy, but also a number of highly-paid managers in the economic and government sectors. In addition to the economic resources at the rulers' disposal, the state, political parties and the media serve as instruments for this ruling elite. The leaders in these areas exercise control over the political system. Soviet observers find it difficult to accept the concept of pluralism in the West German society because of these aspects. To them, the German political system seems to take the form of a conglomerate of oligarchies, as an interdependence between capital, government, employers' associations, media monopolies and a series of interest groups whose common objective is to maintain political and economic power in this country. The overwhelming majority of the West German population appears to be economically dependent and politically helpless in the face of this oligarchy. In this political scene, neither the parties nor the German parliament plays a major role. Instead, the parties are subjected to the influence of various interest groups who attempt to use them for their own purposes.[34]

In this framework, the CDU/CSU represents the interests of monopoly capital, big business, Catholicism and other conservative and neoliberal interest groups, without overlooking the importance of the middle class.[35] Due to the heterogeneity of the Christian-democratic parties, there is the problem of integrating differing interests and satisfying various standpoints regarding particular issues. Both propaganda and academic orientations have been emphasized by Soviet authors. While the propagandistic portrayal dominates the general literature, the academic literature does lend a relatively balanced interpretation.[36]

There is a substantial difference in the view of the Social-democratic party. While the SPD was still in power, the USSR had hoped that it could consolidate its position domestically. Such an expectation resulted from the sociological and demographic changes and the popularity enjoyed by the SPD owing to its policies. The election outcome of 1983 was a disappointing surprise for the Soviets. The West German domestic political scene had received a false interpretation in Moscow, particularly with regard to the high hopes for the West German peace movement.

The inability of the SPD to further consolidate power is seen to be due primarily to the economic crisis in the early 1980s and above all to the failure of the party leadership's domestic policy. The main reason here seems to be the problem of reconciling word with deed. They were unable to fulfil the promises made to their voters. Consequently, they were also held responsible for the fact that the negative effects of the economic crisis had been suffered by the working class.[37]

Throughout 1985, there were renewed Soviet hopes for another turning point in the Federal Republic. Here it seemed clear that the rightist trends of the CDU/CSU in domestic and social policy and the parties' subservience to Washington in foreign policy have caused them to lose their footing. The SPD, on the other hand, "is constantly seeking ways to diminish the military confrontation in Europe to ensure peace and security on the continent..."[38] The leaders of this party appear to have a more sensible perspective from the Soviet point of view.

The incorrect Soviet assessments regarding West German domestic policy in the early 1980s[39] seem to have been repeated recently. Their propaganda portrays an image of growing intolerance of the governing coalition and increasing protest among the population. This means that "anyone who questions Kohl's domestic and foreign policy can be considered a constitutional enemy."[40] Opponents of the government are forbidden to study or hold a job. "Militarism" and "revanchism" (i.e. tendencies for a revision of the territorial results of World War II) are encouraged and the social security of the living standard diminishes.

In this regard, there exists a certain amount of hope for the Greens. The expectation that this party could dislodge the FDP from third place was expressed early on.[41] Just recently, during a reception for the Greens, the Soviet leadership emphasized the growing importance of this party in relation to various mass movements.[42] In comparison, the FDP receives very little mention in Soviet literature. It is considered to be a bourgeois-liberal party, representing the interests of small business, civil servants, white-collar workers, craftsmen and farmers as well as large capital, which advocates a balanced foreign policy.[43]

In Moscow, one was aware of a trend in which the CDU/CSU has continued to lose popularity. "The majority of the people in the FRG sympathize with the opposition parties, the SPD, the Greens, many members of the FDP, as well as nonparliamentary parties and organizations - the DKP, the unions and the antiwar movement..."[44] Only after the two last Länder elections in 1986, in which the SPD suffered heavy losses, were the Soviets forced to accept that the notion of an SPD-led government in 1987 was illusory.

Assessment of Eastern Bloc Policy and its Aims

Since its founding, the Federal Republic has practiced an Eastern bloc policy that has been incompatible with the interests in Moscow. The policies of each Federal government have been judged in terms of the degree of the possible damage to Soviet interests. It was clear to the Soviet leadership that the Federal Republic could use the NATO alliance or its dominance in the EEC to its advantage in Eastern bloc policy. These concerns appeared again as the right-wing National Democratic Party gained popularity during the period of the "Great Coalition" of the CDU/CSU and SPD, 1966-69, and as the Federal Republic refused to recognize the European status quo. The policies of the CDU/CSU-SPD government were viewed with growing skepticism, especially toward the end.

After the 1969 elections, Moscow's new hopes were mixed with apprehension. Perspectives for bilateral relations were improved following the signing of the Moscow agreement in August 1970, which basically brought German acceptance of the territorial status quo in Europe. Specifically, there was the consideration that this agreement would improve the chance for a European security conference. It was not until after the ratification of the Eastern bloc treaties[45] that the Soviets began to have positive expectations for bilateral relations. At the same time, Soviet authors noted a growing West German independence vis-a-vis America. This posed, however, no great threat to German-American relations.

West German efforts to expand trade with the Eastern bloc received overwhelming acclaim. In addition to political expectations, hopes for economic cooperation with the Federal Republic were strengthened in Moscow after the Eastern bloc agreements. The signing of the Final Acts in Helsinki in 1976 and the German-Soviet trade agreement of 1978 confirmed the interdependence between political and economic detente.[46] "The year 1969 opened a new phase in the development of bilateral relations between the USSR and the FRG. This was characterized by the revision in Eastern bloc policy and the realistic basis upon which this policy was practiced."[47]

The cornerstone of such a policy was and still is for Moscow the recognition of the political and territorial status quo in Europe. Since Bonn abandoned its claim on the alteration of the existing borders, there has been more accomplished in the past five years in the area of bilateral relations than in the fifteen years following the establishment of diplomatic relations.[48]

Bonn's recognition of the borders and the sovereignty of the GDR is understood primarily in a security context.[49] This was particularly apparent in the late 1970s as the outlook for continuing detente began to wane. The unwavering position of the Federal Republic in relation to the NATO dual-track decision on deployment of intermediate-range nuclear missiles in Western Europe proved to be a disappointment for the Soviets. This also applied to a lesser extent to the fruits that had been expected from German-Soviet trade. Moscow was convinced "that the state of relations between the USSR and the FRG reflects the character of relations between East and West..."[50] In spite of the disappointment surrounding the West German refusal to renounce the dual-track decision, the deployment of American medium-range missiles did not have a negative influence on Soviet policy toward the Federal republic. The importance of the Eastern agreements is continually stressed by Soviet policymakers.

Moscow was obviously not prepared for the domestic policy change or the election outcome in Bonn in 1983. Chancellor Kohl and his party were claiming that the German question was open.[51] This government's continuation of Eastern bloc policy was a reassuring sign in the area of security and it was also understood as an expression of the general sentiment within the country. Kohl's visit in 1983 was therefore a disappointment for Soviet expectations, particularly the chancellor's announcement that he would continue to aim for German unity.[52] The Soviet reactions here do not necessarily reflect those of the Soviet campaign against West German revanchism, which began in the spring of 1984 with an article in the CPSU publication "Kommunist."[53] This campaign was not directed primarily at the Federal Republic—its purpose was to discipline the Soviet allies. Moscow was becoming anxious about the intentions of Eastern bloc party leaders to travel to West Germany. In the cases of General Secretaries Honecker and Zhivkov, Soviet foreign policy, then, succeeded in preventing the planned visits to the Federal Republic.

The Soviet reference to West German revanchism often served superior state interests. Ordinarily, there is a distinction made between the "forces of revenge within the FRG" and the policies of that country in general. This view was expressed in a Spiegel interview by a staff member of the Central Committee of the CPSU, who stated that the FRG is not a "revengeful" country.[54]

The rightist-nationalist forces are seen as particularly dangerous with their double strategy which calls for military strength and a weakening of the USSR to overcome the German division.[55] Aside from the "resettlers" (those people expelled from their homes in 1945 by Polish authorities) it is above all the leading circles of the union parties who are labeled "revengers." A similar view of the Kohl government is not entirely out of the question. "The German-German policy of Mr. Kohl aims for the annexation of the GDR and a revision of the European border...."[56] Such claims also caused concern among West German allies. In this respect, revanchism is obviously not viewed as an exclusively German phenomenon. The foreign ministers of the Warsaw Pact countries spoke of the "dangerous activity of revengeful forces, above all in the FRG." Implicit here is the reference to similar tendencies in other countries.[57] Soviet authors suspect a possible conspiracy along these lines between Bonn and Washington.[58] The Soviet media portray an image of regional West German revanchism in the annexation of the GDR, the encroachment on Poland and the revision of the borders of 1937. A global American revanchism, on the other hand, attempts to turn back the development of the last fifteen years of world politics. As Gorbachev expressed it, in its global objectives, the United States has "re-animated" the West German revenge.[59]

The current Soviet leader, who for a long time refused to use the term "revenge," is very careful with his choice of words. In his speech to the XIth party convention of the SED, he explained that the ruling class in the FRG speaks of an open German question and is capable of revengeful calculations. This can be viewed in the context of Gorbachev's statements on European security policy: No logic could be detected in the West German policy. The government spoke of its love for peace, yet supported the U.S. rearmament policy. Gorbachev made a connection between the West German policy toward America and the claims made on the Eastern bloc. He emphasized the GDR's demand for equality:

Relations with the FRG are important for the Soviet Union. Moreover, on the basis of equality we are ready to develop these for the benefit of both sides. This requires, however, that Bonn's policy represent the interests of peace and security. In this context, I would like to emphasize that we support the GDR's demand of the FRG that relations between them as equal sovereign states correspond to the recognized norms of international law.[60]

In the West, these statements were considered to be a warning to the SED to practice more restraint with its Western policy. The statements also reflect the Soviet uncertainty about the actual ends and means of West German policy. The Soviet historian Ernst Henri has expressed this uncertainty in the "reformist" Soviet newspaper, "Sovetskaya Rossiya": Every form of revenge must be resisted. The Europeans must follow the path to peace, because Europe is the common house. The Eastern policy of the Federal Republic is rather more reflective of the Adenauer era. This is expressed in the U.S. orientation as well as the continuing activities of the West German "revengers." Therefore, we must know whether the politicians who are at the helm in Bonn are truly striving for a lasting peace. "Or are they playing a double game in signs, whose aims are the same as revenge? We have the right to expect an honest and direct answer."[61]

On the other hand, several of Kohl's statements were viewed in a positive light as they appeared in the Soviet media. So it was not only recorded that Kohl attended the annual meeting of the Sudeten resettlers, but also disappointed the most avid "revengers" with his speech.[62] In particular, it was his comment about the common peaceful settlement of security problems between East and West which received the most praise.[63] In the eyes of Moscow, it is obviously the area of security which plays the central role, followed by trade policy. One must not forget "that questions of security build the decisive part of Soviet-German relations."[64] Similar statements were made during a supreme Soviet delegation's visit in Bonn.

This ambivalence in the Soviet statement about West German policy not only reflects the uncertainty and concern about ends and means, but also allows for two further conclusions:

—The Eastern bloc policy of the Federal Republic is judged primarily from a security standpoint in the Soviet Union. (This statement applies to the Eastern bloc policy of every West German government and every Eastern bloc policy conception.)

—The Soviet leadership does not respect the security interests of Western Europe. They do not understand that their security policy causes a great deal of anxiety and leads to countermeasures. Moscow often interprets the West German security policy as the military groundwork of Eastern bloc policy.

The growing team spirit of Kohl's German-American security policy has led to further confusion in Moscow. At the same time, it touches upon an essential aspect of Gorbachev's Western political conception. From the beginning, he pointed out that in the absence of a satisfactory agreement with the United States, he would emphasize the Western European orientation. He seems to believe that he can use the existing contradictions between America and Western Europe to Soviet advantage. For this purpose, he would like to improve the relations between the USSR and Western Europe. In this context, the Soviet leadership must estimate the importance of the Federal Republic.

Gorbachev's Western European orientation does not justify the expectation that the USSR could play the so-called "German card." However, a reconsideration of the past German policy in the Kremlin seems to be underway. For the moment, in spite of its recognized economic and political significance in the framework of Gorbachev's Western political concept, the Federal Republic remains in the background. This does not mean that Gorbachev plans to exclude the Federal Republic. "The Federal Republic, however, has without a doubt lost the role of preferred western partner enjoyed under Brezhnev and Andropov."[65] This is felt not only in Soviet policy but also in its political communication strategy. Thus, in the years between 1970 and 1983, more German-Soviet summits took place than between the USSR and any other Western country. The years between 1980 and 1983 witnessed an intensification of this trend.[66] In the following three years, the USSR practiced restraint in its diplomatic communication strategy. Soviet-German relations were qualitatively and quantitatively reduced to normality. Gorbachev's preferred Western European partners were now France, Italy and Great Britain. Politburo candidate member Boris Yeltsin informed *Die Zeit* that at least for the present, the possibility of a German-Soviet summit is out of the question.[67] Moscow's new ambassador in Bonn expressed a similar view: "In the near future, I believe that relations will take place at a more modest level."[68]

The main reason for this avoidance strategy may be based upon the failure to influence American policy with the help of the Federal Republic. In particular the Kohl government can be counted as the closest American ally. Gorbachev emphasized this point in his televised speech following the Chernobyl accident.[69] In addition, the German question and the Federal Republic played no role whatsoever in the XXVIIth party congress. They were only implicit in the continuing Soviet revanchism campaign. Even the amendment of the party program warns against German revanchism and stresses that the recognition of the status quo in Europe is the precondition for cooperation.

In the Soviet view, Kohl's public insinuations comparing Gorbachev to Nazi propagandist Goebbels during a Newsweek interview serve as a further stumbling block and are interpreted as an expression of "a particular political tendency."[70] Once before, Gobachev supporters suspected that the West German government had aided the opponents of the general secretary during the Soviet inner-party confrontation.[71]

Conclusion

The diplomatic downgrading of the Federal Republic is a result of the Soviet inability to use the German-American contradictions to its own advantage. At the same time, there seems to be a reawakening of the historic mistrust towards German political elites. There would have been a favorable reaction in Moscow if in 1987 there had been the prospect for a policy practiced by the SPD and other mass organizations and movements which would have better suited Soviet security interests. In this respect, the XXVIIth party congress had already laid down the general line: relations with socialist and social democratic parties should be developed. In contrast to the past, contact with Social-democracy and above all the "anti-war movement" has been ascribed a favorable perspective.[72]

These wishes have not been fulfilled. On the other hand, the new Federal government exists and must be dealt with. Gorbachev has repeatedly stated that the Soviet Union must base its policy on reality. "The Soviet leadership is aware of the political and economic importance, of the objective importance of the Federal Republic. It must always bear in mind that its policy of reduction of the East-West conflict and the settlement of disarmament agreements are not probable without or against Bonn."[73] In addition, there has never been any doubt that the Soviets wish to continue the strong trade relationship.

Accordingly, long before the general election, the Soviet foreign minister already suggested how relations might be continued: In spite of the chancellor's statements, relations in the area of economic cooperation as well as the political contacts remained positive. The Soviet Union is said to be in favor of normal mutually advantageous relations.[74] In particular, Chancellor Kohl's declaration on West Germany's preparedness to renounce the Pershings Ia in the 1990's was repeatedly praised in Soviet statements. In the long term, however, the possibility is not excluded that there could be shifts in the prevailing sentiment in

West Germany, which could lead to a change in Bonn's foreign policy, which would better suit Soviet interests.

Notes

1. See at length Jorg-Peter Mentzel and Wolfgang Pfeiler, Deutschlandbilder. *Die Bundesrepublik aus der Sicht der DDR und der Sowjetunion,* Dusseldorf 1972, pp. 11-20, 42-58.

2. Ibid, p. 61.

3. V. I. Lenin, *Polnoe sobranie socinenij,* Moskva, 5th edition 1960-1966, Vol. 41, p. 24; s.a. Vol. 38, p. 169.

4. Cf. ibid, Vol. 27, p. 393.

5. Ibid, Vol. 24, p. 82.

6. Ibid, Vol. 37, pp. 490, 496; Vol. 38, pp. 23, 42, 104; Vol. 44, p. 322; Vol. 45, pp. 108, 403.

7. See at length Wolfgang Pfeiler, Das Deutschlandbild und die Deutschlandpolitik Josef Stalins, in: *Deutschland Archiv* 12/1979.

8. *Enciklopediceskij slovar',* Vol. VIIIa, St. Petersburg 1893; *Enciklopediceskij slovar',* Moskva/St. Petersburg/Odessa, 7th edition (before 1913), Vol. 13 and 14.

9. Institut Mirovoj Ekonomiki i mezdunarodnych Otnosenij/Institut für Internationale Politik und Wirtschaft (eds.), *Federativnaja Respublika Germanii, Moskva 1983.*

10. Cf. S. Mensikov, Za fasadom "edinstva"; *Kapitalizm segodnja, Pravda* Sept. 3, 1984, p. 6; M.S. Gorbacev, *Pravda* Sept. 9, 1984, p. 4; ibid (speech on the XXVIIth congress CPSU), *Pravda* Feb. 26, 1986, p. 1f.

11. Cf. Michael Dobbs, "Soviet Woos U.S. Allies in Europe on Arms Control" *International Herald Tribune* July 15, 1986, p. 1.

12. Cf. S. Mensikov, "'Triada" mezimperialisticeskich protivorecij, *Pravda* July 8, 1986, p. 4.

13. Cf. V.I. Miljukova, *Otnosenija SSSR-FRG i problemy Evropejskoj bezopasnosti 1969-1982 gg.,* Moskva 1983, pp. 220f, 263.

14. Ibid, p. 282.

15. Ibid, p. 259.

16. V. Fedorov, Nekotorye aspekty militarizacii v FRG, in: *Mirovaja ekonomika i mezdunarodnye otnosenija (MEMO)* 5/1982, pp. 122f, 126.

17. Alexander Bovin, Western Europe: "Strategic Concerns" *International Affairs* (Moscow), Dec. 1985, p. 101.

18. A. Tolpegin, Bonns Reaktion auf die Gorbatschow-Erklärung, "Eiertanz der Koalition" *Neue Zeit* (Moscow), 7/1986, pp. 4, 14. For a comprehensive American assessment of the Soviet Union's European policy see John Van Oudenaren, Die sowjetische Politik gegenüber Westeuropa. Einschätzungen

von Entwicklungen im Atlantischen Bündnis, in: *Europa-Archiv* 4/1985, pp. 89-98.

19. Valentin Falin im Gesprach mit Karl D. Bredthauer. Die Bundesrepublik, die Weltmächte und die Nachkriegsordnung in Europa, in: *Blätter für deutsche und internationale Politik*, 1/1985, pp. 26, 17.

20. Cf. in this sense Yu. Shishkov in: *International Affairs* (Moscow), 3/1982, pp. 53-56; M.A. Avakov, Evropejskij sojuz: tendencii i perspektivy, in: *Sovetskoe gosudarstvo i pravo*, 6/1978, pp. 113-118.

21. M. S. Gorbacev (speech in Paris), *Pravda* Oct. 4, 1984, p. 2.

22. B. N. Elcin (speech in Hamburg), *Pravda* May 4, 1986, p. 4.

23. Cf. V. Lapsin, FRG, in: *MEMO* 3/1986, p. 87f.

24. V. Miljukova, op. cit., p. 204.

25. Ibid, p. 217.

26. V. Varnavskij, Strukturnye osobennosti ekonomiki FRG, in: *MEMO* 9/1985, p. 147.

27. Cf. V. Lapsin, op. cit., p. 87ff.

28. Ibid, FRG, in: *MEMO* 3/1985, p. 73.

29. S. Mensikov, Dialektika krizisa, *Pravda* Jan. 3, 1986, p. 4.

30. Cf. I. Basova/L. Volodin/S. Sokol'skij/ V. Senaev, FRG: opasnye tendencii, in: *MEMO* 1/1985, pp. 51, 55.

31. I. Basova et al, op. cit., p. 58f.

32. Cf. V. Lapsin, op. cit., p. 75; op. cit., p. 89.

33. D. Demin, Sovremennyj monopolisticeskij kapitalizm, in: *MEMO* 10/1984, p. 146.

34. Cf. Wolfgang Pfeiler, Die Parteien der Bundesrepublik Deutschland im Urteil der Sowjetunion, in: *Aus Politik und Zeitgeschichte, Beilage zur Wochenzeitung Das Parlament*, B 21/1973.

35. See at length Sergej L. Sokol'skij, Christiansko-demokraticeskij Sojuz v FRG: *Sociologija i politika*, Moskva 1983, chapter I.

36. Ibid, p. 249f.

37. Cf. Vsevolod Ovcinnikov, Sdvig vpravo, *Pravda* March 23, 1986, p. 4.

38. Ju. Jachontov, Protiv "Strategii riska." Schvatka v bundestage FRG, *Pravda* Sept. 30, 1985, p. 3.

39. Cf. Wolfgang Pfeiler, "Des Kremls blindes Fenster. Die CDU im Spiegel der sowjetischen wissenschaftlichen Literatur" Die Politische Meinung July/Aug. 1982, p. 62.

40. Aleksandr Luk'janov, Pozornaja praktika prodolzaetsja, *Pravda* March 31, 1986, p. 5.

41. L. Istjagin, Partija "Zelenych" v politiceskom landsafte FRG, in: *MEMO* 2/1983, pp. 130, 133.

42. Cf. TASS report, *Pravda* April 19, 1986.

43. Politiceskie partii, in: *Strany mira: Kratkij polit.-ekonomiceskij spravocnik*, Moskva 1983, p. 101f.

44. Ju. Jachontov, Vynuzdennye reveransy i podlinnaja poderzka, *Pravda* April 28, 1986, p. 5.

45. Moscow treaty of August 1970, Berlin Four-power agreement of September 1971, treaties with GDR, Poland, and Czechoslovakia.

46. See at length Silke Lent, Die bilateralen Beziehungen zwischen der Bundesrepublik Deutschland und der Sowjetunion 1969-1978. *Erwartungshorizont und Entspannungskonzeptionen aus sowjetischer Sicht*, Bonn 1979, pp. 231-237.

47. V. Miljukova, op. cit., p. 10.

48. Cf. ibid, p. 240.

49. Ibid, pp. 241, 280.

50. Ibid, p. 229.

51. S. Sokol'skij, op. cit., p. 248.

52. Cf. Dusko Doder, "Kremlin Disappointed by Kohl Visit: Officials Irked by Chancellor's Overtures to East Germany" International Herald Tribune July 12, 1983.

53. V. Nekrasov, Vnimanie: Revansizm! in: *Kommunist* 9/1984, p. 126f; s.a. Ju. Jachontov, Kuda drejfuet FRG, *Pravda* April 5, 1985, p. 4.

54. Wadim Sagladin in an interview with Der Spiegel 50/1984, p. 145.

55. Cf. V. Fedorov, Zlovescaja nostalgija, in: *MEMO* 10/1984, p. 118f.

56. Ju. Jachontov, Esli ne uchodit' ot faktov. FRG v nacale goda, Pravda Jan. 8, 1985, p. 4.

57. Kommunike zasedanija Komiteta ministrov inostrannych del gosudarstvucastnikov Varsavskogo Dogovora, *Pravda* March 21, 1986, p. 4.

58. Cf. E. Grigor'ev. Kak v FRG vygorazivajut revansizm, *Pravda* Sept. 1, 1984, p. 4.

59. M.S. Gorbacev (speech), *Pravda* May 9, 1985, p. 1.

60. M.S. Gorbacev (speech), *Pravda* April 19, 1986, p. 2.

61. Radio Moscow (in German language) March 24, 1986.

62. Ju. Jachontov, S tribuny revansistskoj schodki. Vystuplenie kanclera FRG v Mjunchene, *Pravda* May 19, 1985, p. 5.

63. TASS, Vystuplenie G. Kolja, *Pravda* Sept. 21, 1986, p. 5.

64. NOVOSTI (Jakovlev) Aug. 27, 1984, acc. to Monitor-Dienst Deutsche Welle, *Deutscher Teil*, Aug. 28, 1984, p. 1.

65. Fred Oldenburg, Sowjetische Deutschlandpolitik — von Breshnew zu Gorbatschow, in: *Osteuropa*, 5/1985, p. 318.

66. Roland Smith, *Soviet Policy Towards Germany*, Adelphi paper 203, Institute for International and Strategic Studies, London 1985, p. 14.

67. Boris Yeltsin in an interview with *Die Zeit*, May 9, 1986, p. (Politik) 5.

68. Ambassador Julij Kvitsinskij in an interview with Bonner Rundschau, Aug. 8, 1986.

69. M.S. Gorbacev (speech on TV), *Pravda* May 15, 1986, p. 1.

70. (Unsigned article) Opasnyj atavizm, *Pravda* Nov. 27, 1986, p. 4.

71. Cf. Fedor Burlackij in: *Literaturnaja Gazeta* Sept. 10, 1986; Genrich Borovik (on Soviet TV), Oct. 5, 1986, acc. to Monitor-Dienst Deutsche Welle, *Allgemeiner Teil,* Oct. 6, 1986, p. 7; Valentin Falin, acc. to Monitor-Dienst Deutsche Welle, *Allgemeiner Teil,* Oct. 7, 1986, p. 6.

72. Programma Kommunisticeskoj Partii Sovetskogo Sojuza, *Pravda* March 7, 1986, p. 8. The final edition of this program — as compared to the draft of October 1985 (*Pravda* Oct. 26, 1985) - omits the term 'opportunism', which is regularly used as a synonym for Socialist or Social-democratic parties.

73. Fred Oldenburg, Das Verhaltnis Moskau-Bonn unter Gorbatschow, in: *Osteuropa,* 8-9/1986, p. 786.

74. Eduard Sevardnadze, TASS-report of Nov. 10, 1986.

7

The German Question
from an
East European Perspective

Andrzej Korbonski

Introduction

More than forty years after the end of World War II, memories of
the German occupation of, and behavior in, Eastern Europe still
often generate considerable excitement and even fear in the
region, suggesting that the "German Question" continues to be an important item on the East European political agenda. In light of the emo-
tional character of that issue, it is tempting to disregard the basic rules
of political analysis and to engage in a highly charged polemical exercise. This temptation must be resisted not only because rhetoric is hardly a substitute for rational analysis but also because the "German Question," as seen from different East European capitals, lends itself to a
thorough examination of the available facts, and of the motivations and
objectives of the participating actors on both sides of the Elbe.

Two definitional issues must be settled first. To begin with, the
concept of *die Deutsche Frage* is simply too broad to be of much use for
our investigation. Since it means different things to different people, it
is important to come up with a concept largely devoid of serious am-
biguities. I propose to break it down in four parts: I will first refer to
Germany in its historical perspective, as a country that over at least two
centuries has exerted considerable influence in Europe, both East and
West; secondly, I shall confine the question to the role and influence of
the Federal Republic, and shall do the same for the German Democratic
Republic in part three. Finally, I shall assume that the "German Ques-

tion" in the second half of the 1980s refers to the problem of intra-German relations involving both German states.

The second definitional issue concerns the notion of Eastern Europe. It is increasingly difficult to define Eastern Europe accurately. On the one hand, the eight countries—Albania, Bulgaria, Czechoslovakia, East Germany, Hungary, Poland, Romania and Yugoslavia—not only are located in a well-defined geographical area of Europe but also share several essential features, including political and economic structures and institutions; patterns of socio-economic changes; except for Albania and Yugoslavia, membership in two important regional organizations, the Warsaw Treaty Organization (WTO) and the Council for Mutual Economic Assistance (CMEA); and to a great extent a common historical heritage, especially since World War II. On the other hand, the differences among the individual countries are less easily observable, but increasingly significant, as revealed by the very different reactions to Gorbachev's policies. They derive from many deeply rooted cultural and socio-economic phenomena that have created national political cultures which continue to influence the respective countries' foreign and domestic policies, even after more than four decades of Communist efforts to eradicate or weaken them.

Rather than examine the attitude of *all* East European states toward the "German Question," I shall focus on the two neighbors of both German states—Czechoslovakia and Poland—and treat the remaining East European countries selectively. The reasons for it are mostly historical and geopolitical. Until 1945 the relations between Czechoslovakia, Poland and Germany were characterized by a high degree of hostility, which continued, at least nominally, until the late 1960s with regard to the Federal Republic. Following the postwar division of Germany, Czechoslovakia, Poland and the German Democratic Republic became known as the "Northern Tier" or the "Iron Triangle" within the Warsaw Pact, representing a major source of military, political and economic support for the Soviet Union. The relationship between East Germany and the remaining East European countries, although occasionally quite close in the past, has never achieved the kind of importance and intensity that characterized the interaction between Prague, Warsaw and Berlin both before and after World War II.

Finally, in referring to attitudes and perceptions I shall try, whenever necessary, to differentiate between elite and mass phenomena. In many cases they were congruent, with official attitudes and policies reflecting popular sentiments. In other cases there was occasionally a wide gap between the opinions and activities of the rulers and those of the ruled, as illustrated, for example, by the attitude toward East Germany.

Germany and Eastern Europe Between the Wars

Much has been written about the relationship between Germany and Eastern Europe in the past and one is hard put to say anything new or original about it. Rather than analyze the major turning points in that relationship during the 18th and 19th centuries, I decided to limit the discussion to the period between the end of World War I in November 1918 and Germany's defeat in World War II in May 1945.

One thing that emerges rather clearly from the analysis is that the fate of Germany, in both the Weimar and Nazi editions, was closely linked with the fate of interwar Eastern Europe. It could not really be otherwise. In the early part of the period, what appeared to be a "new" Germany confronted a number of "new" East European states, notably Czechoslovakia, Poland and Yugoslavia. None of the four countries was really "new": in fact all of them have had a glorious history going back several centuries. However, for reasons that need not detain us here, all of them emerged from the First World War as essentially new entities saddled with a multiplicity of problems which made it impossible for them to reach some kind of a *modus vivendi* and which ultimately led to a bloody confrontation in World War II.

By hindsight, it is clear that the Weimar Republic never accepted the provisions of the Versailles Treaty of which Poland was the main beneficiary in Eastern Europe. Hence, a meaningful reconciliation between Berlin and Warsaw was never seriously contemplated by either side. Even before the Nazi takeover in 1933, the Weimar Republic continued to view Poland as a temporary *Saison-Staat*, proclaiming its determination to recover the lost provinces of *Pommern, Posen,* and *Schlesien.* In this context the denunciation of Versailles by Hitler represented a logical continuation of a campaign initiated by his democratic predecessors.

The new Poland, on the one hand aspiring to the status of a European power, and on the other insecure in the knowledge of the inherent weakness of a multinational state, became particularly sensitive to the policy of German revanchism and from the start assumed a distrustful if not a hostile stance vis-à-vis Weimar. Traditional Polish-German enmity was exacerbated by German attempts to stir up the various national minorities against Warsaw, contributing to the growing ill-feeling between the two states.

The situation was quite different with respect to Czechoslovakia, the only democratic country in Eastern Europe. Unlike Poland, Czechoslovakia did not acquire any German territory after 1918 and if the country's ruling elite harbored any anti-German feelings, they tended to be directed against Vienna rather than Berlin. The record shows that until the beginning of the Nazi propaganda campaign in the late 1930s, the *Sudetendeutschen* appeared quite loyal to Prague and enjoyed political and civil freedoms provided by the democratic regime.

The other East European countries tended to be rather friendly toward Germany. This was certainly true for Bulgaria, the "Prussia of the Balkans," and for Romania, partly for dynastic and historical reasons, as well as for Hungary which saw itself and Germany as the chief victims of the Versailles arrangement. While Albania gravitated toward Italy, some of the provinces of Yugoslavia, notably Croatia, looked toward Germany and/or Italy for support against the hegemony of Serbia.

There is no doubt that in the 1930s all the above countries became economically strongly dependent on Germany, which cornered the markets in southeastern Europe. Germany dramatically expanded its import of new materials and foodstuffs from the region, accumulating large import surpluses, establishing bilateral clearing accounts, and delaying payments, thus tying the area closely to the Third Reich. World War II provided the background for further German exploitation of occupied territories in Eastern Europe, resulting in a massive transfer of resources that made a significant contribution to the German war effort.

The German policy and behavior in Eastern Europe during World War II is well known and needs no elaboration. The occupation was particularly harsh in Poland and in some parts of Yugoslavia and relatively mild in Bohemia and and Moravia. Bulgaria, Hungary and Romania largely escaped the worst effects of being forced into the German orbit and the same was true for the puppet states of Croatia and Slovakia.

This differentiated policy greatly influenced subsequent national attitudes toward both German states. The traditional Polish-German enmity increased significantly as a result of the war. There was also a visible growth of anti-German feelings in Czechoslovakia, which could not easily forget Munich and the creation of the Protectorate in March 1939, despite rather benign German occupation policy during the war.

To conclude, the end of World War II did not really witness any lasting changes in East European perceptions of, and attitudes toward, Germany. If anything, the war tended to deepen the already existing division within Eastern Europe generated by the differences in national attitudes and perceptions. The hatred between the Poles and the Germans escalated dramatically, accompanied by a rise in enmity among the Czechs, Serbs, and Germans. On the other hand, the traditional pro-German feelings in the rest of the Balkans and in Hungary remained essentially unchanged, official hostile propaganda notwithstanding. This phenomenon was to have interesting repercussions in the future.

The Federal Republic and Eastern Europe

The relationship between the Federal Republic and Eastern Europe since 1948 may be divided into three different phases. Phase one, which began with the formal establishment of the *Bundesrepublik* in 1948, concluded with the first attempt at an *Ostpolitik* in 1967. Stage two terminated with the imposition of martial law in Poland in December 1981, which seemed to put an end to the rapidly growing rapprochement between Bonn and its past and present adversaries in Eastern Europe. Phase three, which is still with us, has not lasted long enough to allow for a definite statement or even an informed judgment.

The four years which preceded the formal division of Germany and the establishment of the Federal Republic contributed to further alienation between Western Germany, at that time still under Allied occupation, and Poland and Czechoslovakia. The wartime experiences, which were bad enough, were augmented by the suffering of millions of Germans expelled *en masse* from Poland and Czechoslovakia. A large part of the refugees settled in Western Germany and soon became a vocal spokesman and articulator of revanchist interests. Its sheer numbers made it a powerful political force to be reckoned with even in 1987, especially by the CDU-CSU government in the Federal Republic.

The formation of the Federal Republic was greeted with considerable anger by the East Europeans, which was hardly surprising, considering that the division of Germany occurred at the height of both the Cold War and Stalinist hegemony in Eastern Europe. Also, predictably, the Western decision to rearm West Germany in the wake of the Korean War was seen by some of the East European countries as a sign of the revival of German revanchism less than a decade after the end of World War II, and the same applied to the entry of the Federal Republic in NATO in 1955. While the official reaction was articulated by the ruling oligarchy, presumably on Soviet orders, it may be speculated that for once there was a good deal of congruence between the views of the East European regimes and those of the masses, most of which remembered quite well the German excesses of World War II.

The decade separating the mid-1950s and the beginning of West German *Ostpolitik* in the mid-1960s witnessed an increasing heterogeneity in Eastern Europe that allowed some countries in the region a degree of elbow room in their domestic and foreign policies. On the one hand, the upheavals in Hungary and Poland in 1956, followed by Albania's defection from the orbit of Moscow to that of Beijing in 1961, and culminating in Romania's declaration of economic independence from the USSR in 1963, made it clear to the West that Eastern Europe should no longer be treated as a monolith. This meant that the road to Warsaw or Prague no longer had to lead through Moscow and that, at least in theory, Bonn could approach the individual East European countries directly. The process of destalinization with its implications took a long time to be recognized as offering new opportunities for "bridge building" and "peaceful engagement." In this respect, the Federal Republic proved more prescient than the United States and France, which began to emulate West German policy several years later. The West German initiative was rather surprising since as long as Chancellor Adenauer was in charge, Bonn's policy toward Eastern Europe was largely determined by the so-called "Hallstein Doctrine," which was intended to isolate the DDR and which left West Germany with little room for maneuver vis-à-vis the individual countries in the region. Nonetheless, the victory of the SPD-FDP coalition suggested that the West German electorate was ready for a change and was willing to give *Ostpolitik* a try.

The story of *Ostpolitik* I and II has been dealt with extensively in the literature and only some conclusions will be mentioned here.[1] As is well known, the first attempts at normalizing relations between Bonn and the East European capitals proved only partly successful, with Bucharest alone showing interest in establishing diplomatic relations with the Federal Republic. Nonetheless, this development spelled the demise of the "Hallstein Doctrine," which had presented probably the most serious obstacle to normalization.

The Soviet intervention in Czechoslovakia in 1968 appeared to destroy the chances of an early reconciliation. Yet in hindsight, it appeared that the Soviet invasion, in combination with the escalation of Sino-Soviet conflict, paved the way toward the second round of *Ostpolitik*. This second round proved remarkably successful, as shown in the conclusion of four major treaties between 1970 and 1972: the two treaties between Bonn and Moscow and Warsaw, the Quadripartite Agreement on Berlin and the treaty recognizing the existence of two separate German states.

Insofar as Eastern Europe was concerned, the Warsaw-Bonn Treaty, which, among others, recognized the Oder-Neisse line as the

Polish-German frontier, was probably the most significant. It was certainly the most important for Poland as it not only removed the most sensitive issue in its policy and attitude toward the West, but also weakened the strongest link tying it to the USSR, which from the outset saw itself as the ultimate guarantor of Poland's territorial integrity. Moreover, the defense of "Western" or "Recovered" territories has been traditionally the sole goal that united Communist and non-Communist Poles, and the elimination of that issue was bound to make it difficult for the Warsaw regime to use it as a mobilizing and/or legitimizing device. It was clear that after 1970 the ruling party in Poland had to find a new whipping boy for that purpose, which as the history of the past 18 years shows, was a difficult if not an impossible task. Similarly, there is no doubt that the settlement of the border question affected popular attitudes toward West Germany: more and more Poles began to look at the Federal Republic with different eyes, not as a power-hungry, revanchist state but as a modern European country which was willing to provide Poland with know-how and modern technology.

The Warsaw-Bonn Treaty encouraged other East European states to seek accommodation with West Germany. Albania, Bulgaria and Hungary, not to mention Yugoslavia, had no major claims against Bonn and the normalization proceeded rather smoothly, except for Tirana which waited until 1987 to initiate a serious dialogue with Bonn. The story of Czechoslovakia was somewhat different. In 1968, the supposedly evil West German designs were used as an excuse to legitimize the Soviet military intervention aimed at destroying the "Prague Spring." Moreover, the Munich Agreement of 1938, which approved the secession of Sudetenland and other Czechoslovak territory, had to be formally disavowed by Bonn which, for various reasons, found itself reluctant to do so until several years later.

Still, the early 1970s inaugurated a new era between West Germany and Eastern Europe. They coincided also with U.S.-Soviet and East-West detente which also enhanced the relationship, clearly benefiting both sides. For most of the East Europeans, the Federal Republic became a friend rather than a foe, probably more understanding of, and sympathetic to their plight than France, Britain and the United States. Bonn's willingness to grant credits and, ultimately, to carry a growing burden of hard currency debt, was greatly appreciated by both the leaders and masses in Eastern Europe. On their part, the successive West German governments continued the *Ostpolitik* without much visible opposition among the voters. This was in sharp contrast to the situation of a decade before and represented a striking reversal of traditional attitudes and perceptions on both sides.

The imposition of martial law in Poland in December 1981

provided a good test of the stability of the new relationship. Here again, the experts' predictions proved wrong. It would have been easy for Moscow to blame the Federal Republic for encouraging "Solidarity" and for bringing Poland to a brink of a major crisis. To be sure, there were some sporadic references to Bonn's revanchist stance, but they were not part of an organized campaign. It was interesting to note that the first NATO country to be visited after the coup and given an explanation of the military takeover by a representative of the Polish military regime was West Germany.[2] This may have been due to the unexpectedly lukewarm condemnation of martial law uttered by Chancellor Schmidt during his visit to East Germany. Regardless of the actual reason, the fact that a country which only a decade or so ago was branded as Poland's worst enemy was now being treated in so friendly a manner spoke for itself.

The period since December 1981 witnessed a continuation of previous policies. The tremendous private aid given to Poland by the West German population was only one reflection of the great sympathy felt for Poland in its critical times. Although the Federal Republic was Poland's (and Eastern Europe's) largest creditor, it showed itself less inclined to apply drastic economic sanctions against the region than the United States. As time went on, it was not only the Schmidt government but also the new administration of Helmut Kohl that was inclined to maintain good relations with Eastern Europe, including Poland and East Germany. Foreign Minister Genscher became a familiar figure in East European capitals. His example was eventually followed by his colleagues in Britain, France and Italy, leaving the United States as the only major NATO member refusing to acknowledge the new reality until very recently.

To sum up, the record shows that in the mid-1980s the political leadership in the Federal Republic, regardless of party affiliation, was determined to make good on its earlier expressions of good will toward Eastern Europe and to maintain reasonably good relations with the various countries in the region. That this policy was bound to create difficulties both at home and abroad was illustrated by the cancellation of the visits by Messrs. Honecker of East Germany and Zhivkov of Bulgaria, and by the revival of political activities by the refugee organizations. Still, there is no evidence that the Bonn government, concerned with stirring up a new political controversy, is likely to stray from its policy of reconciliation with Eastern Europe.

158 German Question from an East European Perspective

The German Democratic Republic
and Eastern Europe

From its very beginning, the German Democratic Republic (DDR) has been officially viewed by other East European states as an important, bona fide member of the Communist alliance in Eastern Europe, as a key component of the "Northern Tier" or "Iron Triangle" within the Warsaw Pact, and as a major supplier of technologically advanced goods to the rest of the Council on Mutual Economic Assistance (CMEA). However, this positive official perception of the DDR provided a screen which hid not only the much less favorable attitudes of the East European populations but also frequently less positive views entertained by the East European elites.

Some of the negative attitudes have been deeply rooted in the past. While they affected the popular perception of *both* the Federal Republic and DDR, the latter, if anything, suffered more from its historical past than its counterpart across the Elbe. In the eyes of many East Europeans, the DDR tended to be identified with the old Prussia, which had a special image in Eastern Europe as the most aggressive of the historical German states, certainly more militaristic and anti-Slav than Bavaria or Saxony. This negative image was further reinforced by the DDR's attempts to engage in developing a separate national identity which sought to be built on a historical base that, if only by reason of geography, identified it with Prussia. The frequent use of traditional German symbols, such as military uniforms, and the goose step, gave rise to growing references to a synthesis of Marx and Bismarck, adding fuel to the negative stereotypes of East Germans (alias Prussians) still prevailing in Eastern Europe.

But there were also other factors that contributed to the persisting alienation between DDR and the rest of Eastern Europe. One of them was undoubtedly the favorable treatment accorded the DDR by the Soviet Union. It may be taken for granted that few if any of the East Europeans were aware of the fact that, during the first postwar decade, first the Soviet occupation zone and then the fledgling DDR were forced to transfer huge resources to the USSR in the form of war booty and reparations, suffering more in this respect than the other countries in the region. The fact that despite these obstacles the DDR succeeded in developing a modern industrial state was clearly more of an "economic miracle" than the economic recovery of West Germany, handsomely supported by the Marshall Plan and other forms of U.S. aid.

Be that as it may, the East German economic successes, which put it on top as the most advanced and prosperous country in the region, were greatly resented by the East Europeans, who attributed it not only to Soviet support but also to the significant aid provided by West Germany. There is no question that the aid extended by the Federal Republic in the form of credits and favorable payment arrangements in the so-called "interzonal" trade made a considerable difference, if only by making the DDR a *de facto* member of the European Economic Community, enjoying all the benefits but carrying hardly any obligations accruing from that membership. No other country in Eastern Europe, not even the Soviet Union, enjoyed simultaneously the benefits of both CMEA and the EEC and this fact alone could have hardly been appreciated in the region.

The resentment of higher living standards enjoyed by the citizens of DDR was further augmented by the frequently arrogant behavior of East German tourists swarming around Eastern Europe. Prevented from travelling to the West, the East Germans annually invaded the various East European countries, occupying the best hotels and camping grounds and frequently antagonizing the local population. As a result, the East Germans became generally disliked in Eastern Europe, often more so than the West Germans whose behavior tended to be more acceptable.

There were also some serious antagonisms at the official level. They stemmed from the fact that at least during the first 20 or so years of its existence the DDR, dominated by its undisputed ruler, Walter Ulbricht, was generally perceived as the most loyal ally of Moscow, which saw itself as the guardian of Communist orthodoxy and which acted as a watchdog sniffing for signs of ideological and anti-Soviet heresies. It was the DDR which was highly critical of the events in Hungary and Poland in 1956 and it was Ulbricht who was the chief instigator and leader of the campaign against Dubcek and the "Prague Spring" in 1968. The fact that a few years later he miscalculated and misjudged Soviet intentions with respect to a rapprochement with West Germany, which brought about his downfall, did not greatly affect the East European perception of the DDR as a die-hard, conservative state strongly opposed to any signs of political liberalization.

While the new leader, Erich Honecker, cut a more sympathetic figure than his predecessor, there were no clear signs of the hardline policy being changed in any significant degree. The fierce anti-"Solidarity" and even anti-Polish campaign during the critical months in 1980-81 only reaffirmed that image, certainly in Poland but most likely also in the rest of Eastern Europe.[3] Thus in the early 1980s the DDR appeared largely isolated in the region. Paradoxically, its closest friend in Central Europe appeared to be its perennial enemy, the Federal Republic.

As time went on, East Germany's relations with the rest of Eastern Europe deteriorated still further. The background was provided by a rapidly changing atmosphere in the region, following Gorbachev's assumption of power in the Kremlin in March of 1985. After a period of some uncertainty regarding Gorbachev's intentions with regard to Eastern Europe, it became clear that the Soviet leader was much less interested in Moscow's junior allies than in reaching some kind of a rapprochement with the United States and initiating a process of far-reaching domestic reforms in the Soviet Union. Gorbachev's seeming indifference was thus interpreted by some of the East European leaders as giving them a free hand to voice their own opinions and pursue their own policies without the Kremlin's interference. With the exception of Hungary and Poland this meant in essence maintaining a conservative course emphasizing the status quo, which the various leaders pursued in the past two decades with Soviet imprimatur.

One could easily imagine the astonished reaction of the East European leaders to Gorbachev's policy of *glasnost* and to his announcement of extensive political and economic reforms in the USSR. The highly negative response to Gorbachev's ideas in most of the East European countries headed by the East Germany was not really surprising.[4] After all, the current leaders in East Berlin and elsewhere managed to stay in power for a long time by adhering to cautious and conservative policies, by towing Moscow's line, which until recently excluded the possibility of meaningful reforms, and by developing an extraordinary sensitivity which allowed them to divine and predict changes in the Kremlin.

It is now quite obvious that East Germany has assumed the leadership of an anti-Gorbachev league in Eastern Europe. While it is much too early to talk about a formal split within the Warsaw alliance, it is becoming clear that relations between the DDR and some of the East European countries are likely to deteriorate, more so now that Moscow apparently disclaims any desire to continue imposing its leadership on unruly allies. A good illustration of the changing situation is a quarrel between Poland and East Germany over territorial waters around Szczecin and Swinoujscie, which may yet escalate into a full-blown conflict between Warsaw and East Berlin.[5]

The rapidly improving relations between the two German states, if anything, increased the resentment and fear in some East European countries. While some of the latter applauded Honecker's desire to maintain the policy of detente vis-à-vis Western Europe despite the significant worsening of U.S.-Soviet relations, others most likely envied the DDR's ability to obtain large loans while the rest of the region was largely deprived of Western largesse. The incipient split in Eastern Europe came to the fore in the course of 1984, even prior to the cancellation of Honecker's visit to West Germany in September of that year. The DDR's independent stance was supported by Hungary and Romania and loudly criticized by the Soviet Union and Czecho-slovakia, with Poland and Bulgaria largely maintaining diplomatic silence. It was an interesting case of a *renversement des alliances* with traditional friends such as the DDR and Czechoslovakia finding themselves on the opposite sides of the barricade.[6]

To conclude, it is clear that in the second half of the 1980s, the DDR remains a controversial member of the Soviet alliance system in Eastern Europe. It is equally clear that its economic successes have been greatly resented by East European leaders and populations alike and there are no indications that this largely negative image enjoyed by the DDR is likely to change greatly in the foreseeable future.

Eastern Europe and German-German Relations

It may be assumed that while Eastern Europe as a whole welcomed the destruction of Nazi Germany in 1945, it most likely greeted the subsequent division between East and West Germany with either indifference or with some suspicion. On the one hand, most of the East European countries believed, not unlike their West European counterparts, that the division was only temporary and that sooner rather than later, the two parts of Germany would be reunited once again. On the other hand, the concern of Poland and Czechoslovakia in particular was to keep either the divided or united Germany militarily weak so that it could not reclaim the territory lost to its East European neighbors.

This rather benign attitude began to change in the mid-1950s. The reasons for it included the remarkable economic recovery of West Germany, the rearmament of the Federal Republic and its entry into NATO, and the perception of the Adenauer government as essentially hostile to Eastern Europe and eager to overthrow the existing status quo. As long as West Germany was disarmed and economically weak it presented no major threat; all this, however, had changed ten years after the end of World War II. The specter of a powerful Bundesrepublik, supported by the United States and the rest of NATO, most likely instilled considerable fear throughout Eastern Europe.

Because of that, both the East European elites and the masses began to look at the division of Germany with different eyes. It soon became clear that the division carried several important advantages for Eastern Europe, especially for Poland and Czechoslovakia, which for obvious reasons were particularly sensitive to any policy changes affecting the status quo. Apart from weakening Germany militarily and economically, the existence of a separate East German state, strongly linked with both the Warsaw Pact and CMEA, provided a powerful guarantee of the existing territorial arrangement in Central and Eastern Europe which most of the East European states were eager to maintain indefinitely. For Poland in particular, the DDR acted as a shield or a buffer zone against possible West German revanchism. East Germany recognized the Oder-Neisse Line as a permanent Polish-German frontier as early as 1950 and as long as the DDR remained a separate state, the perennial Polish fears of seeing its Western Provinces being returned to a united Germany were largely, if not completely, assuaged.

All this meant that Eastern Europe became a strong supporter of the division of Germany, opposed to any moves that might lead to a rapprochement and possible unification of the two German states. Thus they welcomed the continuing hostility between East Berlin and Bonn, even when in every respect they tended to detest Walter Ulbricht and his insistence on orthodoxy and absolute obedience to Moscow. Except for Romania, all the East European countries rejected West German *Ostpolitik* in 1966-67.

Another critical turning point affecting East European perception of German unity occurred between 1970 and 1972. Of the various treaties concluded during that period, one of the most important was the treaty between Bonn and Warsaw, which seemed to settle the question of the Oder-Neisse Line as the border line between Poland and Germany. After this treaty was signed the division of Germany lost some of its salience for Eastern Europe as West Germany was no longer seriously perceived as a revanchist power. Nonetheless, it may be assumed that the other three treaties signed between 1970-1972 were welcomed by those East European countries which were concerned with the preservation of the postwar territorial arrangement in Eastern Europe. The same was true for the European Security Conference which produced the Final Act that specifically mentioned the inviolability of existing frontiers in Europe.

In the mid-1970s, all signs pointed to a period of stability in Eastern Europe, which of course included the division of Germany. However, this was not to be. The rather unexpected change in the existing situation was triggered off by two actors who until then were believed to be strongly committed to the preservation of the status quo. One of them was the Soviet Union, the other East Germany.

Over the years, the attitude of the Kremlin toward German unity tended to be ambivalent. In the early postwar years, the USSR appeared on the one hand to be a champion of that unity, yet on the other hand, it also proceeded rapidly to Sovietize its zone of occupation. Following the establishment of two German states in 1948-49, Stalin tried in his famous offer of March 1952 to fend off West Germany's integration with the North Atlantic Alliance by agreeing to unite both parts of Germany on the condition that the new German state would remain neutral. There were indications that a year later, after Stalin's death, Lavrentii Beria entertained similar thoughts prior to his demise.

For the next decade or so, Moscow did not return to the question of German unification. Shortly before his ouster in 1964, Nikita Khrushchev tried to revive the idea. While earlier Soviet overtures vis-à-vis West Germany did not cause much concern in Eastern Europe, there is evidence that Khrushchev's 1964 initiative created considerable apprehension, particularly in Poland. As is well known, the Poles have been traditionally highly sensitive to any possible Soviet-German collusion and nowhere were the memories of Rapallo and the Molotov-Ribbentrop Treaty stronger than in Warsaw.

The failure of Khrushchev's policy was obviously greeted with relief in Warsaw but the relief was rather short-lived. Following the signing of the Bonn-Moscow treaty in 1970, relations between the Soviet Union and the Federal Republic began to improve at a rapid pace, culminating in Leonid Brezhnev's well-advertised visit to Bonn in 1974. There is no doubt that the policy of Soviet-West German rapprochement caused renewed worry in East Berlin and Warsaw, and Brezhnev had to reassure his two important allies that the USSR did not contemplate any radical departures from its previous policy.

The next event that generated considerable excitement in Eastern Europe was the emergence of the "Solidarity" movement and the ensuing political crisis in Poland. As was to be expected, the DDR was particularly critical of the developments in Warsaw for fear of the "Polish disease" spreading westward. It was also clear that Moscow was faced with the dilemma: to invade or not to invade Poland. In the wake of the imposition of martial law in Warsaw in December 1981, persistent rumors began to circulate in Poland suggesting that the military takeover under General Jaruzelski was a last minute effort to prevent a joint attempt by the Soviet Union and East Germany to transfer Poland's Western Territories to the DDR as part of a larger scheme to achieve German unification. West Germany's agreement to become a part of a united albeit demilitarized and neutral Germany was to be bought with the return of the territories east of the Oder-Neisse Line. It was Jaruzelski's coup that threw a monkey wrench into the cabal and hence he ought to have been regarded as a hero rather than a villain for preventing another partition of Poland.[7]

While the rumors were obviously far-fetched, they were apparently believed by some Poles, testimony to the long-standing Polish paranoia concerning Germany. Hence, it was not surprising that in 1984 Poland did not join Hungary and Romania in supporting the East German effort to continue the policy of detente vis-à-vis the Federal Republic. Ordinarily, Warsaw would have most likely endorsed the policy of rapprochement with Bonn, but the fact that this policy was opposed by Moscow meant that the Polish fears of another Soviet-German collusion could be laid aside for the time being. On the other hand, Honecker's postponed visit to Bonn in September 1987 caused hardly any ripples in Warsaw, suggesting that Poland has become more relaxed about the dialogue between the two German states.

To conclude, it appears that by and large Eastern Europe in the mid-1980s supports permanent division of Germany and views with suspicion any moves by either the DDR or the USSR toward West Germany that contain references to German unity. While each state has its own reasons, all East European countries, including Czechoslovakia and Poland, are in favor of good relations with West Germany but, together with their West European counterparts, notably France and Italy, clearly prefer to see Germany divided for as long as possible.

Conclusion

The above analysis suggests that the past forty years have witnessed striking changes in the East European attitudes to, and perceptions of, the so-called "German Question."

While the early postwar period was characterized by considerable fear, mistrust and enmity, the past 20 years or so have seen a significant change in this respect. Although there is still a residual of fear and mistrust, the new generation of the East Europeans tends to look at West Germany not principally as an eternal enemy but as a source of economic aid and even support for their political aspirations. To some extent, paradoxically, West Germany enjoys considerable popularity in the region, certainly more so than East Germany despite the latter's membership in WTO and CMEA.

Insofar as the division of Germany is concerned, the East Europeans essentially favor it. On the other hand, there is hardly a consensus with regard to improved relations between the two German states. While some of the countries in the region see the rapprochement between Bonn and East Berlin as being in their interest, others are afraid that close contact between East and West Germany might ultimately result in German unity and an important change in the existing *status quo,* with all its negative consequences.

Notes

1. For an excellent study of Bonn's *Ostpolitik* prior to 1968, see Fritz Ermath, "Internationalism, Security, and Legitimacy: The Challenge to Soviet Interests in East Europe, 1964-1968," *RAND MEMORANDUM RM-5909-PR* (Santa Monica, CA: RAND Corporation, March 1969).

2. Polish Deputy Prime Minister, Mieczyslaw Rakowski, a close confidante of General Jaruzelski, visited Bonn on December 30, 1981, less than three weeks after the military coup.

3. For a latest insider's account of the Polish crisis, including East German involvement, see "Wojna z narodem widziana od srodka" Kultura (Paris) No. 4/475, April 1987, pp. 3-57.

4. Charles Gati, "Gorbachev and Eastern Europe" *Foreign Affairs* vol. 65, no. 5, Summer 1987, pp. 958-975.

5. "The Polish-GDR Dispute over Territorial Waters" *Radio Free Europe Research* vol. 12, no. 35, September 4, 1987.

6. For a comprehensive discussion, see Ronald D. Asmus, comp., "East Berlin and Moscow: the Documentation of a Dispute" *RFE Occasional Papers* No. 1, 1985.

7. Personal interviews in Warsaw, Summer 1982.

8

West German Foreign Policy and the Bifurcation of the Western Security Regime

Mary N. Hampton

There is no doubt that the Federal Republic of Germany (FRG) occupies a very different position today between East and West than it did in the late 1940s and 1950s. The issues that foster debate concern West Germany's current role in the East-West relationship and an explanation of how that role evolved. These two issues will be addressed by focusing on the evolution of the postwar Western security regime and the effect such development has had on West German relations within the Western alliance and with the East bloc. Specifically, I argue that Bonn's continued participation in, and adaptation to, the Western security regime has over time altered the position of the FRG in East-West and West-West relations but that this development reveals mixed blessings for current and future West German foreign policy.

Notwithstanding Kenneth Waltz's claim that the postwar bipolar system remains fundamentally unaltered,[1] most theorists of international relations acknowledge and seek to explain the decline of the U.S. and the parallel relative increase in power of other international actors. A recurring question in this line of inquiry is the role played by international regimes in affecting state behavior and outcomes in the international system, and thus the relationship of international regimes to systemic change itself. Regimes are interpreted by analysts such as Robert O. Keohane as intervening variables that "may affect actors' behavior in classic systemic ways by altering the incentives and opportunities that face them."[2] Accepting the collective definition agreed upon at the conference on regimes held in Palm Springs during 1980-81, where regimes are "sets of implicit or explicit principles, norms, rules and decision-making procedures around which actors' expectations converge in a given area of international relations," I seek to explain how middle-sized states, specifically the FRG, have benefited from participation in the postwar Western security regime, and how Bonn has been able to translate these benefits into real gains in its ability to influence outcomes in the international system.

Focusing on the evolution of the Western alliance as a security regime reveals two essential facets of the postwar Western security relationship regarding the role of middle-sized states such as the FRG that are often overlooked in the traditional alliance literature: a) the alliance was from the outset intended to be more than a traditional military pact and thus was infused with principles other than those based on narrowly defined military considerations; and b) the development of the alliance as a regime determined that the political goal of political cohesion would often heavily influence outcomes in Western security policy- and agenda-setting. Specifically, by tracing the FRG's participation in the initially U.S.-led Western security regime from the early years of NATO's inception, through the detente years and into the present, I will show how the alliance as regime has over time empowered states other than the initial regime leader.

The definitional aspects of the alliance as regime are as follows. The common interests among participants in the Western alliance or security regime were from the outset twofold and related: the attainment of security in the face of the Soviet threat and the advancement of peace and stability in Europe. This second aspect of commonly held Western security goals is central to understanding my proposition that the alliance has operated from the outset differently than a strict military pact; that an important component of the relationship involves a primarily positive political objective. The guiding documents of the Western security regime are the North Atlantic Treaty and the semi-annual North Atlantic Council Communiques. The most important functioning organ of the regime, both as set out in the North Atlantic Treaty and in practice, is the North Atlantic Council. The governing norms emerge clearly from alliance documents and literature as collective security and stability in Europe; both are explicitly stated in the Preamble to the North Atlantic Treaty. The regime principles include the voluntary association of sovereign states, non-coercion and non-discrimination among allies, and equality of status among member states. In a word, reciprocity is a fundamental principle within the alliance. The rules of the regime include timely consultation among allies concerning issues of common importance and the regularity of information exchange and assembly. The rules are carried out procedurally through a formalized network of regularly scheduled committee and advisory meetings and through ad hoc meetings and consultations among alliance officials, heads of state, national ministers and other recognized national leaders.

By appealing at different junctures to the norms, rules and procedures encompassing the security regime, such as to the principle of equal status among member states, Bonn has been able increasingly to achieve its own interests and concomitantly to enhance its position of influence in the regime. Since the late 1970s, West German foreign policymakers have accrued much political power and influence through maintenance and leadership of West European detente with the East Bloc in the aftermath of Washington's retreat into a more confrontational posture. The Western security regime has thus become bifurcated, with Bonn and Washington performing as regime leaders at two distinct levels. This process has led to a situation in which trans-Atlantic discord persists, although the high costs of "exit" have to date precluded serious efforts at fundamentally altering the security regime.

The consequent unruly nature of the security regime combined with the increased competitiveness and conflict within other areas of Western relations present a real dilemma for managing interstate cooperation by leaders in Bonn and other Western capitals. The lack of policy coordination in a host of issue areas, such as development policy, energy policy, and more recently containment of terrorist activity, threatens to unravel further the already strained consensus around which the postwar Western allies have operated.

The prominent economic and political position of West Germany, both regionally within the context of Europe and internationally, continues to assure it an important role in West-West, East-West and North-South relations. The riddle for Bonn will be how to maintain the stability of the already shaken postwar Western security regime upon which West German influence largely rests without forfeiting its interests in this area as well as in those where consensus does not exist, and thus where conflicts of interest are certain to emerge or increase. Finally, balancing the successes achieved through Bonn's prominent position in the East-West relationship with the increasingly politicized content of the NATO relationship will be a difficult task for West German leadership, including both the internal and external dimensions of these often contradictory requirements.

The Historical Origins of
the Western Security Regime

What establishes the alliance as a regime is that it was intended from the start to prescribe the limits within which its members could act in areas of security commonly established. These historical origins of the Western security regime will be covered briefly.

As the clearly predominant power at the close of World War II, the U.S. was able in large part to specify the design of the postwar system, or at least of its Western half. Working on the already existing and diversely intense common interests of the U.S. and Western Europe vis-a-vis the USSR and stability in Europe, the emerging Western security regime was initially orchestrated and led by Washington. Reflective of the overall pattern of America's postwar plans was the constant tension between what George Kennan calls the "universalist" and the "particularist" approaches to international politics. Inherent in the Western security regime were the features of what Kennan in 1948 observed to be the universalistic approach of American foreign policy. This approach

...looks to the solution of international problems by providing a universalistic pattern of rules and procedures which would be applicable to all countries, or at least to all countries prepared to join, in an identical way ... It assumes that if all countries could be induced to subscribe to certain standard rules of behavior, the ugly realities - the power aspirations, the ugly prejudices,... would be forced to recede behind the protecting curtain of accepted legal restraint, and that the problems of our foreign policy could thus be reduced to the familiar terms of parliamentary procedure and majority decision.3

The organizing features of the postwar Western security regime conform quite well to Kennan's depiction and have heavily informed the evolution of the regime. The reliance on consultation, parliamentary procedure, and cooperation among partners as ends in themselves are, in fact, the qualities of the Western alliance that allow it so readily to be viewed as an international regime. It is also the basis for my argument that participation in the security regime empowers from the outset states other than the hegemon or regime initiator. That is, these other states acquire immediately the status of partner and can themselves submit the actions of the regime leader, the U.S., to the standards of behavior they accept; this flows from the universalistic principles embodied in the regime. The claim is not that the U.S. therefore lost its lead completely in directing Western security policy from 1949 onwards, nor that it has since refrained from acting unilaterally. As Egon Bahr, the Brandt-era foreign-policy advisor, has put it, "even among equals, some are more equal than others."[4]

Nevertheless, the code of behavior established for all through the security regime and the immediate access to policymaking granted to all members secures at least the potential for influence in policy formulation and outcome. The regime, then, acts as an avenue by which actors other than the U.S. can influence allied policy and direction. The allies are also empowered in that they and the U.S. can be called to account for "cheating" on the rules of the game, or on the rules and principles of the regime. That the regime has survived intact so long and, as will be argued more fully below, will probably survive a good deal longer, is evidence of widespread adherence to the regime's code of behavior and of my proposition that the goal of political cohesion among the allies has often taken precedence over particularistically defined military interests; so is continued strong support of the regime among such middle-sized members as West Germany.

The Security Regime: 1948-1963

As a defeated, dismembered, and highly vulnerable state, West Germany's integration in the immediate postwar years into the newly-created bipolar organizational scheme was of paramount importance to Bonn's foreign policymakers. In winning the difficult domestic debate concerning the contours of West Germany's role between East and West, Chancellor Konrad Adenauer successfully steered a course of Western integration led under largely American auspices, seeking to exact in this process, "the highest political price for voluntary collaboration."[5] In this regard, Adenauer realized the inherent weakness of the FRG's position at the close of World War II and therefore sought the regaining of Bonn's freedom of action and the resolution of German reunification through the establishment of a solid foundation in the Western bloc.[6] As will be shown, the regime characteristics already established in the Western security relationship greatly facilitated this endeavor.

An important element in Bonn's relationship to the Western powers, particularly to the U.S., was Adenauer's early conviction that West German political and military integration into NATO, including rearmament, was essential for the eventual realization of national sovereignty. As early as 1949, Adenauer sent up a trial balloon concerning German rearmament through an interview with the Cleveland

Plain Dealer. Although the bid was premature, as revealed by negative reactions in France and England as well as domestically, Adenauer's efforts were vindicated a year later in 1950 with the outbreak of the Korean War.[7] As a new "Red Scare" swept through Western capitals, the U.S. and England agreed that the rearming of the FRG was now vital to Western defense. There is evidence to suggest that many in the U.S. were already committed to some form of West German rearmament in 1949.[8] On October 26, 1954, West Germany was admitted to NATO and to the West European Union upon conclusion of the Paris Treaties and the agreements went into force in 1955.

During the West German quest for integration, the element of reciprocity as a fundamental principle to which Adenauer could and did appeal was crucial. Much of the work in political science and history on this period has stressed the near absence of choice and maneuverability on Bonn's part concerning West German allegiance to the West, and thereby implicitly or explicitly supports neorealist assumptions about postwar Western security relations. For example, many analysts and observers view Chancellor Konrad Adenauer's Western integration policy as an *ersatz*, or substitute, for West German autonomy and sovereignty.[9] I interpret the situation quite differently. Through its integration policy, Bonn was able to achieve much national sovereignty and gain influence within the West by appealing to the regime principles of sovereignty, non-discrimination, non-coercion and equality of status that had already been established in the Western security relationship. This highly successful strategy is alluded to in Josef Joffe's observation that, "Adenauer's entire diplomacy was devoted to transmuting the constraints imposed unilaterally by the victors into mutual controls shared voluntarily by all."[10] The existence of established norms and principles guiding Western relations greatly facilitated Adenauer's ability to accept West Germany's integration only on terms that were commensurate with these principles.

Much like Harold Nicolson's analysis of French strategy in gaining re-admittance as a great power in the immediate post-Napoleonic war period,[11] the examination of post-World War II relations via the regime approach reveals similarily that Adenauer was quite successful in using allied concessions to the FRG "as a lever for lifting the restraints upon German statehood and freedom."[12] Already by 1952, Bonn had regained much national autonomy over its domestic situation through such developments as the establishment of the Basic Law (1949), the Petersburg Agreements (1949) and the Bonn Accords (1952). Adenauer persisted each step of the way in insisting on equality of status for the Federal Republic if the West was to gain complete West German loyalty to the Western community. Especially after the outbreak of the Korean

War, when West German rearmament appeared increasingly critical to a majority in the Western community, the United States explicitly promoted and supported Adenauer's pursuit of West German membership in the Western community based on equal and non-discriminatory terms, often against great French resistance.[13]

The success of Adenauer's policy, which culminated with the London and Paris Agreements of 1954, is fundamentally tied to the operating principles of the security regime. The perceived necessity of winning the FRG as a loyal Western ally gained immediacy once the Korean War broke out. According to the explicit principles underwriting the West's formulation of the alliance, an ally must be a sovereign and voluntarily participating state. The sovereignty and equal status which West German foreign policymakers sought could therefore be legitimately expected and demanded prior to West German accession to the alliance.

A historical example from the mid-1950s illustrates West Europe's, and particularly Adenauer's, ability to influence outcomes in allied policy by appealing to the principle of reciprocity. The Federal Republic acceded to NATO in 1954 with the signing of the Paris Agreements. In return for renouncing the use of force and the production of nuclear weapons on its soil, the FRG received the guarantee that U.S. and British conventional forces would remain on the Continent indefinitely and the formal acceptance by the Western allies of the issues of German reunification and the German borders as alliance responsibilities. As the U.S. began developing its "New Look" strategy under the Eisenhower Administration, which envisioned a decreased reliance on conventional forces and an increased strategic nuclear posture, intra-allied strains resulted.

Furor among the allies resulted from the unofficial publication of the Radford Plan in the New York Times during July of 1956. The plan, in keeping with the "New Look," envisioned the reduction of American conventional forces by some 800,000, and included much of the European contingent. The plan was perceived by many West Europeans, especially Adenauer, as directly undercutting the quid-pro-quo established in 1954 and the United States was consequently directly confronted with the issue in NATO. Responding to accusations that the Radford Plan indicated a unilateral change of military doctrine by the U.S., Lt. General Johnson stated before the NATO Standing Group and the Military Committee that

...we recognize that the Military Committee is the authority which determines the strategic guidance on which force goals are based. Changes to the force structure must be made in the manner prescribed in the NATO documents.[14]

The troops were not removed from Europe and, as Eisenhower was later to reminisce, "every time he had tried to do something about bringing our troops back, Secretaries Dulles and Herter had pled with him with tears in their eyes not to talk about any withdrawal of American forces from Europe."[15] Bonn's central role in influencing Washington's position was reflected during a high-level meeting of the Eisenhower Administration during October of 1956:

> The President opened by saying that he felt very definitely that we cannot take divisions out of Europe at this time. The effect on Adenauer would be unacceptably damaging. He could not agree with a Defense position contemplating such reductions, and statements to this effect at this time. [16]

Thus, within a decade following the cessation of hostilities, the FRG's foreign policy leaders had helped achieve West German integration within the Western security regime and on terms largely beneficial to Bonn. While it is clear that West German security aspirations vis-a-vis the Soviet bloc were in fundamental agreement with those of the regime initiator and bloc leader, the U.S., during this period, it is also evident that Bonn's course of persistently appealing to the governing principles of the Western security relationship directly influenced Western security policy.

However, the years leading to Adenauer's resignation in 1963 revealed already the nascent underlying discord in the security regime that would become more pronounced in the 1970s and 1980s. Problems already evident that would continually resurface included friction regarding the rules of the regime, such as that of political consultation among allies, and diverging interpretations concerning the best means for assuring Western security and stability in Europe. A related area of tension surfacing early in the trans-Atlantic relationship was the West German and West European fear of American military "decoupling" and "abandonment" and the corresponding American distrust of "entanglement" in a continental war.[17] For example, U.S. handling of the Berlin crisis from 1958-1961 raised anew Bonn's suspicions of an American abandonment of the security guarantee and revealed once again Washington's fear of entanglement. The timid responses of the Eisenhower and Kennedy administrations during the course of events directly undercut Adenauer's reliance on the Western "policy of strength" toward the East bloc.[18] In particular, Kennedy's nonresponse to the erection of the Berlin Wall in 1961 would leave a lasting impression on Adenauer and future West German foreign policymakers such as Willy Brandt, the governing mayor of West Berlin at the time.

The Security Regime: 1963-1969

The years 1963-1969 represented a period of transition in the Western security regime. From the trans-Atlantic controversy surrounding the American introduction of flexible response under the Kennedy Administration to the related extension of the regime to incorporate detente, these years witnessed the continuation of old grievances and the introduction of new procedures and rules for managing the regime.

The increase in Soviet military capabilities, particularly in the nuclear field and the drive to the "brink" during the Cuban missile crisis convinced policymakers in Washington and elsewhere in the West that more flexibility was needed in the East-West military relationship. De Gaulle's exclamation to Washington's ambassador during the missile crisis, "are you consulting or informing me?" indicated the heightened West European distrust of the American monopoly of nuclear policy. As a result, the first half of the 1960s witnessed the development of the doctrine of flexible response. Because the plan was conceived in a shroud of secrecy and introduced by Washington without prior allied consultation, discord was once again sparked between the U.S. and its West European allies. The often heated trans-Atlantic debate that followed made clear the concern in Bonn and other West European capitals about the form of the U.S. security guarantee, since the doctrine was perceived by many as invoking the possibility of a prolonged conventional war being fought on European soil. The controversy surrounding flexible response is viewed by some analysts as an important catalyst for De Gaulle's decision to withdraw France from NATO's formal military structure in 1966.[19]

The perception was taking shape in Western capitals that corresponding political changes must be wrought in the East-West relationship to coincide with those being forged in the military sphere. Beginning approximately with the signing of the Test Ban Treaty in 1963, the United States took the Western lead in encouraging greater intra-bloc communication and cooperation. By December, 1963, President Lyndon B. Johnson pledged that "the United States was ready to proceed immediately with the search for further East-West agreements to continue the work begun in the Moscow test-ban treaty."[20]

Recognition of the changed international environment tested the cohesion of the Western alliance. Realizing the limits of the Western allegiance to the policy of strength, Bonn joined the rest of Western Europe in becoming increasingly restless with U.S. leadership in the

East-West relationship. Although considered an anathema to Adenauer, the detente initiatives of Washington and Paris found a cautious but interested audience among West German foreign policymakers, which became keener after Adenauer's political demise in 1963. Gerhard Schroeder's "policy of movement" was an attempt in the early to mid- 1960s to open up communication channels eastward without forfeiting the goals of the Hallstein Doctrine, a cornerstone of West German foreign policy under Adenauer.[21] The policy attempted to encourage and take advantage of East bloc pluralism, while maintaining the German Democratic Republic (GDR) and the Soviet Union in isolation, as advocated by the Hallstein Doctrine. This last imperative of the policy, however, led rather to the increasing isolation of the FRG both in the East bloc and within the West, and such a policy was more and more out of step with Western approaches to inter-bloc relations. What Melvin Croan characterizes as Bonn's "selective detente" policy was to give way to intensified efforts at fostering detente under the Grand Coalition in 1966.[22]

The year 1966 was in large part a watershed in West German foreign policy. Following President Lyndon B. Johnson's "bridge-building" speech of 1965, the Kiesinger government was to release in 1966 its German "Peace Note." Without explicitly detailing specific changes in foreign policy, the note was issued mainly to herald a new receptivity in Bonn toward its relations with the East bloc. As Helga Haftendorn states, "Bonn was tired of being constantly reviled by the East and repeatedly pressured by the West to develop its own Ostpolitik."[23] Likewise in that year, at the Party Congress of the other partner in the Grand Coalition, the Social Democratic Party (SPD), the future course of SPD policy toward the East bloc and Europe was debated and outlined.[24] Reflecting the reassessed foreign policy interests of such leaders as Willy Brandt, foreign minister under the Grand Coalition, Helmut Schmidt and Herbert Wehner, the outlook of future SPD policy coalesced well with statements made by the U.S. President Johnson in 1966:

> Nothing is more important than peace. We must improve the East-West enviroment in order to achieve the unification of Germany in the context of a larger, peaceful, and prosperous Europe. Our task is to achieve a reconciliation with the East—a shift from the narrow concept of coexistence to the broader vision of peaceful engagement.[25]

The early 1960s, then, witnessed the beginning of a new set of trans-Atlantic misgivings and the search for a new consensus around which to pursue best the dual common interests of the security regime. The period is one of heightened activity and consultation among regime members. Alongside de Gaulle's continued assault and his push for a specifically defined West European, if not French, detente with the Soviets, the U.S., West Germany and other West Europeans sought the means with which to re-invigorate the security regime.

Rather than ending in crisis, this period turned out to be a period of transition for the Western security regime. U.S. military preponderance was weakened by the mid-1960s and no longer capable of supplying the remedy of a Western approach to the East bloc. Within the general Western push toward a vaguely defined detente posture, and with the U.S. unable or unwilling to take the lead in establishing the framework for a new Western consensus due both to the distraction of the Vietnam War and to the increase in Soviet military capabilities, the West Europeans, and specifically the West Germans, were now in a position to exert new influence and enshrine their specific interests in the regime. By 1966, the FRG had defined an Ostpolitik that conformed to the broad detente aspirations of Western security interests. Beginning in 1969, under the leadership of Chancellor Willy Brandt, the West Germans would develop the most consistent Western detente policy and increase substantially their influence in Western security policymaking.

The period of regime change wherein a new rallying point for the Western security consensus was actively pursued culminated in 1967 with the North Atlantic Council's endorsement of the Harmel Report. The Report, or Harmel Exercise, was initiated in 1966 by the Belgian Foreign Minister Pierre Harmel. There was a great deal of West German input in the exercise, and Willy Brandt was particularly influential in the formulation of the report.[26] Its purpose was to "...study the future tasks which face the alliance, and its procedures for fulfilling them in order to strengthen the alliance as a factor for durable peace."[27]

As a counterweight to the more defensive and military aspects of the alliance, the Harmel Report held that "military security and a policy of detente are not contradictory but complementary."[28] Alongside codifying detente as the second prong in the Western security regime, the report reiterated duties, rules and procedures that had been points of irritation since the regime's inception. The avowal that "the practice of frank and timely consultations needs to be deepened and improved" is one such example.[29] More importantly, the Harmel Report aims at achieving stability in Europe, one of the central principles of the Western security regime, by promoting the "use of the alliance constructively in the interest of detente."[30] Therefore, the solution reached in 1967 to avoid the potential of disintegration in the regime was the embodiment of detente in the regime as the second component alongside defense. The change reflects what John Ruggie calls a norm-governed regime change, or one in which the norms and principles, and therefore the foundations, of the regime remain intact but wherein the regime's methods of implementation are revised to accommodate an altered political environment.[31]

By its codification in the security regime, the Harmel Report would have tremendous implications for the future of the West-West and East-West relationships. The incorporation of detente into the Western security regime reflected an important change in one of the regime's implicit rules. Until the mid-1960s, an implicit agreement existed wherein the United States assured West European security through its nuclear guarantee and Continental conventional troop commitment in exchange for a West German conventional commitment and a deferrence to Washington's leadership in defining the political boundaries of the East-West relationship. This fact is particularly important for understanding the West German position prior to 1967. Not only had the U.S. basically supported Adenauer's "policy of strength" as part of the Western security understanding vis-a-vis the East bloc, a posture which was defunct by the early 1960s; as stated earlier, the U.S. and the Western allies had also assumed the solution of the German reunification question as a formal component of the Western alliance by 1954 in exchange for Bonn's renunciation of force on the border and reunification issues. Until the early 1960s, the reunification issue had been established within the contours of the "policy of strength" posture. Therefore, by the mid-1960s, the reciprocal relationship within the security regime was threatened in two issue-areas from Bonn's perspective. In order to maintain the relationship according to the original principles that governed the Western security regime, then, a new set of understandings was essential. The adoption of the Harmel Report represents in large part the concretization of the new Western understanding and, not surprisingly, was particularly sensitive to the West German position.

From 1967 onward, the process of empowerment of states other than the regime initiator, the United States, reaches fruition, especially in the case of the Federal Republic. Whereas beforehand West Germany supported wholeheartedly maintenance of the security regime because of its adherence to the common purposes of the regime and the opportunities made available to it through the act of regime participation, the West Germans and West Europeans generally played a much greater role in determining the direction and implementation of regime policy hereafter. Because the consensus of the regime through the 1950s had been predicated on US military preponderance, as manifested by the massive retaliation doctrine and the Western "policy of strength," the Federal Republic was necessarily constrained in its approaches toward

the East bloc and more specifically toward East Germany. Once it became clear in the early and mid-1960s, however, that the Federal
Republic's specific interest in the "German question" could no longer be
satisfied through the Western "policy of strength", new directions were
sought by Bonn's leadership in its relations to the East bloc. The influence of Willy Brandt and the SPD in establishing this new direction
has already been alluded to with regard to the Harmel Report. While
West Germany has remained dependent on the U.S. military guarantee
since 1967, the assertiveness of Bonn's leadership in helping to institu-
tionalize detente into the security regime allowed it to pursue
legitimately specific national goals without endangering its relations to
other Western allies and without raising great concern about West German motives. In other words, Bonn and other West European capitals
benefitted much from the action taken in 1967 which explicitly divided
the tools of the alliance into military *and* political components. Although there was fear in some Western capitals and in the East
bloc concerning West German intentions, which will be dealt with
below, Bonn was able to accomplish much through its Ostpolitik because
in large part its pursuit of the policy now fell well within the rules of the
game that West German leaders had helped establish in the Western
security regime. The pursuit of Ostpolitik encouraged West German
leadership over time to be "less inclined to accept unquestioningly
Washington's leadership in the 'management' of East-West detente",
and more inclined to feel itself capable in this area, especially given the
increased ability to realize potential West German economic and political power in the relationship.[32]

The Security Regime: 1969-Present:
The Process of Regime Bifurcation

Beginning in 1969 with the SPD/FDP coalition government under
the leadership of Brandt, West German policy toward the East bloc
changed fundamentally. The series of treaties and agreements signed by
Bonn and East bloc governments, from the Moscow Treaty in 1970 to
the Basic Treaty with the GDR in 1973, served in large part to lessen
the contraints under which West German regional and international
relations had operated for twenty years. The political and diplomatic
benefits included the decline of Bonn's international isolation resulting
from the dictates of the Hallstein Doctrine. Bonn's signing of renunciation of force agreements with East bloc states also smoothed the way for

better inter-bloc relations and dampened suspicions of West German revisionism.

While the new Ostpolitik corresponded to the general Western push toward detente, particularly after 1967, it is important to recognize that Ostpolitik was tailored by Bonn to fit the uniqueness of West Germany's international position. Bonn's Ostpolitik was controversial from the outset. As noted above, West German interest in detente was motivated as much by special economic and political incentives as by military considerations, although these were certainly important. For the U.S., however, the impulse toward detente derived primarily from military-strategic and global considerations. Thus, while Bonn and Washington came to share an interest in the detente component of the security regime, the underlying national interests were quite different.

The already strong domestic economic incentives for an "opening to the East" were given new expression with Ostpolitik, particularly among West Germany's export-oriented businesses.[33] The long tradtion of German trade with the East was restored in the 1970s and the 1980s, when *Osthandel* became an extremely important ingredient in the FRG's relations with the East bloc. Between the years 1970 and 1974, for example, FRG-Soviet trade already grew at an annual rate of 42 percent.[34] Thus, economic gain was an important element of the FRG's pursuit of detente.

A third and equally crucial element of West German Ostpolitik was and remains the corresponding gains in *Deutschlandpolitik*, or in German-German relations. Aside from the tremendous economic benefits developed through more openness, as witnessed by the fact that the FRG is the GDR's and the East bloc's leading trading partner in the West, Ostpolitik enabled the governments of West and East Germany to reach a number of agreements facilitating greater human and cultural contact across the borders. This development is of utmost importance to West Germans and remains a cornerstone of Bonn's eastward policy.[35]

Turning specifically to the effects of Ostpolitik on the FRG's role in the West, participation in detente would enhance substantially Bonn's influence in the alliance. The FRG's changing role and the increase in West German maneuverability were perceived in Washington. For example, in contrast to earlier years when potential conflict between the U.S. and the FRG was usually met with words of assurance and support from Washington, the germinating doubts among American leaders concerning Brandt's handling of Ostpolitik inspired a visit by Brandt to Washington where he had "...hopes of clarifying his intentions to an increasingly nervous American administration. In 1970, it was Bonn rather than Washington whose assurances were directly sought."[36]

What policymakers in Washington and other Western capitals feared was the rapidity with which the Brandt/Scheel government pressed on, or what Dean Acheson more bluntly described as Brandt's "mad race to Moscow."[37] Secondly, the uniquely German features of Ostpolitik caused some suspicion as to the motives of its West German architects; Henry Kissinger, for one, wondered whether Ostpolitik would "turn into a new form of classic German nationalism.[38] However, the Brandt/Scheel government could rely on the established precedent of detente and its stature as a component of the Western security regime in continuing its course of Ostpolitik.

From the Brandt/Scheel years onward, West Germany's participation in detente left a permanent imprint on Bonn's foreign policy interests and on domestic perception concerning the FRG's international role. While the military/defense component of the security regime remained an essential element of West German security, the interests concretized by Ostpolitik/Deutschlandpolitik eventually forged a deep and far-reaching domestic consensus among the West German public and political/economic elites. From the initial explosive debates surrounding Brandt's Ostpolitik in 1969 and continuing into the early 1970s,[39] a consensus has since evolved. A recent illustrative example was the promulgation of the largest "swing credit" deal to the GDR in postwar history by the Christian Social Union's (CSU) Franz Josef Strauss, one of the most conservative of West Germany's major political figures. That West German leadership, be it under SPD or CDU auspices, has pressed onward with its Ostpolitik during the period of declining American interest in detente is further testimony to this consensus.

The U.S., on the other hand, became increasingly disillusioned with detente by the mid-1970s. Because of the failed linkage effects of Washington's detente efforts and the continued Soviet military buildup, U.S. interest in the detente component of the security regime waned as renewed interest in focusing on the defense element increased. Further, U.S. economic interest in the East-West relationship was always bound more closely to strategic consideration than was the West German case, and as James R. Kurth notes, the central industrial and financial sectors that supported detente in the late 1960s, such as the automobile industry, lost interest by 1975.[40] Therefore, whereas the West German experience with detente was largely positive, that of the U.S. was negative.

The playing out of intra-alliance security debates during the 1970s and 1980s reveals how significant the benefits accrued by Bonn in the detente process have been, and reveals likewise the increasing rift in trans-Atlantic relations concerning detente. During the tenure of

Helmut Schmidt, for example, policymakers in Washington were on occasion vexed with what they perceived as Bonn's tendency to pursue an active East-West policy without prior confirmation from or consultation with the United States. Besides the Carter Administration's resentment of Schmidt's offer to assume the role of mediator between Washington and Moscow, his trip to Moscow in the wake of the Soviet invasion of Afghanistan received a chilly reception in the U.S. capital.[41] The efforts of Schmidt's SPD/FDP coalition government to continue encouraging greater East-West dialogue are further reflected by the fact that throughout the 1970s and 1980s, West German policymakers have continued promoting the Mutual Balanced Force Reduction talks, of which Schmidt has dubbed himself the "father,"[42] and the CSCE process. This West German position has persisted into the Reagan Administration. West German influence was present in President Reagan's decision to reenter the detente process with his advocacy of the "Zero option" in 1982, a phrase actually coined by Schmidt.[43] After the changeover of the West German government in 1983 from the SPD/FDP coalition government to that of the CDU/CSU/FDP, pressure from Helmut Kohl's government for more progress in detente was also in evidence. West German and West European influence, for example, were cited by Kohl's security advisor, Horst Teltschick, as major contributors to the U.S. proposals at the INF talks in Geneva, at the Geneva negotiations for banning chemical weapons and at the MBFR talks in Vienna.[44]

Most recently, the inter-allied debate over the correct interpretation of the ABM Treaty and its relationship to the Strategic Defense Initiative (SDI) has reflected the continued divergence of U.S. and West European security postures as well as the continued West European pressure on Washington to adhere to detente-influenced policies. In the face of persistent West European, and especially West German, pressure for continuing detente in East-West relations, particularly in the area of arms control, Richard Perle warned in Washington that "the objectives of the alliance are being subordinated to arms control."[45] A reading of North Atlantic Council Communiques throughout this period attests to the success of the West Germans and West Europeans in largely thwarting U.S. efforts to undermine the detente process agreed upon in the 1967 Harmel Report.[46] A statement made by West German Chancellor Helmut Kohl during his November 1986 visit to Washington is instructive:

The central issues of East-West relations are freedom and security. But peace cannot be genuinely shaped without confidence-building and cooperation. According to the Alliance Harmel Concept, the quest for secure defense capacity has to be supplemented by efforts to reduce differences in East-West relations through dialogue and cooperation.[47]

The 1970s and 1980s seemed to be to some degree a replay of the 1960s in the alliance, the difference being that it is now West Germany trying to prod the U.S. to activate a detente policy rather than vice-versa. Because the FRG has arguably developed the most consistent Western detente policy, it has actively tried to rally West Europe to its cause as well. As one observer perhaps overstates:

Germany has been trying quite successfully in recent years to persuade the rest of Europe to share its national interests by rallying the smaller European countries as well as France around the cause of European detente. In effect the German game is to turn Deutsche Ostpolitik into Europaeische Ostpolitik.[48]

In sum, during the 1970s and into the 1980s, the Western security regime was exhibiting the symptoms of bifurcation despite the allied efforts of the mid-1960s to arrive at a new rallying point for the security consensus. Because the perceptions of and related benefits to be accrued from detente differed significantly in the U.S. and in Western Europe, and especially in the FRG, the mutual understanding reached in the 1967 Harmel Report was not long-lived. The positive benefits achieved by the FRG resulted in Bonn's leaders being unwilling to sacrifice the gains made through West German participation in the detente component of the regime, even with the deterioration in super-power relations. The benefits accrued have ranged from economic gain in East bloc trade to closer political cooperation with the GDR that facilitates greater interpersonal contact across the border, and finally to the domestic perception that the FRG has gained an important degree of control over its East bloc affairs. This is not to belittle the continued support of the FRG for the defense component of the security regime. By way of a few examples, it should be remembered that the whole issue of INF as a central alliance issue was first raised by Schmidt, that the subsequent controversial decision to place intermediate range missiles on West German soil was accepted by Kohl, and that the FRG maintains the strongest conventional forces in Western Europe. Rather, what has developed in the security regime indicates a process wherein Washington has largely retreated into its predominantly military leadership position, and the FRG has been ascending as the central advocate of the detente component. Two related observations of Henry Kissinger allude to the phenomenon of regime bifurcation: "I do not believe in divisible detente in the sense that one side does the defense and the other side does the negotiating...that Europe should have a monopoly on detente and America a monopoly on defense."[49]

"In 1968, at Rejkavek, NATO developed the theory—which I believe is totally wrong—that the alliance is as much an instrument of detente as it is of defense... NATO is not equipped to be an instrument of detente."[50]

On Continued Bifurcation:
Dissonance in the Regime

The potential danger for the continued maintenance of the Western security regime, then, is not fundamental disagreement on the original common purposes of the regime participants, but rather growing contention over the means of how best to achieve those objectives. Since the second common goal has from the beginning been stability in Europe as well as security against the Soviet threat, the two not necessarily contradictory methods of realizing those concerns, that is, defense and detente, have recently begun to jeopardize the common trans-Atlantic understanding of how best to achieve them.

For example, one of the consequences of regime bifurcation has been a change on both sides of the Atlantic concerning threat perceptions. In examining public opinion polls taken in the FRG where respondents were asked, "do you think that the USSR (East) is a threat to us or don't you think so?", the perception of the Soviet Union as a serious threat moved from a high of 81 percent of those with firm opinions in 1952 to 47 percent in the same category for 1983. Correspondingly, those with firm opinions in 1952 who viewed the Soviets as no threat were only 19 percent compared to 53 percent in 1983.[51] Between the years 1980-1983, respondents who felt that the U.S. was as much "a danger to world peace" as the Soviet Union rose from 14 percent to 34 percent.[52] Most recently, a 1987 poll reveals that 49 percent of those polled finds the Soviet leader Mikhail Gorbachev to be "more concerned about the securing of peace and disarmament," while only 9 percent interpreted President Reagan as such; 30 percent answered "both."[53]

Equally important, however, is the fact that a great majority of respondents have consistently held that membership in an "unchanged NATO" is preferrable to some other alternative (i.e., a strengthened NATO or exit from NATO), and that the existence of American troops in the FRG "improve peace."[54] Such results indicate that the West German public holds both components of the security regime to be essential, but views at the same time the perceived U.S. inclination to emphasize the military/defense element as dangerous. American respondents between the years of 1978 and 1983 believed by over 60 percent that the Soviet Union "seeks global domination."[55] While a majority of American respondents do still adhere to the idea of arms control, such findings indicate that American suspicions of the Soviet Union have been escalating since the late 1970s. In large part, these suspicions and the policies they have supported revolve around perceptions of the Soviet military, and thus strategic, threat.

That leaders in Washington and Bonn diverge in their interpretations of the security threat was made vividly clear during the pipeline controversy in 1982. The overwhelming West European denial of Reagan's call for sanctions, and Washington's eventual retreat from its demands, emphasizes both the increased independence of the FRG and Western Europe in setting the agenda for the East-West relationship and the fact that Bonn is less willing and able after 20 years of beneficial participation in detente to disrupt that process. This case is even more revealing when compared with a similar incident in 1963 wherein the West German government finally complied with U.S. demands.[56]

Clearly, regime bifurcation and the consequent differences in security threat perceptions have had spillover effects in other areas, such as allied management of technology transfer issues. Washington and its allies have disagreed on this issue throughout the postwar years, since the U.S. government has been traditionally much more active than its West European counterparts at intervention in the private domain to meet national security objectives.[57] Yet discord in recent years has been growing due to new policies pursued by Washington in mitigating the perceived negative effects of technology transfer. For example, recent efforts to place increased restrictions on American exports to non-Communist countries to "prevent American critical technology from slipping indirectly to the Soviet Union" gives the Defense Department for the first time "the right to review systematically so-called West-West export control cases, and to recommend denial on national security grounds."[58] Since the Eisenhower years and until recently, the guiding stricture had been to avoid restrictions that would interrupt or negatively affect West-West trade relations.[59]

There is currently also related concern among West Germans and West Europeans for the increased restrictions of the Coordinating Committee for Multilateral Export Controls (COCOM), the means by which the allies jointly control technology transfer that is eastward bound. While there have always been accusations that the U.S. holds too strict an interpretation for this agenda, such suspicions have become widespread. These suspicions became particularly acute once SDI became an allied issue. Besides the host of trans-Atlantic grievances raised by SDI, including the fears of some West Germans that SDI was another American attempt to decouple and that SDI would undermine or outright challenge the ABM Treaty and arms control in general, a point of central concern was the issue of technology transfer restrictions. After heated domestic debate over whether or not to participate in the program, Kohl's coalition government agreed upon limited West German involvement. The drawn-out negotiating process that then followed in Washington confirmed prevalent fears about how restrictive U.S. control would be.[60] U.S. concern over sensitive technology making its way to the East bloc will most likely be heightened as the West Germans and West Europeans continue to promulgate the idea of using the Conference on Security and Cooperation in Europe (CSCE) as a forum for East-West economic and technological agreement, a concept with which the U.S. was in general agreement in 1975.[61]

Thus, alongside the economic competitiveness among Western allies in recent years, the consequences of bifurcation in the Western security regime have been to stymy cooperation further. Given the dissimilar emphasis of the U.S. and the FRG on the defense and detente components of the regime, a divergent perception of the security threat has emerged. This phenomenon has already had an impact in areas other than the management of the security regime itself and has in fact spilled over into other areas of Western collective activity, such as the management of technology transfer. Another trouble-spot now brewing that is related to regime bifurcation is the increasingly divergent trans-Atlantic positions regarding the use of military force as a legitimate political policy.

Future West German Foreign Policy: Managing Dissonance

Based on the arguments presented in this paper, it appears clear that Bonn will not forfeit its commitment to a continued East-West detente process. Economic exchange with the East bloc continues to rise, German-German relations remain a cornerstone of West German policy and the FRG continues its position of influence in the West. The pressures to maintain these interests while not undermining the Western security regime have presented and will continue to present a challenge to West German leadership. As has been argued throughout the paper, the Western security regime has been one of the pillars of West German influence and its existance has guaranteed at crucial moments the central principles of equality of status, non-coercion and non-discrimination among member states. The stability of the security regime rests presently upon the high costs of "exit" by any of its members.

While the accumulation of West German international influence has been predicated on its position as a regime participant, and thus on multilateralism, that increased influence amid allied discord has created domestic demands for a West German foreign policy more commensurate with the traditional goals of national sovereignty and international autonomy. In recent years, domestic preferences for a "go it alone" West German foreign policy have found expression in segments of both the right and the left. On the left, the inclination varies in intensity, from the SPD's Oskar Lafontaine, who until very recently favored a Gaullist solution or a West German exit from NATO's formal military organization, to large segments of the Greens who advocate a neutral position for both Germanies outside the blocs.[62] Interestingly, a public opinion poll taken in 1984 reveals 45 percent of SPD respondents favoring neutrality to 54 percent favoring alliance, and 73 percent of Green respondents favoring neutrality to 25 percent favoring alliance.[63]

Although such opinions do not form the majority of West German preferences, as the continued commitment to NATO by the majority indicates, pressures to alleviate the persisting conflicts and the dissonance of the bifurcated security regime will continue. The more that dissonance spills over into other areas of allied activity, the stronger the domestic pressures will be for some resolution.

From all sides of the West German political spectrum comes a renewed interest in consolidating a more coherent and unified West European security entity.[64] The rejuvenated efforts of the West European Union (WEU), the promise of Eureka, and the recent French-West German bilateral defense efforts are indicative that the process is underway. The pursuit of a West European front is likely to continue, although it faces serious obstacles. One obstacle again concerns West German domestic politics. While the main current of West German interests would view a West European security community in a manner similar to Kennedy's "second pillar" vision, where "the strengthening of Europe and the consolidation of the alliance are interdependent," the parameters of a trans-Atlantic community possessing a strong West European component are not yet clearly defined.[65] A second obstacle to be overcome is the persistent reverting to national solutions among West European states during crises, such as during the 1973 oil crisis and over SDI.

In conclusion, then, the Western security regime will most likely continue intact into the future, despite the recent bifurcation of tasks and the increased unilateralism of recent U.S. policy. The likelihood is, however, that another norm-governed regime change will be initiated in an effort to orchestrate better the Western approach to the dual interests of stability in Europe and security against the Soviet threat. There have been promptings in this direction both from Washington and from Western Europe in the recent past. The second possibility, and one that has recently begun to manifest itself, albeit sporadically, is that there will be a re-rallying around the consensus reached in 1967. The West Europeans' urgings to rekindle American detente efforts have been not completely lacking in success,[66] and as recent North Atlantic Council Communiques as well as real Western policy achievements indicate, the East-West relationship has not deviated completely from the general guidelines established in the Harmel Report. A West German policy which successfully balances achieved West German priorities in West-West and East-West relations suggests that Bonn must somehow continue to manage the often competing dictates of defense and detente, especially evident in the current period of regime bifurcation. Because its now substantial role in world affairs is in large part a consequence of Bonn's historical membership in, support of, and influence on the Western security regime, the costs of complete regime erosion would be high. Therefore, the delicate balancing act of achieving detente and defense in foreign policy amid foreign and domestic dissonance, of managing the spillover effects of regime bifurcation into other areas, and of deflecting pressures and temptations emanating from Moscow, witnessed before and during INF deployment, will most likely set the foreign policy agenda in Bonn for some time to come.

Notes

1. Kenneth Waltz, *Theory of International Politics* (Reading, MA: Addison-Wesley Publishing Co., 1979).

2. Robert O. Keohane, ed., *Neorealism and Its Critics* (N.Y.: Columbia University Press, 1986), p. 22.

3. George Kennan, quoted in Thomas H. Etzold and John Lewis Gaddis, eds., *Containment: Documents on American Policy and Strategy, 1945-1950* (New York: Columbia University Press, 1978), pp. 97-98.

4. Bahr, Egon, in background interview, Bonn, 1985.

5. Josef Joffe, "The Foreign Policy of the German Federal Republic," in Roy C. Macridis, ed., *Foreign Policy in World Politics* (Englewood Cliffs: Prentice-Hall, Inc., 1976), p. 24.

6. See Konrad Adenauer's statements in Hans Edgar Jahn, *Die Deutsche Frage-1945-bis heute* (Mainz: Hase und Koehler Verlag, 1985), p. 267.

7. Alfred Grosser, *The Western Alliance* (N.Y.: Vintage Books, 1982), p. 81.

8. Cf. George Kennan, *Memoirs: 1925-1950* (New York: Bantam Books, 1969), p. 472.

9. This position was pervasive in many of the background interviews I conducted in Bonn, 1985 and 1986. Dr. Alfred Blumenfeld was particularly helpful on this point.

10. Josef Joffe, "The Foreign Policy of the Federal Republic of Germany," in Roy C. Macridis, ed., *Foreign Policy in World Politics* (Englewood Cliffs: Prentice-Hall, Inc., 1985, 6th edition), p.79.

11. Harold Nicolson, *The Congress of Vienna: A Study in Allied Unity, 1812-1822* (N.Y.: Viking Press, 1968), esp. pp. 134-147.

12. Joffe, "The Foreign Policy," 1985, op. cit., p. 124.

13. Cf. "Memorandum of a Conversation, by Russell Fessenden of the Office of European Affairs," in William Z. Slany, Editor in Chief, *Foreign Relations of the United States, 1952-1954. Volume V, Part 2* (Washington: United States Government Printing Office, 1983), p. 1259.

14. Lt. Gen. Johnson, quoted in Paul E. Zinner, ed. *Documents on American Foreign Relations, 1956* (New York: Harper and Brothers, 1957), p. 109.

15. Allen W. Dulles, in CIA, Office of the Director, "Memorandum for the President," (Aug. 22, 1961), p. 7.

16. "Memorandum of Conference with the President, Washington, October 2, 1956," in William Z. Slany, Ed. in Chief, *Foreign Relations of the United States, 1955-1957*. Volume IV (Washington: United States Government Printing Office, 1986) p. 99.

17. Cf. David N. Schwartz, *NATO's Nuclear Dilemmas* (Washington, D.C.: The Brookings Institution, 1983), pp. 2-5. See also Richard Sinnreich, "NATO's Doctrinal Dilemmas," in *Orbis,* vol. 19, No. 2 (Summer 1975).

18. Marion Grafin Doenhoff, *Deutsche Aussenpolitik von Adenauer bis Brandt* (Hamburg: Christian Wagner Verlag, 1970), pp. 157-159.

19. Schwartz, *NATO's Nuclear Dilemmas,* pp. 156-177.

20. Richard P. Stebbins, *The United States in World Affairs, 1963* (Published for the Council on Foreign Relations by Harper and Row, N.Y., 1964), p. 90.

21. Melvin Croan, "Dilemmas of Ostpolitik," in Peter H. Merkl, ed., *West German Foreign Policy: Dilemmas and Directions* (Chicago: The Chicago Council on Foreign Relations, 1982), pp. 39-40.

22. Ibid.

23. Helga Haftendorn, *Security and Detente: Conflicting Priorities in German Foreign Policy* (N.Y.: Praeger Publishers, 1985), p. 167.

24. Cf. Peter Bender, *Neue Ostpolitik. Vom Mauerbau bis zum Moskauer Vertrag* (Munich: Deutscher Taschenbuch Verlag GmbH and Co., 1986), pp. 130-133. Also, Jahn, *Die Deutsche Frage,* p. 345-353.

25. President Lyndon B. Johnson, "Address by President Johnson to the National Editorial Writers Conference... 1966," in Richard P. Stebbins, ed., *Documents on American Foreign Relations, 1966* (N.Y.: Harper and Row Publishers, 1967), p. 77.

26. Cf. Willy Brandt, "Fuer ein geregelts Nebeneinander," in *Aussenpolitik, Deutschlandpolitik, Europapolitik* (Berlin: Berlin Verlag, 1968), p. 86. See also Haftendorn, *Security and Detente,* p. 120. Jonathan Dean, in his study, *Watershed in Europe,* goes so far as to claim that Brandt actually initiated the exercise. See his *Watershed in Europe (Lexington Books, 1987), p. 102.*

27. "Annex to Communique," in Stebbins, *Documents, 1966,* p. 110.

28. Ibid.

29. Ibid.

30. Ibid., pp. 110-111.

31. John G. Ruggie, "International regimes, transactions, and change: embedded liberalism in the postwar economic order" *International Organization,* V. 36, No. 2 (Spring 1982), p. 384.

32. Paul M. Johnson, "Washington and Bonn: Dimension of Change in Bilateral Relations," *International Organization* vol. 34 (Autumn, 1979), p. 471. Also emphasized in background interviews with Willy Brandt and Egon Bahr, Bonn, 1985.

33. Angela Stent Yergin, *East-West Technology Transfer: European Perspectives* (Beverly Hills: Sage Publishers, 1980), p. 22.

34. Friedrich Levid and Jan Stankovsky, *Industrial Cooperation Between East and West* (White Plains: M.E. Sharpe, Inc., 1979), p. 188. Also Dietrich Andre Loeber, *East-West Trade* (Dobbs Ferry: Oceana Publications, Inc., 1977), pp. 18-20.

35. Wilhelm Grewe, "Die Aussenpolitik der Bundesrepublik Deutschland," in Karl Kaiser and Hans-Peter Schwartz, eds., *Weltpolitik: Strukturen-Akture-Perspektiven* (Bonn: Bundeszentrale fuer politische Bildung, 1985, Band 217), pp. 306-308.

36. Johnson, "Washington and Bonn," p. 470.

37. Richard J. Barnet, *The Alliance* (N.Y.: Simon and Schuster, 1983), p. 294.

38. Henry Kissinger, *The White House Years* (Toronto: Little, Brown and Co., 1979), p. 409.

39. Jahn, *Die deutsche Frage*, pp. 416-513.

40. James R. Kurth, "The Political Consequences of the Product Cycle" *International Organization* 33 (1 Winter 1979), p. 32. See also Michael Mastanduno, "Trade as a Strategic Weapon: The American State and East-West Trade Policy During the Hegemonic Period," unpublished manuscript.

41. Barnet, *The Alliance*, p. 409. Also Zbigniew Brzezinski, *Power and Principle* (N.Y.: Farrar, Straus, Giroux, 1985), p. 176.

42. Dean, *Watershed in Europe*, p. 102.

43. Strobe Talbott, *Deadly Gambits* (N.Y.: Vintage Books, 1985), p. 56.

44. Horst Teltschick, cited in Wolfram F. Hanrieder, "Arms Control and the FRG," in Wolfram F. Hanrieder, ed., *Technology, Strategy, and Arms Control* (Boulder: Westview Press, 1986) p. 63.

45. Talbott, *Deadly Gambits*, p. 178.

46. On continued allied emphasis on the MBFR, the CSCE, and the commitment to the Harmel Report, see Council Communiques from, among others, December '79, June '83, and December '85.

47. Helmut Kohl, "The Role of the Federal Republic of Germany in International Affairs as We Move Towards the Year 2000," speech given to the Chicago Council on Foreign Relations, quoted in *Statements and Speeches*, V. IX, No. 18 (October 23, 1986), p. 4.

48. Pierre Lallouche, "Does NATO have a Future?" *The Washington Quarterly* (Summer 1982), p. 49.

49. Barnet, *The Alliance*, p. 409.

50. Henry Kissinger, *For the Record* (Boston: Little, Brown and Company, 1982), p. 243.

51. Hans Rattinger, "The Federal Republic of Germany: Much Ado About Nothing" in Gregory Flynn and Hans Rattinger, eds., *The Public and Atlantic Defense* (New Jersey: Rowman and Allanheld, 1985), p. 118.

52. Gebhard Schweigler, "Anti-Americanism in German Public Opinion," in *America's Image in Germany and Europe* (Washington: Friedrich Ebert Stiftung, Washington Office, 1985), p. 21.

53. Forsa Institute poll cited in "Gorbachev Outpolls Reagan in West Germany" *New York Times*, May 17, 1987, p. 18.

54. Schweigler, "Anti-Americanism," p. 27.

55. William Schneider, "Peace and Strength: American Public Opinion on National Security," in Flynn and Rattinger, *The Public,* p. 327. While Schneider convincingly uses results of different public opinion polls to show that Americans are still committed to defense and peace, they also reveal that Americans have become increasingly concerned about defense preparedness at the same time that the ideological conflict between East and West was reemphasized. Thus, in his discussion, Schneider remarks that for Americans, "what motivated the surge of international assertiveness in 1980 was a sense of military vulnerability and anti-Soviet hostility. Americans suddenly realised that it was in their own interest to fortify the anti-Soviet military alliance." (p. 361).

56. Angela Stent, *Soviet Energy and Western Europe* (Washington: Praeger Publishers, 1981) p. 23.

57. Mastanduno, "Trade as a Strategic Weapon," p. 44.

58. Ibid.

59. Ibid.

60. Cf. Dr. Olaf Feldmann, "Ost und West bei der Sicherung des Friedens in einem Boot," in fdk tagesdienst, FDP-Fraktion im Deutschen Bundestag, No. 584, 5 June, 1986, p. 3. See also discussion of alliance aspects and SDI's relationship to the ABM Treaty in Claus Richter, "Strategische Verteidigungsinitiative (SDI): Kriegsfuehrung oder Kreigsverhinderung?" in *Aus Politik und Zeit Geschichte: Beilage zur Wochen Zeitung das Parlament* April 6, 1985, pp. 7-14. Further, Wolfram Hanrieder, in "Arms Control and the FRG", states that the SDI program reveals a U.S. perception that a "'fortress America' is a feasible and desirable U.S. geopolitical option" (p. 62). For a discussion of the domestic and bilateral negotiation process concerning West German participation in SDI, see Steven J. Breyman, "The Strategic Defense Initiative and the Federal Republic of Germany: Political, Economic, and Strategic Implications," paper delivered at 1986 Annual Meeting of the American Political Science Association, Washington, D.C., August 28-31, 1986.

61. Cf. Prof. Horst Ehmke, "Europe's technological self-assertion," paper given at Den Haag, den 24 mai, 1985. See also Dr. Olaf Feldman, "Ost-West Wirtschaftsbeziehungen Sind Beitrag zur Friedenssicherung." Interestingly, Hans-Dietrich Genscher had recommended in the summer of 1986 that the European Research Coordination Agency (Eureka) be used to promote East-West technological cooperation. Since then, such advocacy has been moved once again into the CSCE process.

62. Background interview with Oskar Lafontaine, July 5, 1985. See also *Die Gruenen, The Program of the Green Party of the Federal Republic of Germany* (Bonn: Die Gruenen, Colmantstrasse 36, 5300 Bonn 1) p. 19. Their program states that to realize the goal of "peace and disarmament" in West German foreign policy, "the principle of peace must immediately begin with the dissolution of military blocs, above all, of NATO and the Warsaw Pact".

63. Schweigler, "Anti-Americanism," p. 26.

64. Cf. Dr. Hans-Gert Poettering, "Die Emanzipation Europas in der Sicher-heitspolitik," in Europa Als Auftrag, CDU/CSU Fraktion im Deutschen Bundestag, Heft 2, May 2, 1985. Also, this development was advocated in the majority of background interviews conducted in Bonn in 1985-86.

65. Kohl, "The Role of the Federal Republic," p. 3.

66. Cf. comments of Horst Teltschick quoted in Wolfram F. Hanrieder, "Arms Control and the FRG," in Wolfram F. Hanrieder, ed., *Technology, Strategy, and Arms Control* (Boulder: Westview Press, 1986) p. 63.

9

On the Potential for Forging a U.S.-FRG Policy Consensus Vis-à-Vis the Soviet Union

Werner Kaltefleiter

Domestic Political Decision-Making and Foreign Policy Definition of Interests

The definition of a country's foreign political aims is generally a function of its domestic political decision-making processes. It results from the interplay between political elites and public opinion, under the basic conditions set by the respective political system. The perceptions of elites and public opinion influence as well as limit the process of political decision-making. The perceptions of public opinion provide the framework within which the elites can transform their perceptions into action; at the same time, however, the elites are generally in a position to influence the perceptions of public opinion, thus adding to their own liberty of action.

The rules and norms of a given political system determine the way in which this happens. A country's foreign policy is decisively coined by its domestic political structure. Compared to other political issues, foreign policy decision-making knows three distinctive features:

1. More than with domestic political issues, the liberty of action is limited by the power options of the respective country.
2. Among the three sources of political information available to the public—personal experience, discussions with friends and acquaintances, the mass media—only the mass media are relevant to foreign policy because there is generally no far-reaching per-

sonal experience in the field of foreign policy. Tourist experiences do not compensate for that deficiency, as tourist gatherings at the beach do not provide information on the political situation of a country. Consequently, opinions on foreign policy issues, especially with regard to day-to-day politics, are generally much less stable.

3. The partner in foreign affairs will always try to influence decision-making with regard to issues of relevance to foreign policy.

Analyses of the foreign policy decision-making processes mostly focus their attention on the concept of "national interests". However, this is not a fixed quantity objectively predetermined on the outside. On the one hand, the definition of "national interests" is the result of domestic political decision-making processes and, thus, it can be subject to changes in the course of time. On the other hand, however, in every situation there will be a set of variables which, at least for medium-term periods, will remain constant and/or with regard to which there is a broad consensus in a society. Such issues, which are not significantly controversial among the parties, also exist with regard to domestic politics—usually questions regarding a country's constitution belong to that category. This broad consensus conveys the impression that one is dealing with a predetermined constant. However, there are numerous examples in domestic and foreign policy where sets of opinions that had been constant for decades suddenly experienced profound changes.

Some of the variables which, in the process of foreign policy decision-making, are normally constant for longer periods of time are:

— the geopolitical situation;
— power options;
— the value system of a society; and
— domestic political structures.

Those foreign political areas that are determined by these variables and that are generally noncontroversial, at least for a certain period of time, can then be defined as "national interests" for the respective period. In addition, there exist a great number of variables whose influence on foreign policy decision-making is controversial and change over time as a result of pluralistic decision-making processes. For example, among these are:

— the assessment of (changing) foreign politicians;
— the effectiveness of exterior influences;
— the position of opinion leaders;
— the perceived relevance of individual events; and
— the threat perception.

Following the separation of variables relevant to foreign policy decision-making into those of medium-term constancy and those which will change more frequently, basically four constellations are possible for the relations between two countries. In case the short- and medium-term variables result in parallel definitions of interests on both sides, relations will be characterized by consensus. Correspondingly, conflict situations will be the result of a constellation in which both groups of variables produce contrasting definitions of interests. These are fields which are more or less unequivocal. More interesting, however, are cases in which the short- and medium-term variables result in different definitions of interests in both countries. If, in contrast to short-term variables, medium-term ones do coincide, this will result in a tense situation, which, however, will end in a phase of consensus. If, however, only the short-term variables coincide, in contrast to medium-term ones, presently relaxed relations will lead to a period of conflicts.

Diagram I			
variables of short-term effectiveness \\ variables of medium-term effectiveness		parallel interests	diverging interests
parallel perception		consensus	short-term consensus long-term conflict
diverging perception		long-term consensus short-term conflict	conflict

Definition of Interests in the U.S. and the Federal Republic of Germany

Applying the above-mentioned model to German-American relations, one must first define the medium-term constant variables in regard to the definition of interests in the foreign affairs of both countries, in general, and vis-à-vis the Soviet Union, in particular. In doing so, one will soon discover one basic difference between the United States and the Federal Republic: In view of the completely different power options of both countries, their relations to one another are much more important to the Federal Republic than to the U.S. Consequently, medium-term constant factors are of greater significance for the Federal Republic of Germany. It is, however, highly probable that short-term variables will arise which to some extent will rebel against the "dictate" of national interests. Moreover, there are medium-term constant variables in the American foreign policy decision-making process which are only indirectly relevant to U.S. policies vis-à-vis the Federal Republic. These can change the priorities of American policies in such a way that, even towards the Federal Republic, some political reorientation can become possible. On the whole, however, the American definition of interests vis-à-vis the Federal Republic remains constant.

First and foremost, the Federal Republic's interests are determined by its domestic political structures and geopolitical position. Maintaining the standards of a free society is the highest priority for the Federal Republic. This is true for elites as well as for the general public. West Germany's geopolitical position at the border of the Soviet empire illustrates the immediate threats facing it as a free society. Consequently, the Federal Republic's alliance with the U.S. dominates its definition of interests.

Numerous individual political decisions resulted from that definition: Western integration, build-up of the Federal armed forces, deployment of American troops, decades of payments to the U.S. to finance these troops, execution of the NATO dual-track decision and, most recently, the formalization of the FRG's participation in the SDI project. These decisions all followed from the Federal Republic's geopolitical and structural position, and reflect some 30 years of continuity of German foreign policy in this field, regardless of who was in power in Bonn. The basic perception of the Soviet Union also results from this constellation: The Soviet Union is primarily perceived as "the threat" to national integrity and the democratic domestic structure. However, this basic perception has become more sophisticated over the course of the Federal Republic's history.

Another result of its geopolitical position is the fact that Germany's interest in a war-preventing strategy is absolute. The settlement of conflicts in Central Europe by military means would jeopardize the very existence of the Federal Republic. From this position also follows a second element in the perception of the Soviet Union: To avoid war, the alliance is of crucial importance, but a second reassurance is desired. Therefore, forms of "detente" vis-à-vis the Soviet Union are sought. Detente is understood as a lasting change of atmosphere which will finally lead to a solution of the political problems. Here, of course, exists a wide range of opinions: what does change of atmosphere mean? On the one side, the establishment of diplomatic relations with Moscow in 1956 by Konrad Adenauer can be mentioned. At the other extreme is the concept, propagated by the Social Democratic Party in recent years, of a security partnership with the Soviet Union. The approach of detente follows from the geopolitical setting. The version of the detente concept depends on the understanding of the character of the Soviet system and of the related threat perception.

The search for detente, which in its modest version is bipartisan, and the Soviet response to these efforts has changed the perception of the Soviet Union. More and more, the perceived threat has decreased and the Soviet Union has become regarded as a superpower without expansionist ambitions. This perception, of course, is controversial. Part of public opinion calls it wishful thinking. Most recently, about 48 percent perceived the Soviet threat as big or very big. In 1962, the figure was 63 percent, while in 1974 it was only 35 percent. Fifty percent consider the Soviet threat unimportant. This shows that today German public opinion is split on this issue. The perceived threat with regard to the Soviet Union is the variable which most reliably explains other attitudes with regard to foreign affairs.

But when it comes to the essentials of German foreign policy, this split becomes irrelevant. Even in 1983, during the hot debate on the dual-track decision, about 80 percent favored the presence of American troops in Germany, and 91 percent wanted the FRG to be a member of NATO, either in the present structure (76 percent) or in a modified structure (15 percent). These figures have been rather stable since the early 1960s, despite the changing threat perception. To sum up: A huge majority favors the alliance, but even that majority shows significant and changing threat perceptions over time.

Still another consequence of the Federal Republic of Germany's geopolitical position—which also includes the existence of a divided Germany—are the continued efforts to improve relations with Eastern neighbors. In general, this means attempts to ignore the existence of a systemic conflict between pluralistic democracy and totalitarian communist dictatorship. Attempts to circumvent this conflict by way of bilateral relations are made in order to contribute to the improvement of living conditions of people in the GDR and other countries of Eastern Europe. As a consequence of this, trade with East bloc countries is given a higher priority by the Federal Republic of Germany than by its allies.

This, of course, has also influenced the perceived threat towards the Soviet Union.

Finally, the geopolitical position and the limited power options of the FRG, as well as the value structures of its society—which, in turn, are inseparably linked to the results of historical experience—lead to a far-reaching renunciation of a global political orientation in favor of a regional one. For the Federal Republic of Germany, global politics means careful participation in a preferably world-wide system of free trade, with the aim of securing its own import requirements and chances of export. This also implies ignoring Soviet political activities outside Europe. Even the Soviet invasion of Afghanistan has had only a marginal effect on the perception of threat within the FRG.

The medium-term constant American definition of interests is characterized by the global rivalry with the Soviet Union. As the result of World War II, these two countries are the leading powers of the systemic conflict, and this has been acknowledged by every American administration since the days of President Harry S. Truman. It is the basis for the American perception of the Soviet Union. Their rivalry consists of a political-structural dimension and a power-political dimension. Both dimensions require American engagement in Europe. The political-structural dimension results in an understanding of the North Atlantic Alliance as an alliance of democracy, in general, and it leads to an American obligation—embedded in the American value system—to support European democracies against threats from the Soviet Union. The power-political dimension implies that Europe's economic, technological and demographic potential is of decisive importance to the global rivalry. Without Europe on its side, the U.S. would be reduced to number two in the global contest. Within the context of the American engagement in Europe, the Federal Republic of Germany takes a key position due to its geopolitical position and its economic-technological leading role.

The global character of the Soviet-American rivalry, however, also means that U.S. foreign policy will always be more than just its policies towards Germany alone or even Europe; correspondingly, European interests will always have to compete with the interests of other regions with regard to the definition of American foreign policy interests. This also implies that the American perception of the Soviet Union is derived from the global behavior of the Soviet Union, with the European theater playing an important, but not exclusive, role.

Since the difference of strength between the U.S. and the Soviet Union has, on the whole, ceased to exist, to an increasing extent the American engagement in Europe no longer has only protective functions, but is coupled with American expectations of European support with regard to external areas of conflict. In this context, the Federal Republic is usually mentioned first, mainly due to its economic strength.

This also explains the American approach to detente as an instrument to settle specific problems: the arms race, nuclear proliferation and, if possible, also the global expansionism of the Soviet Union. If this instrument does not prove to be successful, American policymakers have been prepared to give up and try another tool, which does not exclude the possibility of returning to detente if the other approach fails. This is a contrast to the broadly accepted European attitude that there is no alternative to detente.

It should be mentioned that neither the European nor the American understanding of detente is compatible with the Soviet concept of peaceful coexistence. Peaceful coexistence is a dynamic concept to change the correlation of forces, for the time being not by military means, but always with the option of using military means if this seems to be adequate. In addition, peaceful coexistence is only directed towards the major Western countries and does not exclude the use of military power against Third World countries. The development of the military and political balance during the 1970s, which can be called the decade of detente, shows how successfully the Soviets have played this game: talking with the West, organizing a substantial military build-up and expanding in the Third World at the same time.

As a consequence of the global character of the American-Soviet rivalry, the U.S. is often forced to cooperate with states whose domestic political structures correspond neither to American nor to European standards.

Finally, America's role as a superpower means that the U.S. is interested, first and foremost, in avoiding a nuclear confrontation, because only such a confrontation could jeopardize the country's existence. For a superpower, limited conventional use of armed forces is a realistic power option, as has been shown on numerous occasions, but direct use of force against the Soviet Union has always been avoided.

This overview of the American and German definition of interests results in medium-term parallel interests, which are basically determined by the perception of the Soviet Union as a threat: Germany's interest in the alliance with the United States corresponds to the American interest in having the Federal Republic, and thus Europe as a whole, on its side in the global rivalry. Because this is the dominating definition of interests for both sides, which ultimately follows from the structure of the international system, it can be characterized as stable in the medium term. This, however, does not mean that there are no diverging interests. Three problematic fields can be deduced from the medium-term effective variables of definitions of interest.

First, the global approach of American policy contrasts with Bonn's renunciation of global orientation. This is most clearly demonstrated when the U.S. expects support in external regions of conflict. Here, the disputes concerning policies towards the Caribbean and the Middle East serve as the most illustrative examples. The same is true for the European and especially the German efforts with regard to detente and the resulting change in the perception of the Soviet Union: If the United States considers reduced cooperation with Eastern Europe or the Soviet Union appropriate due to overriding global considerations, conflicting attitudes are unavoidable. In this context, the boycott of the 1980 Olympic Games and the controversies concerning the natural gas pipeline deal can be given as examples. Conflicts like these are a general problem of American-European politics. Whether European countries, or indeed any of them, are prepared to cooperate, and on what issues, and to what extent they intend to cooperate, all depends on short-term effective variables.

Second, whenever the United States is willing to cooperate uncritically with dictatorships of a different color because of the global rivalry with the Soviet Union, this will burden the alliance due to its political-structural dimension as an alliance of democracies. The American engagement in Vietnam, the support given to the Shah of Iran as well as various South American dictators, and the temporary tolerance of dictatorial systems in Turkey, Greece, Spain and Portugal are characteristic examples. These conflicts led to different perceptions of the Soviet Union. By cooperating with dictatorships, the United States is reducing the moral disqualification of the Soviet Union and contributing to the development of an equal evaluation of the Soviet Union and the United States as simply two superpowers.

Third, while the Federal Republic of Germany is interested in war-preventing strategies because of its geopolitical position, the American interest would be to limit military conflicts regionally and to conventional means. Until today, this has been a more or less theoretical discussion in Europe, which especially influenced the strategic debate on whether to lower or to raise the so-called nuclear threshold. Characteristically, the German Chancellor Helmut Schmidt is the father of the NATO dual-track decision, while the American General Bernard Rogers (like his predecessors and successor as SACEUR) pointedly calls for greater conventional efforts. However, these contrasting strategies, based upon geopolitical positions, have also influenced foreign policy thinking. The use of military power, wherever it occurs, will be judged with extreme criticism in West Germany, and, because of its democratic structure, standards applied to the United States will be much more critical than those applied to the totalitarian Soviet Union. West

Germany's reactions to American policies vis-à-vis Vietnam, Grenada and Libya are well-known examples of these kinds of conflicts. The result is the strengthening of the perception of the Soviet Union simply as a superpower similar to the United States.

These three fields of conflict—support in external regions of conflict, evaluation of dictatorial partners and of conventional power options—are like satellites circling around essentially stable relations within the alliance. The stability is based on the solid support for the alliance, and times of conflict coincide with changing perceptions of the Soviet Union. In addition, there are short-term effective variables which can either support the consensus or sharpen conflicts. Here, personal relations often play a special role in the atmosphere of international relations. There have been periods when the American perceptions of the Soviet Union were more "European" than those of the Europeans themselves (at the beginning of the Carter Administration), or when the German perception was more "American" than that of the United States at the same period of time (the conflict between Adenauer and Kennedy). The image of politicians conveyed in the press or expressed through public opinion in the other country is no less important, which often reduces the liberty of action of one's own government. The importance especially of Soviet attempts to influence public opinion in the countries concerned also cannot be overlooked. A long chain of examples reaches from the "spirit of Camp David," triggered by Khrushchev's visit to Eisenhower, to the support given to the peace movements. But above all the inability of the peace movements to prevent the NATO dual-track decision demonstrates that although such short-term effective variables can lead to political turbulence, in the final analysis they will not achieve much more.

This definition of interests in German foreign policy and its implications for American-German relations are reflected in a study on the perceptions of the German elite in foreign policy conducted by the Institute of Political Science at Mannheim University in 1982 (Table 1). The study shows that strong and continuous American-German cooperation is mostly desired in defense and in policy towards the East bloc, that the desire for such strong cooperation is much higher than the expected degree of cooperation, and that the desire and the expectations for such cooperation are much higher in a situation of crisis. In other words, in those fields of central relevance to the security of the FRG, defense and Eastern policy, the desire and expectations for strong cooperation are highest; the same is the case in a situation of crisis, which obviously means that the security issue dominates perceptions. In other policy areas, especially when no crisis is perceived, the expected

TABLE 1
DESIRED AND EXPECTED SITUATION
IN AMERICAN-GERMAN RELATIONS
ELITE PERCEPTIONS 1982

Field of Policy	Desired Cooperation		Expected Cooperation	
	strong and continuous(%)	strong in crisis(%)	strong and continuous(%)	strong in crisis(%)
Defense Policy	89.9	8.2	65.0	30.9
Foreign Policy	53.8	27.6	17.3	45.9
Policy towards the East ("Ostpolitik")	83.2	9.8	37.2	50.2
Economic Policy	68.1	17.8	22.9	33.8

degree of cooperation is lower. The same picture is shown if the question is raised with regard to American-European relations.

To sum up: the understanding of the Soviet threat against the free societies of Western Europe is the basic field of agreement between the U.S. and the FRG. This agreement dominates American-German relations. Nonetheless, there are disagreements on how to meet the Soviet challenge: on whether military posture should be based on conventional defense or should rely on nuclear deterrence; on the use of political cooperation, e.g. detente, with the Soviet Union in Europe as part of a global arrangement, as opposed to the European attempt to keep such regional cooperation free of global entanglement; and on whether to use economic cooperation as a tool in the global confrontation or as a goal in itself and as a means of stabilizing political cooperation in Europe. In these three areas, the U.S. wants to achieve global containment of Soviet expansionism while Germany's interest is directed to the European theater.

These fields of disagreement have long troubled American relations with Germany and more broadly with Europe. This is part of the history of the alliance and should not be exaggerated, given the fundamental agreement on the Soviet threat. However, in recent years the situation has changed to a certain degree: the frustration on the American side is no longer restricted to a small foreign policy elite but has reached broader parts of the American public. The American public has reacted angrily to the lack of European support for U.S. actions in the Caribbean and against international terrorism. The irrational anti-Americanism from prominent members of the peace movements and

Policy areas towards the USSR	military confrontations in Europe	political cooperation in Europe	economic cooperation	global containment
Diagram II				
U.S. policy	conventional defense	instrumental	instrumental	yes
FRG policy	nuclear deterrence	principal	goal in itself	no

also of the democratic left in Europe has raised questions in the U.S. about the value of the alliance. This is linked to the general mood that the Europeans should spend more on defense. Whether this development can be controlled or whether it will lead to a unilateral reduction of American forces is still too early to be judged. But given the strong common interests, both sides are well advised to watch this development very carefully.

Options for Future Developments

For the future development of relations between the U.S. and the Federal Republic of Germany and towards the Soviet Union, it is important that interests are basically parallel and stable, as has been demonstrated by the continued high support for the deployment of American troops in Germany and for alliance membership.

Hence it follows that relations between the U.S. and the Federal Republic are, in the course of time, changing between two kinds of relations. At root is a far-reaching consensus between both governments in which the medium-term effective variables dominate the definition of interests with regard to political decision-making. Such situations, however, are unstable in that they can always be replaced by originally secondary divergencies of interests which can suddenly become the focus of public attention. Nevertheless, due to the basically stable parallel interests, these conflicts can always be settled or their discussion can be prevented. Thus, these situations will after some time be replaced by a phase during which parallel definitions of interests dominate foreign policy perceptions. In most cases, there is a direct connection to relations with the Soviet Union: The more tense these are perceived to be by the Federal Republic, the lower will be the relative importance of conflicts with the U.S. In turn, perceived detente will increase attention given to divergencies in German-American relations. This is especially true if the threat perceptions are different, that is, if the Federal Republic perceives detente while the U.S. senses tensions. From the German point of view, the U.S. could then assume the role of an international trouble-maker. Especially since President Reagan's inauguration, this has been the case on a number of occasions.

Among these periodic conflicts, those resulting from short-term political constellations are much less important than those which are due to divergencies concerning medium-term variables. Parallel domestic political structures are one of the most important reference points for the stability of mutual relations and attitudes towards the Soviet Union. As the central variable, this cannot—and, according to value perceptions on both sides, should not—be changed, just as the geopolitical position and the power options cannot be altered. Consequently, the variable which could possibly be changed is above all based in the value system of a society. In a more concrete sense, this means that the regional orientation of the Federal Republic's political perceptions and the rejection of almost any power option are the variables which are most pronouncedly in conflict with American value perceptions. As a superpower, the U.S. cannot adapt to the Federal Republic's attitude with regard to these questions. The conflicts resulting from these divergencies can only be settled by changes on the German side.

In this context, it is important to realize that as an *economic* power, the Federal Republic of Germany has been following internationally recognized, responsible and globally-oriented policies for decades. In allusion to Germany's economic capacities and its general political role, some fifteen years ago the magazine *Der Spiegel* awarded it the title of "world power against its will." Naturally, the Federal Republic of Germany can never become a real world power, but to participate in global politics as a member of the alliance is a real option. This, of course, would require a perception of the Soviet Union based on global Soviet behavior.

The Federal Republic's regional orientation and rejection of power options is not only a consequence of its geopolitical position and its limited power options. The consequences of a megalomania which had led to two World Wars and the German catastrophies connected with them are clearly part of Germany's historical memory and a significant factor in its current policies.

Nevertheless, the question remains whether the conclusions drawn by the Federal Republic from these historical experiences are inevitable and unchangeable. The renunciation of global orientations, of a global perception of its own interests as well as of international politics, in many ways contradicts German long-term interests. This is also true for consequent rejection of power options, for example, with regard to the problem of securing raw material and energy supplies. Naturally, the Federal Republic of Germany can never give its policies a global orientation or make use of power options in national isolation. What is important is whether the FRG is prepared to take part in global orientation within the alliance with the U.S. and within a concept of burden-sharing. The U.S., the Federal Republic of Germany, and Japan account for one-third of world trade, which results in significant parallel interests for the three countries in this global arena.

The decisive resistance against such a reorientation of German policies follows from the basic patterns of public opinion; here, the perceptions of the elites and the general public coincide. In order to change this, a systematic learning process will be necessary, which can only be carried out by the political elites in the course of one generation. To do so, political leadership is required. In that sense, the Federal Republic still lives in a "post-war" period, even more than 40 years after the end of World War II. The U.S. can support the Federal Republic in that learning process; instead of criticizing Europe, in general, and Germany, in particular, for its structural parochial attitude, the U.S. should help it approach global tasks, before these assume the character of major crises, and help it achieve successful firsts when globally approaching international politics. The special role which, for example, the Federal Republic of Germany played and still plays with regard to the stabilization of Turkey is one possible precedent. The same is true for the German participation in the space program and in the SDI efforts, which will also offer manifold chances in this field.

It is of central importance that the U.S. contribution to that learning process is not perceived as tutelage. Part of a global political orientation must be a global orientation of public thinking. Without a certain pride in one's own achievements in international politics, this can never be obtained. Here, a soccer world-cup success will not be enough.

Such a development, however, requires a learning process for the United States as well. Naturally, the readiness of a superpower to consult regional powers in an adequate fashion is not very pronounced, and, in particular, the behavior of many European regional powers during important crisis situations did not exactly increase U.S. preparedness for consultations. But it is worth trying to let at least some regional powers develop into responsible partners of tomorrow by way of privileged consultations. Given its potential, the Federal Republic of Germany could be such a partner. If the FRG ever grew into such a role, this would change its perception of the Soviet Union: Regional options for cooperation would become less important than the global confrontation. Such a development, of course, would not exclude further differences in the U.S.-German perception of the Soviet Union, but those differences would be based on issues of day-to-day politics, and not, as it is the case in the present situation, on differences which follow from medium-term constant variables.

What does this mean for the future of U.S.-FRG agreements and disagreements on East-West relations? Three scenarios can be imagined:

a) The frustration in the U.S. over European parochialism, lack of global support and anti-American sentiments leads to a substantial reduction of American forces from Europe. The result will be an encouragement of those political groups in Germany—and most likely also in the other countries—favoring accommodation with the Soviet Union. This will lead to a steady political penetration of Western Europe by the Soviet Union. Not war and military defeat, but anticipated political self-subjection describes the end of this road. The gap between American and European understanding of the Soviet Union will increase.

b) Germany and Europe will recover from World War II in a moral and political sense, will start to think in global political categories and will be prepared to share worldwide responsibility with the United States. This would imply an effective and lasting containment of the Soviet Union and even the beginning of a decline of the Soviet Empire. Differences over details may characterize American-German relations under this scenario, too, but they will not matter. The vision of making the world safe for democracy will unite the free societies on both sides of the Atlantic.

c) The worst cases on both sides can be avoided, but nothing more: no troop reduction and no socialist/neutralist party will come to power in a major European country. The German SPD, of course, will return to power but only after having returned to a middle-of-the-road policy, which will not happen before the 1990s. Germans will be shocked by American self-assuredness of a Reagan-style government and will be exasperated by the inconsistency of a Carter-style administration. Americans will be disappointed by the allies' lack of support in their global competition with the Soviet Union. But both sides know to define their interest: keeping the troubled alliance alive.

What is the likelihood of these scenarios? The answer is obvious. The first is wishful thinking Moscow-style and the second is a Western illusion. The third is unpleasant, full of crises, embarrassments and disappointing events, but also free of catastrophe. This is reality.

The INF Negotiations

All this is the result of 30 years of experience with the Federal Republic as a member of the Western alliance. However, with the Reykjavik summit in late 1986 and during the following discussions regarding new arms control negotiations in the field of medium-range systems with short and longer ranges, perspectives began to form which seemed to leave room for a new situation. With the acceptance by both sides of a zero-zero option, German interests have been fundamentally violated. Now that these proposals have become reality, this means:

1. The nuclear coupling between Europe and the U.S. brought about by the deployment of Pershing IIs and ground-launched cruise missiles since 1983 will break up, and a nuclear war, limited to the European theater while leaving the Soviet Union as a sanctuary, will become possible.

2. The Federal Republic (and the GDR) will be threatened by the continued existence of nuclear systems with ranges up to 500 km, to a far greater extent than the other members of the alliance. This will jeopardize solidarity among the alliance members, as demonstrated by the other members' rejection of the German demand for immediate inclusion of short-range systems in the negotiations. The interests of the non-German alliance partners are obvious: they want a minimum of nuclear deterrence, without being threatened by nuclear weapons themselves.

3. All aspects of the Federal Republic's possible role as a nuclear firebreak in Europe contradict German interests, reducing the nuclear threshold and jeopardizing the physical existence of the Federal Republic of Germany in case of conflicts.

4. The conventional imbalance will gain strategic importance without the smallest signs of efforts being made to neutralize the imbalance. The traditional strategy of NATO to compensate the conventional imbalance by nuclear options will be eroded.

5. Effective defense against the second and third attacking echelons of the Warsaw Pact will no longer be possible, which draws into question the credibility of conventional forward defense. With systems of ranges up to 500 km on both sides, the Warsaw Pact

can still reach all targets which are crucial for conventional forward defense in the Federal Republic and around it, thus preventing conventional forward defense. On the other hand, the Warsaw Pact will be allowed an unthreatened deployment area for its second and third echelons which would be out of reach for systems with ranges up to 500 km. This follows from the dual asymmetry, the geopolitical and the political one, between defender and aggressor.

6. Even if the problem of nuclear short-range systems can be solved—that the Soviet Union has a superiority of fifteen to one—this would also only make Europe safe for a conventional war, something which has been the case often enough in Europe's history.

The argument that credible deterrence and the coupling between the U.S. and Europe would remain intact because of the continued deployment of American forces and other nuclear systems does not sound very convincing: The American troops—and all other alliance troops as well—do not suffice to guarantee conventional stability, and the remaining nuclear threat to central military installations severely devalues the strength of the defender. With regard to the other nuclear systems, one has to keep three points in mind:

— the intercontinental strategic systems are balanced by the strategic parity between the superpowers;
— the sea-launched systems lack sufficient accuracy to be of operational use; and
— the air-based systems do not have a realistic chance of penetration.

It seems astonishing that major parts of the German public welcome the agreement on a zero-zero option as a breakthrough, despite these grave disadvantages. This can only be understood in the context of the political erosion of the consensus regarding all kinds of nuclear strategies among the German and other European publics. Arms control no longer is a political instrument to reach security, but has become an end in itself. Therefore, one can now observe in the Federal Republic the paradox that massive violations of one's own interests are celebrated as successes.

Although the INF Treaty has been signed, the severe violations of the interests of the Federal Republic of Germany are at present only discussed within a small circle of experts. However, after the agreement enters into force, one should not have any illusions about whether the Soviets would make immediate use of their newly won position to employ threats and political pressure against Europe and, first and foremost, against the Federal Republic, in order to underline that both have become zones of reduced security. One may ask what kind of awakening among the German public will follow and what it will imply for the role of the Federal Republic within the alliance and for American-German relations. However, it seems to be prudent only to raise this question and not to answer it. One only has to keep in mind that German neutralists, from the left and the right, have always maintained that the U.S. is not a reliable partner. This arms control agreement has not yet become reality, but when it does, the likely consequences are clear for all to see.

What can be done to limit the damage of the INF Treaty? Nonratification by the American Senate is no solution because this would destroy the European trust in the reliability of American politics—this follows from the gap between European interests and the public desire for arms control. This gap is the result of a basic confusion: It is the existence of certain weapons that is perceived as the threat, not the existence of political systems like that of the Soviet Union which have prepared to use these weapons. The only solution is to couple the entering into force of this treaty with an agreement on short-range nuclear systems and on conventional and chemical weapons. This is the common interest of the United States and Europe, in general, and Germany, in particular. Whether the existing confusion on both sides of the Atlantic will allow the realization of these common interests, however, is doubtful. The remaining hope is that the Soviet Union will try to exploit its advantages too soon and thereby offer effective medicine against Western confusion—as has been the case several times since 1945.

Books in the CISA Book Series include:

#1. William C. Potter, Editor, *Verification and SALT* (Westview Press, 1980).

#2. Bennett Ramberg, *Destruction of Nuclear Energy Facilities in War: The Problem and Implications* (Lexington Books, 1980); revised and reissued as *Nuclear Power Plants as Weapons for the Enemy: An Unrecognized Military Peril* (University of California Press, 1984).

#3. Paul Jabber, *Not by War Alone: Security and Arms Control in the Middle East* (University of California Press, 1981).

#4. Roman Kolkowicz and Andrzej Korbonski, Editors, *Soldiers, Peasants, and Bureaucrats* (Allen & Unwin, 1982).

#5. William C. Potter, *Nuclear Power and Nonproliferation: An Interdisciplinary Perspective* (Oelgeschlager, Gunn, and Hain, 1982).

#6. Steven L. Spiegel, Editor, *The Middle East and the Western Alliance* (Allen & Unwin, 1982).

#7. Dagobert L. Brito, Michael D. Intriligator, and Adele E. Wick, Editors, *Strategies for Managing Nuclear Proliferation—Economic and Political Issues* (Lexington Books, 1983).

#8. Bernard Brodie, Michael D. Intriligator, and Roman Kolkowicz, Editors, *National Security and International Stability* (Oelgeschlager, Gunn and Hain, 1983).

#9. Raju G.C. Thomas, Editor, *The Great Power Triangle and Asian Security* (Lexington Books, 1983).

#10 R.D. Tschirgi, *The Politics of Indecision: Origins and Implications of American Involvement with the Palestine Problem* (Praeger, 1983).

#11. Giacomo Luciani, Editor, *The Mediterranean Region: Economic Inter-dependence and the Future of Society* (Croom Helm (London & Canberra) and St. Martin's Press (NY), 1984).

#12. Roman Kolkowicz and Neil Joeck, Editors, *Arms Control and International Security* (Westview Press, 1984).

#13. Jiri Valenta and William C. Potter, Editors, *Soviet Decision-making for National Security* (Allen & Unwin, 1984).

#14. William C. Potter, Editor, *Verification and Arms Control*, (Lexington Books, 1985).

#15. Rodney Jones, Joseph Pilat, Cesare Merlini, and William C. Potter, Editors, *The Nuclear Suppliers and Nonproliferation: Dilemmas and Policy Choices* (Lexington Books, 1985).

#16. Gerald Bender, James Coleman, and Richard Sklar, Editors, *African Crisis Areas and U.S. Foreign Policy* (University of California Press, 1985).

#17. Bennett Ramberg, *Global Nuclear Energy Risks: The Search for Preventive Medicine* (Westview Press, 1986).

#18. Neil Joeck, Editor, *Strategic Consequences of Nuclear Proliferation in South Asia* (Frank Cass, 1986).

#19. Raju G.C. Thomas, *Indian Security Policy* (Princeton University Press, 1986).

#20. Steven Spiegel, Mark Heller, and Jacob Goldberg, Editors, *Soviet-American Competition in the Middle East* (Lexington Books, 1987).

#21. Roman Kolkowicz, Editor, *The Logic of Nuclear Terror* (Allen & Unwin, 1987).

#22. Roman Kolkowicz, Editor, *Dilemmas of Nuclear Deterrence* (Frank Cass, 1987).

#23. Michael D. Intriligator and Hans-Adolf Jacobsen, Editors, *East-West Conflict: Elite Perceptions and Political Options*, (Westview Press, 1986).

#24. Marco Carnovale and William C. Potter, Editors, *Continuity and Change in Soviet–East European Relations: Implications for the West* (Westview Press, forthcoming).

#25. William C. Potter, Editor, *The Emerging Nuclear Suppliers and Nonproliferation* (forthcoming).